Naturalism and the Frontiers of Legal Science

Dia-Logos

Schriften zu Philosophie und Sozialwissenschaften
Studies in Philosophy and Social Sciences

Edited by
Piotr W. Juchacz

Vol. 29

Tomasz Pietrzykowski

Naturalism and the Frontiers of Legal Science

Translated by Krystyna Warchał

Bibliographic Information published by the Deutsche Nationalbibliothek
The Deutsche Nationalbibliothek lists this publication in the Deutsche Nationalbibliografie; detailed bibliographic data is available in the internet at http://dnb.d-nb.de.

Library of Congress Cataloging-in-Publication Data
A CIP catalog record for this book has been applied for at the Library of Congress.

This publication was financially supported by University of Silesia
In Katowice, Poland.

UNIVERSITY OF SILESIA
IN KATOWICE

This work has been reviewed by José Manuel Aroso Linhares (University of Coimbra, Institute for Legal Research)

ISSN 1619-005X
ISBN 978-3-631-84498-4 (Print)
ISBN 978-3-631-85330-6 (E-PDF)
ISBN 978-3-631-85331-3 (EPUB)
ISBN 978-3-631-85332-0 (MOBI)
DOI 10.3726/b18343

Peter Lang – Berlin · Berlin · Bruxelles · New York ·
Oxford · Warszawa · Wien

This publication has been peer reviewed.

www.peterlang.com

Contents

Introduction: The background of methodological discussions in legal sciences

One of the most important characteristics of the development that has been taking place over the past several centuries is the increase in the prestige and importance of science as the most credible source of knowledge about reality. This process of the "disenchantment of the world," to use Max Weber's term, gained impetus during the scientific revolution of the sixteenth and seventeenth centuries,[1] with the Copernican turn in astronomy marking its symbolic starting point, and Newton's laws of motion – its closure. Other major figures of the time were Francis Bacon and Galileo. Bacon is credited with undertaking a systematic reflection on the empirical foundations of knowledge, which he presented in *Novum Organum* of 1620. This work was to replace the long-dominant Aristotelian-scholastic approach to explaining reality, which based on syllogistic reasoning from fundamental truths and logically necessary principles.

Bacon contrasted this method with inductive reasoning, which took single observations as the point of departure and aimed at conclusions in the form of generalisations corresponding to empirically observable laws of nature.[2] Bacon recommended cautious induction and careful elimination of typical cognitive errors ("idols") which interfered with empirical reasoning. This was supposed to counteract the human propensity to yield too easily to flights of imagination and to erect various intellectual structures which proved remote from reality. Knowledge derives from sound and arduous investigation of facts and consists in formulating only such conclusions as these facts can support. According to Bacon, human understanding needs no wings but "lead and weights."[3]

Galileo's experiments and observations not only paved the way for a number of breakthrough discoveries which abolished beliefs so far accepted as "obvious

1 For more details, see, e.g., A.R. Hall, *The Scientific Revolution, 1500–1800: The Formation of the Modern Scientific Attitude* (London: Longmans, Green, 1954).

2 For more details, see T. Kotarbiński, "Myśl przewodnia metodologii Franciszka Bacona. Program Bacona" [The Guiding Thought of Francis Bacon's Methodology. Bacon's Program], in Kotarbiński, *Szkice z historii filozofii i logiki* [Sketches from the History of Philosophy and Logic] (Warszawa: Państwowe Wydawnictwo Naukowe, 1979), pp. 104ff and 134ff.

3 "[W]e do not need to give men's understanding wings, but rather lead and weights, to check every leap and flight. And this has not been done before; but when it shall be done, we may have better hope of the sciences;" F. Bacon, *The New Organon*, eds. L. Jardine and M. Silverthorne (Cambridge, Cambridge University Press, 2000), p. 83.

truths," but also laid foundations for the mechanical-mathematical model of nature, crowned by Newton's great synthesis of the laws of classical mechanics. It is Newton's *Mathematical Principles of Natural Philosophy* (1687) that formed the cornerstone for the modern scientific method, explaining what appeared to be a variety of motion phenomena with several relatively simple and basic principles, formulated in a way which is precise, consistent, and open to empirical verification.

The triumphant advance of science which this revolution had started continued through centuries of breakthroughs in chemistry (eighteenth century) and biology (nineteenth century) and the impressive development of computer science (twentieth century). These changes led to a major transformation in the foundations of scholarly thinking and in the way of life of nearly all human societies (the industrial revolution, electricity, medicine, transportation, and telecommunication). As a result, scientific cognition itself became for many the most desirable, if not the only credible, source of knowledge about reality. It was explicitly juxtaposed with non-scientific views, in particular, with superstitions, unfounded beliefs, fruitless speculations, and naive projections of human expectations and wishes.

In philosophy, this scientism culminated in the logical positivism of the Vienna Circle, preceded by the nineteenth-century positivism of August Comte and the eighteenth-century mechanical philosophy developed by Pierre Laplace and Julien La Mettrie, rooted in the thought of Thomas Hobbes.[4] In Comte's classical positivism, the realisation that knowledge rests exclusively on the empirical observation of facts and cause-effect relations that bind them together marks the moment when humanity becomes "mature." This is the closing stage of the centuries-long process of overcoming infantile theological and religious explanations and lay rationalist metaphysics that later replace them. For Comte, the fact that humanity entered the final positive phase meant that fantasies and speculations had to be abandoned for objective scientific knowledge about facts – knowledge which provided a thorough explanation of the world and its processes.

The object of knowledge is reality in its entirety, with its particular levels studied by interrelated scientific disciplines. Ultimately, these disciplines form a whole, where the more basic sciences serve as the foundation for those addressing more complex phenomena. In this way, entire knowledge is based on

---

4 On the history of mechanism in philosophy and in science, see a comprehensive and in-depth account by M. Heller and J. Życiński, *Wszechświat - maszyna czy myśl? Filozofia mechanicyzmu - powstanie, rozwój, upadek.* [The Universe - Machine or Thought? The Philosophy of Mechanicism - Rise, Development, Decline] (Kraków: Polskie Towarzystwo Teologiczne, 1988).

mathematics, through astronomy, physics, chemistry, and biology, to sociology, the study of society. As one moves along the scale, the degree of generality of the phenomena studied by individual disciplines decreases, while their complexity grows. They form a continuum, where the order

> is determined by the degree of simplicity, or, what comes to the same thing, of generality of their phenomena. Hence results their successive dependence, and the greater or lesser facility for being studied.[5]

In later years, Comte extended the list, adding ethics, a philosophical moral doctrine based on objectively observable regularities in human needs and behaviours and in the social processes that these needs and behaviours triggered.[6]

The positivist movement initiated by Comte soon underwent divisions and, for various reasons, began to wither, while scientism, which was thriving over the next decades, abandoned many of the most important ideas proposed by the French founder of positivism.[7] Still, the kernel of his naturalist model of the world – one that construes reality in terms of phenomena which are, in principle, describable by laws discovered by individual sciences concerned with its various levels or aspects – has become part and parcel of the western intellectual tradition, often forming the keystone of the intellectual worldviews of European elites.

The revival of the positivist-oriented "scientific worldview" took place in the first half of the twentieth century, mostly as a result of the activity of a group of scholars known as the Vienna Circle. Many of the ideas they propagated were to a greater or lesser extent inspired by the thought of Ludwig Wittgenstein, one of the most eminent and renowned philosophers of the past century, and his *Tractatus Logico-Philosophicus*, published in 1921.[8] Wittgenstein's position in relation to the Vienna Circle was far from unambiguous, and in the course of time, the philosopher revised and abandoned his earlier views presented in *Tractatus*. Nevertheless, there is no doubt that for many leading representatives

---

5 A. Comte, *The Positive Philosophy of Auguste Comte*, Vol. 1, trans. H. Martineau (Kitchener: Batoche Books, 2000), p. 48.

6 M. Pickering, *August Comte: An Intellectual Biography*, Vol. 3 (Cambridge: Cambridge University Press, 2009), p. 240f; cf. also A.J. Noras, *Kant i Hegel w sporach filozoficznych osiemnastego i dziewiętnastego wieku* [Kant and Hegel in the Philosophical Disputes of the Eighteenth and Nineteenth Centuries] (Katowice: Wydawnictwo Uniwersytetu Śląskiego, 2007), p. 203.

7 For more details, see Noras, *Kant i Hegel…*, pp. 206f.

8 L. Wittgenstein, *Tractatus Logico-Philosophicus* (London: Kegan Paul, Trench, Trubner & Co., Ltd, 1922); available from Project Gutenberg at https://www.gutenberg.org/ebooks/5740.

of the Vienna Circle, they were an important source of inspiration and an object of deep personal fascination, especially after direct contacts with Wittgenstein during his stay in Vienna. It is debatable whether or to what extent the interpretation of *Tractatus* by members of the group was accurate. Still, it is indisputable that the main ideas of logical positivism largely coincided with at least one possible and justifiable reading of the text – one that emerged after months of close reading and discussion, sentence by sentence, of its fragments during the weekly meetings of the Circle.[9]

Tractatus – dubbed a "logical poem" for its unique style – contains claims which were central to the view of science and scientific approach developed by Vienna logical positivism. According to it, the world is the totality of facts. Pictures of facts that people make to themselves are thoughts expressible in the form of propositions. The sense of a proposition, Wittgenstein argues, is the picture of reality – of the fact – that it represents. Thus, only propositions which represent facts have sense. They can be understood because

> [t]o understand a proposition means to know what is the case, if it is true.[10]

Only propositions which have sense can be true or false (that is, they can have a logical value), depending on whether they are accurate representations of the facts to which they correspond. One can, of course, understand a proposition without knowing whether it is true or not. But one can speak of understanding only if the proposition represents a certain state of affairs (a fact), that is, if it "*shows* how things stand, *if* it is true."

A proposition "only asserts something, in so far as it is a picture," that is, in so far as it represents a state of affairs that is the case if it is true.[11] Conclusions that Wittgenstein draws from the above are radical. It is possible to express something only if the propositions used to express it represent a certain state of affairs. And only such propositions can be understood. All other propositions – those that do not represent any facts – are senseless; they may *seem* to have sense, but in fact, they are incomprehensible because there is no sense that can be ascribed to them. This brings Wittgenstein to the following conclusion:

> The totality of true propositions is the total natural science (or the totality of the natural sciences).[12]

---

9 M. Geier, *Der Wiener Kreis* (Hamburg: Rowohlt, 1992), pp. 73–74.
10 Wittgenstein, *Tractatus*…, t. 4.024, p. 41.
11 Ibid., t. 4.03, p. 41.
12 Ibid., t. 4.11, p. 44.

Only such propositions can be understood (only such content is expressible) and determined as true or false, because they can be compared with the states of affairs they represent. Whatever goes beyond a description of facts falls outside what can be thought and intersubjectively communicated.

Thus, good and beauty (ethics and aesthetics) lie beyond the boundaries of the expressible. If the world consists only of facts which simply are the case, their potential value must "lie outside the world," as Wittgenstein puts it. Hence, it rests beyond the boundaries of what can be encapsulated in a thought that has sense and is comprehensible and expressible through language, through propositions which have sense. According to Wittgenstein, "[i]t is clear that ethics cannot be expressed. Ethics are transcendental."[13] The same applies to problems which cannot be resolved by referring to facts that can be ascertained and expressed. Therefore,

> [m]ost propositions and questions, that have been written about philosophical matters, are not false, but senseless. We cannot, therefore, answer questions of this kind at all, but only state their senselessness.[14]

For Wittgenstein, philosophy "is not one of the natural sciences. (The word 'philosophy' must mean something which stands above or below, but not beside the natural sciences.)"[15] Its aim is not to provide knowledge in the form of propositions about facts, but to critically analyse language in order to identify statements which merely pretend to have sense and be comprehensible but, in fact, are senseless (that is, attempt to express something that lies beyond the realm of facts).

> The result of philosophy is not a number of "philosophical propositions," but to make propositions clear. Philosophy should make clear and delimit sharply the thoughts which otherwise are, as it were, opaque and blurred.[16]

The main point of this radical position is to demonstrate that the boundaries of what can be meaningfully expressed are in fact surprisingly tight and come down to whatever can be empirically ascertained as true (and which forms "the totality of the natural sciences"). As a result,

> [t]he right method of philosophy would be this. To say nothing except what can be said, i.e. the propositions of natural science, i.e. something that has nothing to do with

13 Ibid., t. 6.421, p. 88.
14 Ibid., t. 4.003, p. 39.
15 Ibid., t. 4.111, p. 44.
16 Ibid., t. 4.112, p. 44.

> philosophy: and then always, when someone else wished to say something metaphysical, to demonstrate to him that he had given no meaning to certain signs in his propositions. This method would be unsatisfying to the other—he would not have the feeling that we were teaching him philosophy—but it would be the only strictly correct method.[17]

Once we understand the boundaries of the expressible, we are able to fully recognise the senselessness of any attempts to express in language the "mysteries of life" that we consider so important. It turns out that all most important things, including those that fall under ethics and aesthetics, lie outside the scope of language and knowledge of facts that is linguistically expressible. Hence,

> even if all possible scientific questions be answered, the problems of life have still not been touched at all. Of course there is then no question left, and just this is the answer.[18]

Thus, whatever is important cannot be understood, and whatever can be understood is metaphysically insignificant. The impossibility of saying anything that goes beyond verifiable propositions about facts accumulated by science is fundamental and uncancellable, and any mindless, repeated attempts to break through this impassable boundary can only result in an endless stream of nonsense and chaos. This is why, in a short preface to *Tractatus*, Wittgenstein presents his main recommendation, which follows, in his view, from his inquiries: "[w]hat can be said at all can be said clearly; and whereof one cannot speak thereof one must be silent."[19] The truth of the thoughts that lead to this conclusion seems, says Wittgenstein, "unassailable and definitive. I am, therefore, of the opinion that the problems have in essentials been finally solved. And if I am not mistaken in this, then the value of this work secondly consists in the fact that it shows how little has been done when these problems have been solved."[20]

Tractatus was received with great interest by many foremost members of the Vienna Circle, where – in their opinion – similar problems of "the scientific view of the world" (*Wissenschaftliche Weltauffassung*) had for some time been discussed. They shared the view that true knowledge of reality was only constituted

17 Ibid., t. 6.53, p. 90.
18 Ibid., t. 6.52, p. 89.
19 Ibid., p. 23.
20 Ibid., p. 24. Interestingly, Wittgenstein was fully aware of the fact that his own considerations presented in *Tractatus* failed to meet the criteria of comprehensible statements which represented facts, and that they fell within the scope of metaphysics. This is why he added the following reservation: "he who understands me finally recognizes them as senseless, when he has climbed out through them, on them, over them. (He must so to speak throw away the ladder, after he has climbed up on it;)" ibid., t. 6.54, p. 90.

by beliefs that could be expressed in the form of elementary observation statements (so-called protocol propositions). The correspondence between protocol propositions and facts, or the lack of such correspondence, determined whether conclusions drawn from these propositions were true or false. This is also what made such propositions significant (comprehensible), because to understand a proposition meant to know how to determine whether it was true or false (which facts determined its truth or falsehood).[21]

Thus, meaningful propositions are those describing reality in a way that can be reformulated in terms of observation protocol statements or analytic propositions, true by virtue of definition (e.g., "A square has four sides"). The latter, however, perform ancillary function in relation to observation statements, merely indicating the kind of reasoning that is justifiable and thanks to which knowledge consists not only of a list of singular observations but also of the consequences that logically follow from them, generalisations by induction, and others.

In this way, the logical positivists of the Vienna Circle, known also as logical empiricists, reached the conclusion that whatever did not fit their model of scientific knowledge had no cognitive value. Scientific knowledge consists of claims which can be reformulated in terms of empirically verifiable observation statements and of analytical propositions, true by definition. Other statements – including evaluations, regulations, and non-empirical speculations, expressing, in fact, various emotions, longings, beliefs, or hopes – belong to futile, if not harmful, metaphysics, which only pretends to be true knowledge. It may be of great value to human beings and form an important part of their lives, but it does not provide any objective knowledge. Thus, such non-empirical metaphysical considerations are,

> like laughing, lyrics, and music, expressive. They express not so much temporary feelings as permanent emotional or volitional dispositions... Both have no representative function, no theoretical content. A metaphysical proposition, however – as distinguished from a lyrical verse – *seems* to have some, and by this not only is the reader deceived, but the metaphysician himself. He believes that in his metaphysical treaties he has asserted something and is led by this into argument and polemics against propositions of some other metaphysician... The danger lies in the *deceptive* character of

21 "Stating the meaning of a sentence amounts to stating the rules according to which the sentence is to be used, and this is the same as stating the way in which it can be verified (or falsified). The meaning of a proposition is the method of its verification;" M. Schlick, "Meaning and Verification," *The Philosophical Review* 45:4 (1936), p. 341.

> metaphysics; it gives the illusion of knowledge without actually giving any knowledge. This is the reason why we reject it.[22]

It is the task of a reliable, useful philosophy to unmask such pseudo-knowledge and expose it as a collection of meaningless statements amounting to incomprehensible gibberish rather that falsehood (if it is impossible to establish what must be the case for them to be true, they turn out to be objectively incomprehensible). Statements such as: "The limitless is the first substance" (Anaximander) or "The absolute Idea is…, on the one hand, substantial fullness of content and, on the other hand, abstract free volition" (Hegel) would then be classified as metaphysical by the Vienna Circle philosophers, that is, as nonsense passing itself off as profound truths. In fact, however, as Carnap points out, they are "neither true nor false, because they assert nothing."

As a result, like Wittgenstein in *Tractatus*, the Vienna Circle aimed at putting an end to traditional philosophical disputes. Logical positivists maintained that it was possible either to transform them into empirically soluble scientific problems (which is not to say that the problems could indeed be investigated or solved at the current state of knowledge and technology), or to expose them as nonsense metaphysics. According to them, the whole of scientific knowledge forms a uniform building resting on the foundations provided by physics, and physics offers the most elementary language for the description of reality. Consequently, it is in this language that observation protocol statements should be formulated.[23] The language of other sciences can be reduced to statements of physical facts, although phenomena of higher complexity (such as biological organisms or society) may require concepts and theories which match their nature and scale. Nevertheless, reality is ultimately physical in nature, so it must be possible to transform the whole of knowledge into the language of elementary physical observations. Indeed, it was one of the long-term (and never fulfilled) aims of the Vienna Circle to build a system of unified science, where theories concerning various phenomena were translatable into the physicalistic language.

The activity of the Vienna Circle was soon interrupted, first, by the murder of Moritz Schlick, who in organisational matters was the moving spirit of the Circle, and later, by the Anschluss of Austria by the Third Reich, followed by

---

22 R. Carnap, *Philosophy and Logical Syntax* (London: Kegan Paul, Trench, Trubner & Co. Ltd., 1935), pp. 29–31.

23 Throughout the period of activity of the Vienna Circle, disputes continued over the object and structure of such basic observation statements; see A. Koterski, *Spór o zdania protokolarne. "Erkenntnis" i "Analysis" 1932 -1940* [Dispute over Protocol Phrases. "Erkenntnis" and "Analysis" 1932 -1940] (Warszawa: Aletheia, 2002), p. 32.

emigration and dispersion of the majority of leading representatives of Vienna logical positivism. Moreover, the views propagated by the Vienna Circle evoked critical reactions. The most significant criticism came from Karl Popper, a philosopher closely associated with the Circle and called by some logical positivists "the official opposition of the Vienna Circle." As early as in the 1930s, Popper published a book in which he criticised one of the cornerstones of logical empiricism, that is, the tenet that the empirical verifiability of propositions is the criterion of their meaningfulness. According to Popper, this belief leads to two false conclusions. Firstly, it results in treating all considerations that cannot be transformed into observation statements as meaningless nonsense, or "nonsensical twaddle." This stance of logical positivism, Popper argues, can be compared to "trying to kill metaphysics by calling it names." In fact, metaphysics is a valuable area of human thought and many ideas that it nurtured have added to the advancement of science.[24]

Secondly, and more importantly, some fundamental theories of natural science fail the criterion of empirical verifiability as a condition of meaningfulness (comprehensibility) of their claims. As Brian Magee points out, Popper's criticism has convincingly demonstrated that:

> logical positivism claimed to be first and foremost a (indeed the) scientific view of the world, and yet its central tenet, the Verification Principle, wiped out the whole of science.[25]

Laws of science are general – they refer to an infinite number of cases – and the principle of verifiability in their case runs into the problem of induction, well known at least since Hume's time. It consists in the realisation that no number of observations can count as empirical verification of a universal law as formulated by science. No finite number of observations can provide empirical evidence for a claim that refers to an infinite number of possible future events.[26] Under this view, every general scientific law is empirically non-verifiable and must be treated as a metaphysical rather than scientific claim. Thus, as a tool for removing metaphysics from science, the verification principle in fact dealt

24 K. Popper, *The Logic of Scientific Discovery* (London: Routledge, 2005), p. 16.

25 B. Magee, *Confessions of a Philosopher* (New York: Random House, 1997) p. 57.

26 As noticed by Bertrand Russell, the argument that such generalisations from a finite number of observations have so far worked, that is, have so far been confirmed by upcoming future events, is based on a vicious circle, because in an attempt to make induction more reliable, it makes use of inductive reasoning itself.

a heavy blow to the latter. As Magee puts it, "[p]eople began to realise that this glittering new scalpel was, in one operation after another, killing the patient."[27]

Rejecting the verificationist theory of meaning propagated by logical positivists, Popper proposes a different perspective. The real "problem of demarcation," as he calls it, does not consist in distinguishing between meaningful statements and nonsense, but in distinguishing between scientific and non-scientific claims. In particular, it involves the distinction between science and pseudo-science, that is, theories that declare themselves as scientific but in fact are not. Non-scientific statements need not be meaningless, but they lack the cognitive credibility that is attached to scientific claims and hence should not be confused with them (this is why, what poses a real threat to knowledge is not whatever is non-scientific but whatever pretends to be science, namely, pseudo-science). The criterion of demarcation between scientific and non-scientific claims is not empirical verifiability of the former, but their falsifiability.

A claim (or theory) is scientific if there is a possibility to refute it by experience. No number of observations that confirm a particular theory can conclusively establish it as true. However, a single observation that contradicts it is sufficient to falsify it and to refute it as false. Thus, only views formulated in a way that allows empirical falsification deserve to be called science – views for which it is possible to identify observations that might disprove them as false. Beliefs which are empirically non-falsifiable fall outside science, and if they aspire to be scientific, they belong to pseudo-science.

In formulating the idea of falsifiability as a criterion of demarcation of science from non-science, Popper drew inspiration from vivid discussions that continued within various intellectual currents and trends developing in the first decades of the twentieth century. That was the time when Karl Marx's theories (which claimed to offer a "scientific" explanation for the organisation of society and the historical development of humanity) and Sigmund Freud's psychoanalysis were at the height of popularity. At the same time, the very foundation of modern science, that is, Newtonian classical mechanics, was questioned by Einstein's theory of relativity. Popper pointed out the striking difference between Einstein's attitude towards his own theory and the stance taken by proponents of Marxism and Freudianism. Both Marxism and psychoanalysis – like astrology – attracted supporters by their "apparent explanatory power." Popper puts it in the following way:

---

27 Magee, *Confessions…*, p. 57.

> These theories appeared to be able to explain practically everything that happened within the fields to which they referred. The study of any of them seemed to have the effect of an intellectual conversion or revelation, opening your eyes to a new truth hidden from those not yet initiated. Once your eyes were thus opened you saw confirming instances everywhere: the world was full of verifications of the theory. Whatever happened always confirmed it.[28]

They exemplify theories constructed in such a way that their adherents come across an "incessant stream of confirmations," because they account for everything that takes place or could take place. Both the occurrence and non-occurrence of a given fact are equally convincingly explained by them and serve as confirmation of the truth of such theories. The situation is very different with Albert Einstein's theory. Einstein demonstrated what empirical consequences followed from the theory he proposed (very different from those that could be predicted on the basis of previous physical knowledge), pointing out that if observations conducted in appropriate conditions did not correspond to his predictions, his theory would be refuted. The possibility to conduct such observations appeared several years later, during an eclipse of the sun, and Sir Arthur Eddington's expedition, specially organised for this purpose, actually observed phenomena that were in complete agreement with the predictions of the theory of relativity.

For Popper, falsifiability in the sense explained above – understood as susceptibility to empirical refutation – was the key feature of a truly scientific theory. If a theory is constructed in such a way that no observation can disprove it, it does not deserve to be called scientific (but it may belong to pseudo-science). At the same time, no scientific theory can be conclusively validated. Observations which do not falsify a theory make it more probable and function as corroborating evidence, but there is no guarantee that future observations will not refute it.

Thus, in Popper's view, scientific method is hypothetical-deductive in nature. It consists in the formulation of hypotheses and in attempts to conduct observations that would disprove them. The bolder the hypothesis, and the more resistant to falsification, the better it is, because it forbids a greater number of facts which, if observed, would refute it. A hypothesis which few observations could potentially disprove is trivial, and one which does not exclude any observations is scientifically worthless. In other words, each scientific hypothesis must be a prohibition, that is, it must exclude the possibility of some observations, which, if actually made, render it false.[29] At the same time, the less probable a hypothesis

28 K. Popper, *Conjectures and Refutations* (New York: Basic Books), 1962, p. 34.
29 Ibid., p. 37.

is – that is, the greater number of observations can potentially disprove it – the better, as long as it survives attempts at refutation.

As can be seen, Popper's hypothetico-deductive theory of science encourages formulating boldest possible hypotheses and conjectures, and then subjecting them to rigorous and systematic tests, until an empirically refuted hypothesis is replaced by a new one. This view of the method of empirical sciences proved highly influential and gained enormous popularity; in fact, Popper himself claimed that by presenting it, he had "killed" logical positivism. However, his ideas soon met with criticism very similar to that he had raised against Vienna positivism. The most serious challenge came from one of Popper's most famous disciples: Thomas Kuhn, American philosopher of science. According to him, the gravest weakness of Popper's theory of science lies in its glaring incompatibility with actual scientific practice. As Kuhn argued, the history of science demonstrated clearly and unambiguously that

> [i]f any and every failure to fit [theory and data] were ground for theory rejection, all theories ought to be rejected at all times.[30]

The practice of scientific research looks indeed very different. According to Kuhn, each scientific community concerned with a particular discipline develops a set of shared beliefs, fundamental theories, concepts, and models how to properly formulate and solve scientific problems. This is what Kuhn calls the paradigm of the discipline. Thanks to the commonly accepted paradigm, it is possible to ask concrete scientific questions and to search for answers, which together comprises what Kuhn refers to as "normal science."

All research problems that are legitimate in the light of the set of concepts, theories, and methodological models of a particular paradigm are treated as puzzles. Solving the puzzles corresponds to filling in the gaps in knowledge based on that paradigm. Paradigms determine which problems are scientifically legitimate, significant, or solvable. And similarly, research questions which cannot be formulated according to the principles of the prevailing paradigm are considered, within its limits, as illegitimate and unscientific – or simply "the wrong sorts of questions to ask."

As Kuhn argues, over time, within each established paradigm, there appear anomalies: observations, facts, or phenomena that are in conflict with its basic tenets. When the number and significance of such anomalies – observations

30 T. Kuhn, *The Structure of Scientific Revolutions*, 2nd ed., (Chicago: University of Chicago Press, 1970), p. 146.

which cannot be accounted for within the dominant paradigm – pass the critical point, a crisis may follow, leading to a so-called scientific revolution. This is where the period of normal science comes to an end: the previously prevailing paradigm is rejected and replaced by a new one, which can better explain the observations that so far could not be accounted for and were treated as anomalies.

According to Kuhn, a paradigm is not rejected merely as a result of empirical data that contradict it. Such observations can undermine it or question its credibility. However, a true scientific revolution does not take place until theoretical proposals are formulated which can lay the basis for a new, "better" disciplinary paradigm. If they are promising in terms of their ability to explain the available facts and observations (including those that so far were regarded as anomalies), a next stage in the development of science may begin: the stage of a developing crisis and rivalry between competing paradigms, with some scholars abandoning the previously accepted views on the foundations of their discipline, and others staying faithful and seeking to defend them.

Scientific revolutions can be short or very long (sometimes lasting many decades) and end with a victory of one party or the other. What is important is that the competing paradigms are largely incompatible, that is, they apply totally different perspectives to explain the phenomena of a particular discipline. As a result, it is impossible to settle this competition by a simple confrontation of theories and facts. Rather, it is a question of clash and rivalry between two worldviews that offer an entirely different interpretation and explanation of the same phenomena. This is because their defenders refer to arguments that make sense within only one paradigm, in the light of its assumptions and concepts, and this argumentation, obviously, cannot be convincing for supporters of the other, competing paradigm. Thus, the differences of opinions between scholars who work within various paradigms in fact amount to "what is a problem and what a solution."[31]

The degree of attractiveness of a paradigm is not (or not only) a matter of its "past achievement" but rather "future promise." This means in particular that

> [t]he man who embraces a new paradigm at an early stage must often do so in defiance of the evidence provided by problem-solving. He must, that is, have faith that the new paradigm will succeed with the many large problems that confront it, knowing only that the older paradigm has failed with a few. A decision of that kind can only be made on faith.[32]

---

31 Ibid., p. 109.

32 Ibid., p. 158.

The victory of a new paradigm is often a long process, advancing in spite of the fact that "some scientists, particularly the older and more experienced ones, may resist indefinitely."[33] Abandoning an old paradigm and replacing it with a new one lead to another period of normal science, with a particular scientific community, once again, referring to a shared set of basic theories, concepts, methods, and models of formulating and solving specific research problems – or puzzles – of their discipline. Because of scientific revolutions, the process of scientific development is not cumulative; it is only the periods of normal science – practiced within the currently prevailing paradigm – that are cumulative in nature. As a result of a paradigm shift, the so far accumulated knowledge becomes largely outdated and has to be replaced with new theories and explanations. Moreover, what has been considered a legitimate scientific question may now turn out to be a pseudo-problem, misconception, or a blatant error.

This change in worldview – or, more precisely, in the way of thinking about a specific aspect of the world investigated by a particular discipline – involves the necessity to rewrite, in whole or in part, the existing textbooks. This need arises "whenever the language, problem-structure, or standards of normal science change,"[34] because it is through textbooks that the current paradigm is maintained and propagated. The fact that they have to be rewritten following a scientific revolution means that the perspective from which the prior development of knowledge is described changes as well. This results in disguising not only the role but also the very existence of the revolution that has effected in the paradigm shift. Although textbooks usually make references to the history of a particular discipline, the point of view they adopt is that of the paradigm that has produced them. Kuhn puts it as follows:

> Partly by selection and partly by distortion, the scientists of earlier ages are implicitly represented as having worked upon the same set of fixed problems and in accordance with the same set of fixed canons that the most recent revolution in scientific theory and method has made seem scientific.[35]

This is why the development of particular disciplines is often perceived as a linear process of accumulating discoveries, which has gradually (and, so to say, inevitably) brought them to their current shape. This is made possible by a certain reinterpretation of the past (or by writing history backwards, to use Kuhn's phrase), which ignores the fundamental incompatibility of paradigms that follow

33 Ibid., p. 152.
34 Ibid., p. 137.
35 Ibid., p. 138.

one another. Thus, the current paradigm appears to be more than a set of beliefs and research standards of a particular discipline, which an individual must accept to become a member of the community of "serious" scholars. It also appears to be the endpoint of a long process of knowledge development, which, through a series of discoveries and improvements, has led to true knowledge of a particular aspect of reality.

Popper himself tried to refute these objections, arguing that Kuhn described the actual course of scientific development in terms of psychological and sociological aspects of scholarly practice but did not propose a new, "logical" model of scientific method, which was what he had intended to do. Nevertheless, further development of philosophical reflection on science and whatever constitutes it has followed the path taken by Kuhn. For example, Imre Lakatos, another famous student of Popper, supported and amplified Kuhn's criticism of the principle of falsifiability. It is not the case that observations contradicting a theory that is being put to test must inevitably lead to its refutation. Each theory may be almost freely supplemented with additional assumptions, elaborations, and exceptions which make it compatible with new observations. In this way, the task of testing a particular theory is, in a sense, moved to another place, at the moment less vulnerable to falsification. As Lakatos puts it,

> [n]ature may shout *no*, but human ingenuity – contrary to … Popper – may always be able to shout louder.[36]

These additions and modifications give rise to competing chains or clusters of interconnected theories, which Lakatos calls scientific research programmes.[37] They fulfil the same function for scholars who work in their framework as Kuhn's paradigms. They are the foundation and the axis of knowledge and determine which questions or problems are legitimate and which methods of answering or solving them are appropriate. Within one discipline, several research programmes may coexist, each based on entirely or partly different assumptions and offering various explanations for the same phenomenon.

What Kuhn calls normal science is in fact a period of development of a research programme, where apparently inexplicable facts must be accounted for by theories which belong to it or develop within its scope, so that observed anomalies can be treated as verifications confirming the programme. Each research

36 I. Lakatos, "History of Science and its Rational Reconstructions," *Boston Studies in the Philosophy of Science* 8 (1971), p. 100.
37 I. Lakatos, *The Methodology of Scientific Research Programmes* (Cambridge: Cambridge University Press, 1978).

programme consists of a "hard core" and a "protective belt" of auxiliary theories and hypotheses, which are of lesser importance. The hard core is not subject to empirical verification; it cannot be questioned without abandoning the programme. This is why it is protected by a belt of auxiliary hypotheses and theories, which, in case of persistent contradiction with empirical data, can be altered, expanded, or replaced by others. The negative heuristics of a programme prohibits the falsification of its hard core, which means that all anomalies must be neutralised by adopting or refuting auxiliary theories of the outer protective belt.

At the same time, each programme also has its positive heuristics, which specifies what can and should be investigated within its scope, how to formulate research problems to ensure that they are scientific, what methods can be used to solve them, and so on. The positive heuristics makes it possible to systematically revise and modify the protective belt and thus "saves the scientist from becoming confused by the ocean of anomalies,"[38] which surrounds each research programme. Research programmes can be progressive or degenerative, depending on whether they are able to predict new phenomena and explain new observations or, conversely, have no predictive power but merely protect themselves against the pressure of facts that contradict their assumptions.[39] As a result, research programmes which turn out to be more progressive supersede those which are degenerating and whose scientific vitality is on the decline.

The most radical anti-falsificationist stance was taken by Paul Feyerabend, another influential student of Popper. He rejected the view that science proceeded according to predefined methodological schemata and strict rules which were to ensure its scientific character. Feyerabend referred to this view of scientific progress as authoritarian and claimed that, as clearly demonstrated by past developments, the only methodological principle that had actually made it possible was *anything goes*. If scientists had taken into consideration any restrictions forcing them to reject views which contradicted observations or prior theories, the most significant and valuable discoveries, including major scientific breakthroughs, would never have been made.[40]

According to Feyerabend, the history of greatest scientific discoveries has conclusively demonstrated that any attempt to confine research activities to the "application of methods of criticism and proof … would wipe out science as we

---

38 Ibid., p. 50.

39 This is why, according to Lakatos, only a research programme can be scientific; qualifying a single theory as scientific would count as a category error; ibid., p. 42.

40 P. Feyerabend, *Against Method* (London: Verso, 1993), p. 155.

know it, and would never have permitted it to arise."[41] Scientific progress proceeds through presenting and defending hypotheses which in many cases run against what so far has been considered as corresponding with facts and which often violate all norms and canons of scientific inquiry accepted at a given time. More often than not, such hypotheses are rejected, ridiculed, or ignored and are quickly forgotten. But sometimes they prove accurate and initiate a revolution in their domains. The more of such ideas, theories, or suggestions scientists put forward, the better, as it is only through ferment and unrestricted discussion that identification of the best and most promising of them is possible (and, indeed, none of them agrees, or can agree, "with all the facts in its domain"[42]). To ensure an unhindered development,

> a person trying to solve a problem whether in science or elsewhere *must be given complete freedom* and cannot be restricted by any demands, norms, however plausible they may seem to the logician or the philosopher who has thought them out in the privacy of his study.[43]

Feyerabend frequently illustrated his views with the story of the Copernican Revolution and its defence by Galileo. At that time, the heliocentric model of the world – according to which it was the earth, not the sun, that was in permanent motion – stood, as Feyerabend argues, in glaring contradiction with common sense and with what was accepted as obvious and easily observable facts. A popular argument invoked to disprove the Copernican theory involved an experiment with a stone falling from a tower. According to it, if the earth were in motion, a stone falling from a tower would have to hit the ground at a certain distance from its base. This distance would increase with the height of the tower and the time of falling, because during this period of time, the tower – together with the whole earth – would move away from the straight vertical trajectory of the falling stone.[44]

Thus, Copernican heliocentrism was on the one hand "refuted" by a variety of empirical proofs that exposed its fallacy, and on the other defended by Galileo in a way that Feyerabend referred to as "propaganda" and "psychological tricks,"[45] supported merely by invented thought experiments (rather than based on experiment proper). This is why Feyerabend was of the opinion that Galileo's trial by

---

41 Ibid., p. 148.
42 Ibid., p. 39.
43 Ibid., p. 262.
44 Ibid., pp. 55–56.
45 Ibid., p. 65.

the Roman Inquisition should not be interpreted as a confrontation between religious dogmas and "scientific knowledge." On the contrary, it was a confrontation between the most solid and reliable scientific knowledge then available, consistently supporting the geocentric view of the world, and Galileo's speculations, which at that time were dubious and groundless and which were thought to pose a serious threat to the social order.

From this perspective, Feyerabend argues, the Church "acted no differently from modern scientific institutions: universities, schools and even research institutes," as they all take similar measures to deal with views which their authors introduce as revolutionary and for which they cannot present sufficiently solid and convincing evidence. As a result of the first trial, Galileo "was advised to teach Copernicus *as a hypothesis*; he was forbidden to teach it *as a truth*."[46] It is only his perseverance in propagating Copernicanism as a scientifically proven view of the world (together with perjury and mockery of the Pope) that brought about the second trial, as a result of which Galileo, at that time 69, was put under house arrest and his *Dialogue Concerning the Two Chief World Systems, Ptolemaic and Copernican* was placed on the list of prohibited books.

Feyerabend argued that all forms of the mythologisation of science should be rejected, including Popper's falsificationism, which he considered an extreme manifestation of dogmatism. In his opinion, the logical positivism of the Vienna Circle reduced the objectives of philosophy to clinging onto science's coattails, and Kuhn provided scientists with a false alibi that the lack of criticism for the existing views – the paradigm – was the recipe for doing "mature science." Moreover, he questioned the alleged superiority of the scientific view of the world over other modes of perception of reality, pointing out that in modern western societies, science had become a form of religion.

According to Feyerabend, science is not, in principle, superior to other forms of beliefs or cultural practices. It owes its special status to the prejudice of western societies, dogmatically rejecting anything that does not fit the narrow picture of the world which has grown to dominate the Euro-Atlantic culture within the last few centuries. Because of that, science is in a position of undeserved privilege and, while receiving gigantic support, continues to give off an

46 Ibid. p. 132. Feyerabend quotes a very interesting fragment of a letter by Cardinal Bellarmine, the main prosecutor in Galileo's case, where he argues that if there were solid evidence in support of heliocentrism, the Church should admit to an error in the understanding of relevant fragments of the Holy Scripture rather than deny a view that was proved beyond doubt (p. 132, note 17).

aura of exceptionality, which protects its high status and the benefits that go with it. In the past, Feyerabend argues, the separation of church and state became a fact; now it is time for science to become separate from the state. Science should be brought back to the status of one of the possible ways of understanding the world, of a type of practice by a specific group of people. This, in turn, should neutralise the dangers resulting from the growing power of "experts" who control societies, borrowing authority from the mythologised status of science.[47]

Disputes about the methodology of empirical sciences that were underway throughout the twentieth century had little impact on the humanities and social sciences, including legal sciences. Here, discussions focused on their characteristic features and distinctiveness from the natural sciences, that is, historically speaking, on an older problem. The idea that there was a group of "spiritual" sciences (*Geistewissenschaften*), whose object and methods made them significantly distinct from the natural sciences (*Naturwissenschaften*), emerged at the end of the nineteenth century and became known in the history of ideas as the anti-positivist turn. It came as a reaction to the triumphant, radically positivist views of the convergence of object and method of all sciences in the classical formulation by August Comte, later referred to by various versions of scientism (e.g., by Herbert Spencer).

Wilhelm Dilthey was one of the foremost figures of the anti-positivist turn of the end of the nineteenth century. For him, the major difference between *Natur-* and *Geistwissenschaften* lay in the object of inquiry: facts and natural relationships in the case of the former, and the "spiritual" realm of human experience (culture) in the case of the latter. Because the humanities investigate human "expression of life," they rely on the hermeneutic process of *understanding* rather than on explanation in terms of causes and effects. In the case of a poem, painting, or another artefact of culture, this understanding leads ultimately to re-experiencing it, to re-creating a particular thought content in the mind of the receiver (*Nacherlebens*).

This highest form of understanding, however, can only be achieved through complicated processes of elementary forms of understanding, which, for Dilthey, do not attempt to deduce the cause from the effect. Rather, they aim at comprehending the specific relation between the action or object which is an expression of life on the one hand, and that which is being expressed, on the other. In sciences whose object comprises an indelible "humanistic coefficient," to use Florian Znaniecki's term, the appropriate method must consist in comprehending and

47 P. Feyerabend, *Science in a Free Society* (London: New Left Books, 1978).

explaining behaviours of subjects by reconstructing the subjective sense they make of the world. For this reason, Dilthey regarded psychology as a basis for the humanities, much like mathematics and mechanics provided the basis for the natural sciences and physics, respectively.[48]

A slightly different perspective on the separate status of the humanities was developed within the Baden School of Neo-Kantianism. Like Dilthey, its founder Wilhelm Windelband maintained that it was impossible to reduce culture and social life to phenomena that could be described with the methods of the natural sciences. However, he argued that

> an empirical discipline of such significance as psychology is not to be accommodated by the categories of the natural sciences and the humanities; to judge by its subject, it can only be characterized as a humanity, and in a certain sense as the foundation of all the others; but its entire procedure, its methodological arsenal, is from beginning to end that of the natural sciences.[49]

Windelband proposed that, instead of this anachronistic juxtaposition, empirical sciences should be distinguished from cultural studies (*Kulturwissenschaften*), with the major difference consisting in their methods rather than objects of study.

> [D]ie Erfahrungswissenschaften suchen in der Erkenntniss des Wirklichen entweder das Allgemeine in der Form des Naturgesetzes oder das Einzelne in der geschichtlich bestimmten Gestalt; sie betrachten zu einem Teil die immer sich gleichbleibende Form, zum anderen Teil den einmaligen, in sich bestimmten Inhalt des wirklichen Geschehens. Die einen sind Gesetzeswissenschaften, die anderen Ereigniswissenschaften.[50]

Cultural studies are idiographic in that they are not concerned with discovering general principles that govern a certain class of phenomena, but rather aim to understand and describe concrete facts (events) in all their uniqueness. Thus, they are concerned with individual events (*Ereigniswissenschaften*) rather than laws, which are the province of natural studies (*Gesetzeswissenchaften*). At the same time, Windelband emphasised that the juxtaposition of idiographic and

48 See H.A. Hodges, *Wilhelm Dilthey: An Introduction* (Ann Arbor: University of Michigan, 2010), pp. 38–39.

49 W. Windelband, "History and Natural Science," trans. J. Lamiell, *Theory and Psychology* 8 (1894/1998), p. 11; see also A.J. Noras, *Historia neokantyzmu* [History of Neo-Kantianism] (Katowice: Wydawnictwo Uniwersytetu Śląskiego, 2012), pp. 474–475.

50 W. Windelband, "Geschichte und Naturwissenschaft." Rede zum Antritt des Rektorats der Kaiser-Wilhelms-Universität Straßburg gehalten am 1. Mai 1894; available at http://philosophierer.blogspot.com/2014/09/wilhelm-windelband-geschichte-und.html; accessed 3.12.2018.

nomothetic sciences was not ontologically motivated. The same phenomena can be analysed both nomothetically and idiographically; for example, the human being can be studied from the physiological-biological perspective, that is, in terms of general laws of nature, or from the idiographic perspective, that is, as a concrete, unique individual with his or her own distinctive biography.

Heinrich Rickert, Windelband's disciple and a continuator of his thought, "the true father of the Baden School in all its greatness,"[51] reformulated the distinction between idiographic and nomothetic sciences, juxtaposing generalising (*generalisierenden*) sciences on the one hand, and individualising historical (*historisch-individualisierenden*) sciences on the other. Although the distinction between the generalising method, characteristic of the natural sciences, and the individualising method of the sciences of culture is not absolute, it demands that the utopian idea of the universal method should be rejected.

Like Windelband, Rickert regarded this division as purely methodological and did not refer to any differences between the objects of these two types of sciences. The same reality can be described with a focus on universal aspects ("as they have always been") or concrete, historical aspects ("as they really were").[52] Social sciences must belong to individualising sciences because they are concerned with phenomena that are related to values, which makes them unique and irreducible to universal principles described in terms of general laws of nature. It does not mean that social scientists should evaluate their objects; it means that they should take into consideration the complex ways in which the relationship with the domain of values turns a particular object of study from a mere psychophysical unit into a unique element in the domain of culture.

A still different, and perhaps most influential, perspective on the methodological distinctiveness of the humanities and social sciences was proposed by Max Weber, the cofounder of modern sociology. The sociological method he advocated consisted in the interpretive understanding of human behaviours, that is, in the reconstruction of their subjective sense: the goals, aspirations, and motives of the agents. Thus, Weber's "understanding sociology" (*Verstehende Soziologie*) markedly differs from the natural sciences, where phenomena are described and explained, but not in terms of motivations and goals that underlie intentional acts. In the social sciences, the focus is on the recreation of the meaning and

---

51 Noras, *Historia...*, p. 479.

52 S. Schallon, "Zur Dedeutung Heinrich Rickerts 'Die Grenzen der Naturwissenschaftliche Begriffsbildung,'" in Schallon, *Rickert. Texte zur Praktischen Philosophie* (London: Turnshare, 2009), p. xviii.

"structures of sense" behind human actions. This, in turn, requires taking into consideration the context of culture in which they are embedded. On this view, facts form the basis for sociological understanding, but they are only the starting point for further processes of rational interpretation of the cultural meaning of social actions.[53]

Interestingly, according to Weber, history "pursues the causal analysis … of individual, culturally significant actions, structures and personalities," while sociology "seeks general rules about events," classifying various forms of behaviour to types. This makes it possible to formulate sociological "laws," that is generalisations based on "typical probabilities confirmed by observation," which are "both understandable and definite in the highest degree insofar as the typically observed point of action can be understood in terms of the purely rational pursuit of an end."[54]

Weber draws a clear distinction between the description of values which underlie a particular action, and evaluation of the action by the scientist. If the former is essential to humanities research (it is indispensable to understanding), the latter is unacceptable. The basic requirement for any true science, including the humanities and social sciences, is that it should be value-free (the doctrine of *Wertfreiheit* of science), that is, that the description and explanation of the object of study should be neutral with regard to subjective opinions of and evaluation by the scholar. The aim of science is to give an objective, unprejudiced, and value-free description of its object. This holds true also for cases where the object is a human action, that is where the analysis and interpretation must take into account the values which underlie it and which give it its cultural and social sense.

In this respect, there is no difference between the natural sciences and any other field of knowledge. A textbook of astronomy offers no room for ruptures over the beauty of the sky; similarly, sociologists (or any other scientists concerned with human behaviour), who are expected to accurately reconstruct the values relevant to concrete human actions, cannot voice their own opinions on the objects studied – at least as long as they approach them as scientists.[55] The aim is to arrive at understanding, not to acclaim or criticise. Scientists have the right to hold personal opinions and experience emotional reactions to what they describe, but in no way can they reveal them when they act as scientists; in

53 M. Weber, *Economy and Society*, ed. and trans. G. Roth and C. Wittich (New York: Bedminster, 1968).

54 Ibid., p. 18.

55 S. Andreski, *Max Weber's Insights and Errors* (London: Routledge & Kegan Paul, 1984).

particular, they cannot attempt to impose their value judgements ex cathedra, because then they misuse the authority of science to raise their subjective opinions to the status of "scientific truths."[56] This is difficult especially in the case of objects which easily stir emotions. However, the ability to keep apart the emotionless, unbiased description of facts and their evaluation is for Weber a major dividing line separating scientific from non-scientific statements.[57]

Despite the existing controversies over the concept of understanding sociology, the distinction between a methodology which aims at understanding culturally significant facts and that which aims at their mere description, combined with the idea of science as free from the scientist's value judgements, no doubt became an important element of the anti-naturalistic approach to the humanities and social sciences in the twentieth century.[58] It has also had a major impact on the methodological self-awareness of legal sciences, especially on positivist legal dogmatics, where it is still today an important point of reference.

56 M. Weber, "Science as Vocation," in *The Vocation Lectures*, trans. R. Livingstone, ed. D. Owen and T. Strong (Illinois: Hackett Books, 2004).

57 Andreski, *Max Weber's Insights….*

58 Ibid.

1 The methodological characteristics of legal sciences

Any discussion of the need and prospects to naturalise scientific thinking about law must start with formulating a possibly precise understanding of the object and nature of legal sciences. This preliminary issue, as I will argue, to a large extent determines the stance on the question of the practicability and validity of contemporary naturalisation appeals. At the same time, this task comprises problems which are anything but simple or unequivocal. Disputes regarding the essence and methodological assumptions of legal sciences have a long history, and views that can be regarded as commonly accepted and adopted are more than scarce. Thus, we have to start with the problem of the nature and kinds of scientific thinking about law. Only against this background will it be possible to draw some conclusions concerning whether, and to what extent, legal sciences can and should follow the contemporary naturalisation trends in methodology, which are increasingly embracing those areas of knowledge that so far have been regarded as the province of the humanities and systematic reflection on social and cultural phenomena.

The debate over the status and methodology of law as a science started in the nineteenth century. It was triggered by the eclipse of the speculative systems of natural law and their finest achievement, that is, the rationalist legal naturalism of Christian Wolff, inspired by the views of Gottfried Leibniz. The turn of the nineteenth century in Europe saw many deep-going changes in the intellectual and legal culture. On the one hand, it marked the beginning of the era of the codification of law, which resulted in the dominance of written statutory law. This, in turn, meant that lawyers had to focus more closely on the linguistic analysis and dogmatic interpretation of legal texts as the main method of learning law. On the other, the intellectual transformations that came with the Age of Reason severely undermined the confidence in universal systems and unalterable norms of natural law, all of which were based on metaphysical assumptions. David Hume's scepticism played a special role in this respect, as did theories – such as Giambattista Vico's and Montesquieu's – that shed light on the complex relationship between law and various social and cultural factors. Moreover, the beginning of the nineteenth century also saw the rise of a radical utilitarian philosophy, with Bentham's criticism of the very concept of natural rights and the related ideology, which he dubbed "nonsense upon stilts."[1] Finally, it was the time when various natural sciences gained autonomy, adding to the aspirations of law to become a separate, autonomous science, with its own object of study and appropriate research methods.

As a result, it was in the nineteenth century that the process of shaping the methodological framework for legal sciences gained impetus. In particular, the foundation and development of Friedrich Carl von Savigny's historical school and the emergence of positivist, systematic legal dogmatics made it possible to redefine their main objective as a possibly thorough analysis and scientific study of the norms of positive law that are in force in a particular place at a given time. Law started to be treated as a historical phenomenon, the content of which could be rationally reconstructed on the basis of appropriately organised empirical data, that is, laws and codes established by lawmakers and doctrines that evolved around them. In the decades that followed, legal sciences were turning to these sources of data with increasing frequency. Christopher Columbus Langdell, a famous reformer of American jurisprudence and for many years Dean of Harvard Law School, used the following metaphor to encapsulate this idea:

> the work done in the [Law] Library is what the scientific men call original investigation. The Library is to us what a laboratory is to the chemist or the physicist, and what the museum is to the naturalist.[2]

It is the task of the jurist to transform the raw material of law into a coherent, orderly, and understandable system of laws in force *hic et nunc*. This, in turn, requires careful exegesis of particular norms in order to disperse doubts concerning their validity, interpretation, or possible mutual conflicts and to establish relations obtaining between individual regulations, so that potential gaps or contradictions in the data which serve as the object of dogmatic legal analysis can be effectively solved.

This change in thinking laid the ground for the paradigm of legal science as we know it today, marked by positivism, idealism, and formalism. It is positivist in that it takes positive law as its main object of study: human-made laws and other regulations, together with the related judicature and doctrine. Thus, the findings of legal science must be based on empirical facts, that is, on the texts of

1 See J.M. Kelly, *A Short History of Western Legal Theory* (Oxford: Clarendon Press, 1992).

2 C. Langdell, "The Law Library," *49* Annual Reports of the *President* and *Treasurer* of *Harvard College 1873–74* (1875), pp. 63, 67, quoted in R. Danner, "Law Libraries and Laboratories: The Legacies of Langdell and his Metaphor," *Law Library Journal* 107:1 (2015), p. 8.

normative acts, rulings, and other sources of law which are recognised in a particular legal order, and on other relevant documents. For legal science, the object of analysis is, in principle, the content of laws established in concrete historical circumstances, which in that particular place and time formed a legal system.

The idealism of legal science concerns the ways in which it refers to concepts – such as being in effect, norm, legal system, source of law, legislator, legal relation, claim, or legal person – that denote ideal objects or abstract constructs, rather than empirical facts. These are the fundamental tools for the description of "legal reality," which is, in principle, based on obligation (that is, it states what follows from the binding laws) and for this reason does not have to tally with what particular persons actually do in real life. In other words, statements of legal science concern the norms, or models of behaviour that these norms impose, no matter whether or to what extent they are actually followed by people. Thus, what lies at the core of legal statements are not actual acts, but the content of norms that define the binding model of behaviour.

At the same time, the findings of legal science can be considered formalist in that the obligation they express is, in principle, only a restatement of the obligation expressed in law itself. It is the task of the scholar to reconstruct the models of behaviour that form the very content of norms established by the lawmaker (and not by the scholar). Their binding force (or normativity) follows from the fact that they are present – explicitly or implicitly – in the legal text by the lawmaker, regardless of personal opinions of the scholar, who might or might not find them acceptable.

Although the belief that the nineteenth-century jurisprudence of concepts was marked by extreme formalism is to a large extent a product of its later critics, it cannot be doubted that at that time, the task of legal science was primarily limited to formal operations which were to transform empirical legal material into a logical, coherent system based on an ordered network of concepts and an inventory of basic principles that held them together. This is the kind of system that enables legal reasoning and finding solutions in the existing law to cases which have not been directly and explicitly accounted for in the norms. However, another important task of legal science is to methodically develop the existing law, so that the gaps in the legal material are filled in a way which does not disturb the coherence and consistency of the legal system, making it possible to attribute to the lawmaker the solutions that follow from it.

The rise of jurisprudence as a science investigating the content of laws did not proceed without tensions. Fierce discussions were going on about almost all important aspects of nineteenth-century legal sciences, in particular, about the so-called Pandectist methods, the school of exegesis, Savigny's and Puchta's historicism, a radical turn in the views of Rudolf von Ihering and his method of weighing interests, and, finally, the ideas developed within the school of free law (*Freirechtsschule*). Still, the most heated debate was triggered by the radical criticism of the methodological foundations of legal sciences expressed by an outstanding Prussian jurist Julius von Kirchmann in a lecture *Die Wertlosigkeit der Jurisprudenz als Wissenschaft* (The worthlessness of jurisprudence as a body of knowledge).[3] In 1847, at a meeting of the Berlin Law Society, he gave a speech which resonated through German legal circles and which exposed him to years' long political harassment (including relegation to the position of vice-president of a local court of appeal in the town of Racibórz in Upper Silesia, at that time under Prussian administration).

In his speech, Kirchmann argued that no other discipline could boast so much aimless verbosity as legal literature. The object of study for jurists is a provisional, arbitrary, and often random decision of a particular lawmaker, transformed into a text of law which is binding at a given time. For this reason, jurisprudence is scientifically worthless. The "truths" it establishes and propagates turn into "untruths," and vice versa, in the blink of an eye, depending on the whimsy of the lawmaker. What is more, according to Kirchmann, scientific analyses of law are hostile to any advances in legal thought, as they strive to force new phenomena into the so-far applied schemata and categories. A prime example of this practice is the many-century-long tradition of referring to the institutions of Roman law in circumstances with which they are incompatible, in the reality of other times and places. In this way, legal sciences are carrying the burden of the past, unable to break themselves free from its powerful influence.

Legal decision, Kirchmann argues, are based not only in reason but also in the subjective sense of justice. This is what makes legal statements intrinsically different from those made by typical natural sciences, where the truth of a statement does not depend on the scientist's approval. An author who is concerned with legal considerations usually has some preconceptions concerning the validity of relevant claims even before undertaking a "scientific" inquiry into a particular legal problem or regulation. However, this subjective judgement of what is right is never the criterion of truth; rather, Kirchmann maintains, it is the product of upbringing, customs, temperament, and other, similarly contingent circumstances. Problems and findings of legal sciences are therefore servants of chance, coincidence which determines the content of law, and the subjective

3 J. von Kirchmann, *Die Wertlosigkeit der Jurisprudenz als Wissenschaft. Ein Vortrag gehalten in der Juristischen Gesellschaft zu Berlin* (Berlin, 1848).

judgement of the scholar whose statements are supposed to represent scientific legal knowledge.

In their treaties, monographs, commentaries, and exegeses, jurists focus on those fragments of positive law which pose problems or difficulties and turn out to be unclear or incomprehensible.

> Nur ein kleiner Teil davon hat das natürliche Recht zu seinem Gegenstand; neun Zehntel und mehr haben es nur mit den Lücken, Zweideutigkeiten, Widersprüchen, mit dem Unwahren, Veralteten, Willkürlichen der positiven Gesetze zu tun. Die Unkenntnis, die Nachlässigkeit, die Leidenschaft des Gesetzgebers ist ihr Objekt. Selbst das Genie weigert sich nicht, dem Unverstand zu dienen; zu dessen Rechtfertigung all seinen Witz, all seine Gelehrsamkeit aufzubieten. Die Juristen sind durch das positive Gesetz zu Würmern geworden, die nur vom faulen Holz leben; vom gesunden sich abwendend. Es ist nur das kranke, in dem sie nisten und weben.

The value of such efforts focusing on problematic issues of the text of law is negligible, because, as Kirchmann puts it, a few words of the lawmaker can turn whole law libraries into waste paper.

Although Kirchmann's arguments and his scathing tone were obviously products of his times, many of the methodological problems haunting legal sciences that he touched upon in his speech remain controversial after 150 years. At the same time, one cannot disagree with Karl Larenz, who, in a critical commentary to Kirchmann's lecture, points out that the role of jurisprudence and the function it serves for jurists and the legal system are more important than the considerations concerning its status as a science.[4] According to Larenz, the problem of the range of the term science is secondary, and if it were narrowed down to exclude jurisprudence, it would at the same time leave out other *Geisteswissenschaften*. Still, even if one accepts, after Larenz, that all rational efforts to obtain knowledge are scientific provided that they make use of appropriately developed methods of inquiry, well-suited to their objects, and effective mechanisms of controlling the results, the problem of jurisprudence as a science does not appear to be conclusively resolved.

Also today, major critical voices are raised that call into question the scientific value of the dominant paradigm of dogmatic juristic inquiries. For instance, over a century after Kirchmann, explicit criticism was expressed by Stanisław Ehrlich. Ehrlich refers to the views which describe dogmatic disciplines of jurisprudence as "science which explains and systematises applicable law:"

---

4 K. Larenz, *Über die Unentbehrlichkeit der Jurisprudenz als Wissenschaft* (Berlin: Walter de Gruyter & Co., 1966), p. 11.

> dogmatics is a strange science, limited as it is to explaining, commenting, and systematising… it is rash to treat as scientific a skill whose achievements can at any time be erased by a *nonscientific* intervention [original emphasis].… Legal dogmatics is neither a theoretical nor a practical science. It is not a science at all. It is a technical skill in handling legal texts. … What kind of "methods" does this science apply, a science which has limited its field arbitrarily and in advance to normative material, and its research method, to the principles of elementary logic, several interpretive rules that evolved centuries ago through practice, and efforts of so-called common sense. What poor tools these are! And they are sufficient to learn a certain technical skill which is available to any intelligent practitioner, any intelligent specialist. Of course, this kind of skill, which makes it possible to produce commentaries and textbooks, is socially useful. But appeals to usefulness… are not enough to legitimise science.[5]

Ehrlich's arguments elicited a polemical response from Jerzy Wróblewski. Wróblewski convincingly demonstrates that the criteria of scientific inquiry that Ehrlich implicitly applies are nebulous. He also argues that, while the appeal by Ehrlich for legal sciences to "penetrate deep into social processes" is by all means justified, statements about the actual working of law will never be able to replace statements which interpret, systematise, or validate, and which are the result of dogmatic legal considerations.

In time, recurring discussions over the methodological assumptions of legal sciences have considerably mitigated the criticism levelled against ascribing the status of science to particular legal disciplines. Still, they have not contributed much to working out a shared, commonly accepted view of the methodological canon of legal sciences or of jurisprudence as a kind of science.

This situation can be demonstrated by a brief survey of literature on the methodological aspects of legal studies. Irrespective of the existing differences of opinions, the authors often start from divergent assumptions about what a scientific reflection on law is and what constitutes its object. Even such fundamental aspects of jurisprudence as the object and findings that can be obtained from its study remain largely disputable. As a result, there are also major differences in the way the methodological foundations of legal sciences are defined.

In the majority of works, especially those by German authors, the terms juristic methodology (*Juristische Methodenlehre*) and methodology of legal science (*Methodenlehre der Rechtswissenschaft*) – used synonymously – refer to the presentation of problems in and ways of interpreting and applying law, as well as

5 S. Ehrlich, "Kilka uwag w sprawie metodologii nauk prawnych" [Comments on the Methodology of Legal Sciences], *Państwo i Prawo* [State and Law] 11 (1964), pp. 645f.

to the types of reasoning used in solving the difficulties connected with the legal qualification of acts.

In a classical text on the methodological underpinnings of legal science (later editions co-authored by Claus-Wilhelm Canaris), Karl Larenz includes the following main topics: the structure of the normative statement; problems in establishing facts to which a particular law is to be applied; types of interpretation of law and legal reasoning, which makes it possible to apply existing law to unregulated cases; and the construction of legal concepts, elements, and relations that form a legal system.[6] The authors explicitly define legal sciences as investigations into the validity and meaning of positive law.

According to Larenz and Canaris, legal science is normative in that it studies the norms of applicable law. However, its task is to describe these norms (that is, to explain their sense and the consequences that follow from them) rather than formulate norms that might compete with those established by the lawmaker. Still, the findings of legal science, unlike those of the natural sciences (*szientistischen Wissenschaften*), have a direct impact on the object described.[7] It is in this sense that legal science and law – its object – are not fully independent from each other, with the findings of legal science often contributing to the shaping of the content of law, that is, its object.

The object and findings of legal science are, in principle, relativised to a particular legal order, although they need not be limited to it, as, for instance, in comparative studies or in critical analyses of positive law solutions undertaken from a moral or sociotechnical perspective.[8] However, as pointed out by Larenz, the methods of legal science do not permit proposing better legal solutions; this is the province of legal policy, which is based on other sciences (psychology, biology, economics, medicine, empirical social research, and others).

A similar approach to the nature and scope of legal sciences is taken by Reinhold Zippelius. According to him, legal sciences comprise problems and methods of interpretation of law, including linguistic and non-linguistic arguments used to establish the sense of norms which belong to a particular system, issues related to the subsumption of a norm to facts and filling various gaps, as well as problems connected with the range of discretion (margin of decision) left by law to the subjects that apply it.[9] Law is, as Zippelius puts it, a rule of conduct

6 K. Larenz and R. Canaris, *Methodenlehre der Rechtwissenschaft* (Heidelberg–Berlin: Springer, 1992), passim.
7 Ibid., p. 82.
8 Ibid., p. 81.
9 R. Zippelius, *Juristische Methodenlehre* (München: Beck, 1994), passim.

"clothed in words."[10] This means that semantic methods as well as problems of interpretation and elimination of ambiguity from the language of law are of paramount importance to legal studies. At the same time, only those rules of conduct can form law which are appropriately "carried out," that is, those which stand a good chance of being put into practice. For this reason, the methodology of legal sciences must also take into account the problems of actualisation and transformation of legal texts into law in action.[11] Moreover, law as a rule of conduct also serves the administration of justice, which means that legal methodology should make provision for cases which are not regulated and which need to be resolved on the basis of the axiological assumptions of the system.[12]

In a similar vein, Hans-Martin Pawlowski identifies the methodology of legal sciences with the entirety of ways in which jurists resolve the problems of validation, interpretation, and systematisation of applicable law. Thus, legal methodology is an instrument of legal dogmatics, but unlike the latter, it does not refer to particular problems but to the ways of handling specific types of recurrent legal-dogmatic issues in various branches of law.[13]

A similar perspective is taken by Franz Bydlinski, an author of often-cited publications on this subject.[14] According to Bydlinski, the "proper" scope of legal sciences – in contrast to that of the history, sociology, or philosophy of law – involves legal-dogmatic efforts to understand and explain the content of norms which constitute various branches of law. In his view, methods of legal science should allow for finding rational and verifiable solutions to legal problems, that is, for establishing legal consequences of facts or types of facts. Both texts of regulations comprising a legal system and legally relevant facts are the raw material which legal science transforms – using the methods and tools it has developed – into appropriately justified legal statements (that is, solutions to legal problems).[15]

Bydlinski rejects two extreme positions on the nature of jurists' research activity in relation to the content of applicable law. On the one hand, he dismisses the formal-deductive model of legal thinking, where the role of the jurist is limited to logically correct reasoning, as a result of which ready solutions to

10 Ibid., p. 1.
11 Ibid., p. 7.
12 Ibid., pp. 8f and 58f.
13 H.M. Pawlowski, *Methodenlehre für Juristen. Theorie der Norm und des Gesetzes* (Heidelberg: C.F. Müller, 1999), p. 12.
14 F. Bydlinski, *Grundzüge der juristischen Methodenlehre* (Wien: UTB GmbH, 2012).
15 Ibid., p. 17.

particular cases are extracted from legal material. The belief that the system of law contains the only appropriate solution to each legal problem is, according to Bydlinski, not verifiable and thus meaningless, at least as long as the truth of this claim cannot be demonstrated beyond doubt.

On the other hand, he rejects the "realistic-nihilistic" view that decisions made to solve legal problems are in fact random and arbitrary. One cannot claim that the content of regulations does impose any limits on such resolutions. The fact that in particular circumstances there are arguments in favour of various decisions does not imply that those decisions are equally well supported. Actually, in most cases, arguments invoked to support one are weightier than others, making it possible to rationally choose the solution which is better justified than other potentially competing options.[16]

Similarly, Veronique Champeil-Despalts identifies the methodology of legal sciences primarily with the analysis of the language of law and the language about law, including interpretation and systematisation of legal regulations and arguments.[17] By contrast, Jan Smits, a Dutch legal scholar, distinguishes four types of research activities in the field of law: descriptive, normative, empirical, and theoretical. The descriptive approach consists in the doctrinal exposition and systematisation of applicable law, with its alternative models (that is, descriptive but non-doctrinal) including sociological, economic, historical, or comparatist descriptions of law. The empirical approach is very different in nature, focused as it is on the actual effects of law, while the theoretical approach seeks to explain what law is and in what ways it differs from other types of rules.[18]

In methodological terms, as Smits observes, the empirical approach to the study of law makes use of the methods of non-legal sciences, and theoretical investigations "tend to make use of the same methods and techniques of argumentation as the more positive fields of law" (combining them additionally with methods and findings of other fields of knowledge).[19] Although traditionally, the descriptive-doctrinal approach has played the leading role in legal sciences, Smits makes a case for a thoroughgoing revision in this respect, towards a sharper focus on normative challenges: the search for scientific answers to the

16 Ibid., p. 22.

17 V. Champeil-Desplats, *Methodologies du Droit et des Sciences du Droit* (Paris: Dalloz, 2014), passim.

18 J.M. Smits, *The Mind and Method of the Legal Academic* (Cheltenham–Northampton: Edward Elgar Publishing, 2012), pp. 9f.

19 Ibid., pp. 31, 34.

question about what the content of law ought to be like. This can be achieved using the "empirical-normative" method, where

> existing jurisdictions are treated as laboratories for dealing with conflicting normative positions. They show which arguments exist in favor of, and against, any particular solution, which arguments have prevailed elsewhere and how the result has been received in that jurisdiction.

Thus, legal solutions (both statutory and adjudicatory) introduced in various legal orders (including the home legal order) are not treated as binding models of conduct, but as material on the basis of which it is possible to evaluate arguments that speak for or against a particular normative decision. It is the object and the goal of a scientific study of law to weigh the arguments and to find the best solution. The view of legal science as a strictly normative discipline, which uses the empirical-normative method proposed by Smits and focuses on the search for appropriate decisions in dealing with concrete social problems, involves a radical departure from the so-far taken approach to jurisprudence, according to which undertaking efforts to find strictly normative solutions is not its main objective.

Some authors have emphasised the need to distinguish the methodology of legal dogmatics on the one hand, and the methodology of the general theory of law on the other, with the latter focused mainly on the study of law as a phenomenon. This distinction is important because the methodological characteristics of dogmatic approaches within various legal disciplines are largely shaped by the fact that

> we confine ourselves to solving the problems of interpretation and validation from the point of view of a particular legal system, accepting tacitly or explicitly its assumptions and treating them as axioms of our reasoning.[20]

It is the task of the jurist-dogmatist (but to a large extent also the lawyer-practitioner) to explain the decisions of the lawmaker by pointing out the intentions or goals behind them. In an attempt to provide a scientific description of law in the form it was given by the lawmaker, the scholar will strive

> to determine the meaning of norms and the relations between them and to describe their origin and social function, but he or she will also show preference for some judgements and norms rather than others.[21]

---

20 J. Kowalski, W. Lamentowicz, and P. Winczorek, *Teoria państwa i prawa* [Theory of State and Law] (Warszawa: PWN, 1986), p. 29.

21 Ibid., p. 31.

Legal-dogmatic conclusions drawn from such considerations unavoidably go beyond a neutral description of their object and become dependent, to some extent, on the subjective views and judgement of the scholar. Such interference, in turn, must be treated "a foreign body in the system of scientific statements."[22]

Still, the vast majority of statements that comprise the legal-dogmatic knowledge in various legal disciplines are objectively verifiable, and so they represent knowledge that can be regarded as scientific. Moreover, some non-relativised judgements and proposals put forward by scientists-dogmatists can be treated as hypotheses, to be verified – that is, confirmed or refuted – by future social practice connected with the operation of these regulations or legal institutions.[23]

According to these authors, law can be studied not only using dogmatic method, but also using system analysis and comparative methods. In the former case, the legal order is treated as a system composed of certain elements and the relations that obtain between them, which fulfils particular functions in the processing of input data and their transformation into output data.[24] Legal comparative research, in turn, is regarded as a separate method (and not merely "an exemplifying comparison") which is supposed to "construct theory both in the science of law and in the science of state," "discover the laws of and tendencies in the evolution of legal-political institutions," and "discover that which is cognitively most valuable, that is, the direction of changes and the law of changes."[25]

Apart from legal dogmatics, a general theory of law requires some other methodological planes.[26] Its multilevel nature – understood as the ontological complexity of law as an entity and the diversity of methods appropriate to study its different levels – is perhaps the most characteristic idea that emerged in the Polish philosophy of law in the twentieth century. Depending on the adopted approach, various authors distinguish such planes, or levels, as logical-linguistic, sociological, psychological, axiological, and, sometimes, historical and cybernetic (systemic).

On the logical-linguistic plane, a legal phenomenon is studied as a set of statements, primarily those by the lawmaker and included in texts of legal acts and other normative documents (that is, in the language of law).[27] According to Jerzy

22 Ibid.
23 Ibid., p. 40.
24 Ibid., pp. 35–37.
25 Ibid., p. 38.
26 Ibid., pp. 24f.
27 W. Lang, J. Wróblewski, K. Opałek, *Teoria państwa i prawa* [Theory of State and Law] (Warszawa: PWN, 1979), pp. 30f.

Wróblewski, methods typical of the logical-linguistic level of analysis include both formal logics (classical, deontic, and normative logics) and non-formal, descriptivist analysis of legal argumentation and reasoning.

On the sociological plane, an analysis of a legal phenomenon refers to observation, statistical analysis, surveys, and experimental studies. The psychological plane calls for methods that are considered reliable in the field of psychology, including introspection (adopted, for example, by Leon Pietrażycki) and experimental methods developed by behaviourist psychology (interesting attempts in this respect were undertaken by Underhill Moore, one of the foremost representatives of American Legal Realism) and other major directions of psychological studies.

With regard to the axiological plane, usually distinguished in the multilevel approaches to law, Wróblewski observes that without adopting strong assumptions of metaethical cognitivism, the study of law on this level must in fact be limited to the study of evaluative statements – by the lawmaker, subjects of law, or other participants in the legal order. For this reason, such analyses are usually based on logical-linguistic methods.

The idea of the multilevel nature of legal phenomena and its theoretical and methodological consequences were received with reserve by Zygmunt Ziembiński. In his opinion, true methodological differences are related neither to the number of legal disciplines nor to the division of a legal phenomenon into various levels, but to the types of problems that are dealt with in the study of law, which can be of a dogmatic, sociotechnical, or theoretical nature. Problems of each of the types appear – although with varied frequency – in real research practice of both dogmatists in various branches of law and scholars who are concerned with the general theory of law.

Solving dogmatic problems consists in reconstructing fragments of a legal system on the basis of the approach to sources of law it adopts and law-making facts. Reconstructing the norms of conduct refers here to establishing who and in what circumstances may, may not, or must behave in a particular way under binding law.[28] This is why, as Ziembiński points out, "a fully developed normative view of sources of law" must include not only validation rules which specify what acts are regarded as law-making in a given system, but also rules of legal exegesis (including interpretation, inference, and collision rules). Only if taken together can they be used to draw conclusions about the content of norms that

---

28 Z. Ziembiński, *Metodologiczne zagadnienia prawoznawstwa* [Methodological Issues of Jurisprudence (Warszawa: PWN, 1974), pp. 104f.

are binding under the studied system, thus making it possible to make relevant decisions concerning the legal qualification of different types of conduct.

In terms of the methodological approach to solving dogmatic problems, legal science belongs to the humanities. It shares with them the assumption that subjects whose behaviour and artefacts it studies and seeks to explain are rational. This is also the starting point for history, anthropology, and other cultural sciences (such as literary studies).[29] In all these disciplines, the rationality of actions that are to be explained is an idealising assumption which belongs to the "deep structure" of their methodologies, making it possible to ascribe certain intentions, beliefs, and goals to subjects whose actions form the empirical basis for further conclusions.

Founded on the assumption of the lawmaker's rationality, various branches of legal sciences aim at a reconstruction of an orderly, internally consistent system of norms, clear, complete, and free from conflicts, and at the same time well based in the coherent system of values ascribed to the lawmaker and in the known effects produced by the obligation, prohibition, or permission to act in a particular way. In this reconstruction, legal scholars refer to the entirety of facts which in a given legal order are considered as law-making.[30] In juristic practice, this process also allows for adaptive interpretation, which adjusts the content of law to concrete, current problems, ascribing such decisions to the intention of the lawmaker rather than the interpreter.[31]

From this perspective, as Wróblewski remarks, jurisprudence can be seen as necessarily normative insofar as it describes norms, that is, the content of models of conduct. However, its task is not normative with regard to establishing such models, although to some extent, legal science does evaluate and contribute to the formation of norms it aims to describe. The assumption of the lawmaker's rationality (accepted both by the jurist-dogmatist and by the jurist-practitioner) makes it possible to ascribe the results of interpretation directly to the lawmaker, where the lawmaker is a construct rather persons or institutions who are authors of the studied fragments of a legal text.[32]

---

29 L. Nowak, *Próba metodologicznej charakterystyki prawoznawstwa* [An Attempt at a Methodological Characterization of Jurisprudence] (Poznań: Uniwersytet im. Adama Mickiewicza, 1968), p. 74.

30 Ibid., p. 121.

31 As pointed out by L. Nowak, jurists who carry out institutionalised social roles in the process of application of law "pretend that the amendments they introduce to law are already included in it, and that the jurists' task is not to rectify law but to uncover 'its true meaning';" Nowak, *Próba*..., p. 73.

32 J. Wróblewski, W. Lang, S. Zawadzki, *Teoria państwa i prawa* [Theory of State and Law] (Warszawa: PWN, 1979), p. 32.

Apart from dogmatic problems (related to the content of law-making facts), legal sciences deal with sociotechnical and theoretical issues. The former comprise questions about the ways to achieve expected social goals through establishing and implementing law. They appear in legal dogmatics in particular when it is necessary to reduce the margin of decision left by law or to formulate proposals *de lege ferenda* on the basis of an analysis of current law. Theoretical problems, in turn, concern

> the formulation and resolution of statements which comprise the theoretical description of legal phenomena, analysed both from the formal, linguistic perspective (on the "logical-linguistic plane") and from the real-life, extralinguistic perspective (for example, on the "sociological," "psychological," or "economic plane").[33]

Dogmatic problems are the core of all branches of legal sciences. Sociotechnical problems are their natural extension, as they are connected with the search for the best possible shape of law in a specific legal domain, so that it can bring the effects intended by the lawmaker. However, legal sciences are by no means limited to dogmatic and sociotechnical issues; similarly, theoretical issues are not the exclusive domain of the general theory of law.[34] In practice, the range of problems addressed by particular branches of legal sciences includes also relevant theoretical issues, and the general theory of law does not ignore dogmatic and sociotechnical issues.[35]

Thus, the choice of research tools depends primarily on the type of problem that is to be solved, and not on the division into disciplines, which is, to some extent, conventional. Specific methodological challenges in various branches of legal sciences result rather from the relative prominence of various types of research problems they address. Thus, individual branches of legal sciences are dominated by dogmatic questions, the remaining issues being secondary and ancillary; in the general theory of law, the proportion is reversed. Although Ziembiński does not reject the concept of various "research planes" of legal studies, he considers it useful only for theoretical considerations and regards it as a primarily methodological tool. According to him,

> distinguishing between various research planes within the theoretical subject matter of jurisprudence is methodologically quite significant, as it helps to determine from which

---

33 Z. Ziembiński, *Szkice z metodologii szczegółowych nauk prawnych* [Sketches in the Methodology of Particular Legal Sciences] (Warszawa–Poznań: Polska Akademia Nauk, 1983), p. 7.

34 Ibid., p. 37.

35 Z. Ziembiński, in Z. Ziembiński, A. Redelbach, and S. Wronkowska, *Zarys teorii państwa i prawa* [An Outline of the Theory of State and Law] (Warszawa: PWN, 1993), pp. 17–19.

> sciences appropriate research methods can be borrowed and to consider what modifications should be introduced in the application of these methods to the theoretical problems addressed by legal sciences.[36]

At the same time, Ziembiński argues against increasing the number of such planes without necessity or attributing any ontological status to them; rather, he treats them as linguistic (formal) and real-life (sociological and psychological) *aspects* of a legal phenomenon.[37]

Still other assumptions are adopted by authors of a volume based on a symposium on the methodological diversity in legal studies.[38] Its aim is to "draw attention to the wide range of methodological problems and the need to adopt comprehensive approaches in their discussion." In particular, the authors recognise the need to oppose "the trend to apply methods which are currently in vogue," such as "the strong tendency to overestimate the sociological approach in legal sciences," "the practice to exaggerate logical-linguistic problems," and "the firmly established trend to treat the traditional dogmatic approach as the only legitimate approach to the study of law."[39] Among the methods of legal sciences, the authors distinguish and discuss the following approaches: historical, comparative, logical-linguistic, sociological, psychological, statistical, empirical, and cybernetic.[40]

One of the broadest overviews of the methodological issues in legal sciences has been proposed in one of the latest contributions to this field in the Polish literature by Jerzy Stelmach and Bartosz Brożek. The authors distinguish three main approaches to research methods in law.[41] The first consists in rejecting the view that there are any reliable methods used in legal sciences, as exemplified by Kirchmann, the most radical directions in legal realism (e.g., Joseph Hutcheson's intuitionism), the school of free law, or the movement of critical legal studies. The second – the heteronomous perspective – points to the fact

36 Ziembiński, *Metodologiczne zagadnienia…*, p. 80.

37 Ibid., p. 82; Ziembiński, in Ziembiński, Redelbach, Wronkowska, *Zarys…*, pp. 10–14.

38 *Metody badania prawa* [Methods of Studying Law], ed. A. Łopatka (Warszawa–Wrocław–Kraków–Gdańsk: Zakład Narodowy im. Ossolińskich, 1973).

39 A. Łopatka, "Wprowadzenie," in *Metody badania prawa…*, p. 7.

40 The historical approach in legal studies is discussed by H. Olszewski; the comparative approach, by M Rybicki; the logical-linguistic approach, by J. Wróblewski; the sociological and psychological approaches, by M. Borucka-Arctowa, statistical methods, by Z. Rogoziński; the empirical approach, by W. Sokolewicz and S. Zawadzki; and the cybernetic approach, by F. Studnicki.

41 J. Stelmach and B. Brożek, *Metody prawnicze* [Legal Methods] (Kraków: Zakamycze, 2004), pp. 11f.

that in their research practice, legal scholars use methods developed within other fields of knowledge. Examples of this approach include Petrażycki, the law and economics school of thought, and the analytic philosophy of law, which refers to hard and soft methods of language analysis. The third approach assumes that law relies on autonomous research methods, characteristic specifically of legal sciences. Stelmach and Brożek include here Savigny's historical school and representatives of the nineteenth-century *Begriffsjurisprudenz.*

According to Stelmach and Brożek, both methodological nihilism and the belief that there are autonomous research methods in law cannot be defended and must be rejected. Tools of legal sciences are adaptations of research methods developed within other fields of knowledge, adjusted to the specific needs of law. Thus, research practice in legal studies is marked by heteronomy and methodological pluralism, and the adaptation of various methods to law may serve the needs of jurists-practitioners, jurists-dogmatists, or jurists-theoreticians. At the same time, there is no hierarchy of methods used by legal scholars; moreover, decisions concerning the choice of method and its application are made ad hoc, often prompted merely by "habits" of individual interpreters.[42] Among research methods used in law, the authors enumerate logic (including the tools developed by non-classical logics, aspiring to the status of the logic of legal discourse), analysis (linguistic, economic, etc.), argumentation (discourse theory, topoi theory, new rhetoric, etc.), and hermeneutics (especially as an epistemological approach in the interpretation of texts, including legal texts).[43]

***

This brief and rather selective survey demonstrates the vast diversity in the approaches to the methodology of legal sciences and the lack of broad agreement on even the most fundamental issues concerning the nature of jurisprudence and the methods of solving problems it encounters. This situation hinders any effective discussion of the need to naturalise legal sciences and of the prospects and usefulness of reflection on law that refers to ontological and methodological assumptions of naturalism, as the findings obtained by legal scholars depend directly on the adopted understanding of jurisprudence, the type of problems that form the core of its object of study, and the research purposes.

For this reason, it seems necessary to introduce some clarifying distinctions within legal sciences and then, in their light, to identify major differences in the "naturalisation potential" that follow from two fundamentally incompatible

42 Ibid., p. 37.
43 Ibid., passim.

models of scientific reflection on law. This picture is further complicated by the variety of methodological approaches within each of the models; however, I will argue that this diversity is secondary in relation to the essential contrast between the view of jurisprudence as a legal science and as a science of law. Still, various methodological approaches proposed within these two views of jurisprudence also give rise to considerable differences in the validity of naturalisation appeals and in the possible scope of such naturalisation.

2 Legal science and the science of law

The brief survey of literature on the methodological assumptions of legal sciences presented in Chapter 1 reveals such an amount of diversity and controversy in this area that one cannot help but think that jurisprudence has not yet reached the stage of development commonly described as "bringing method to our madness." One of the principal causes of this situation is, I believe, underestimating a fundamental distinction that already appeared in the well-known dispute between Eugen Ehrlich and Hans Kelsen in the beginning of the twentieth century, and that later featured in various directions of twentieth-century juristic thought; a distinction which is of particular significance for the way the model, nature, and methodology of legal sciences are construed.

This distinction refers to the difference between a science determining the content of binding laws on the one hand, and a science of law understood as an empirical phenomenon and part of a certain cultural reality on the other (that is, as a certain complex social practice). In the former understanding of jurisprudence, research results in principle concern what acts are prohibited, obligatory, permitted, etc. according to applicable law.[1] In the latter, in turn, the results concern the origin and organisation of a particular legal order as well as its operation, including, especially, psychological and social processes connected with establishing, interpretation, application, and observance of regulations. These two research ventures differ essentially in their nature, goals, and function and in the methodology they adopt. In this sense, there is no one jurisprudence with its set of methods but two separate approaches to the study of law, each with its own characteristic tasks, methods, and problems. I will argue that they also differ fundamentally in their openness to possible calls for naturalisation, which are sometimes voiced with regard to the field of legal studies.

This methodological landscape of jurisprudence is further complicated by the fact that within these two basic models of legal sciences, there exist many competing (and partly complementary) methodological orientations. They indicate not only what, according to a given author, the "appropriate" way of understanding jurisprudence is, but also what its statements refer to and how they

---

1 For an outline (and an indication of an unmet need) of a comprehensive sociological description of a doctrinal study of law see C. Boulanger, The Comparative Sociology of Legal Doctrine: Thoughts on a Research Program. *German Law Journal, 21*(7) 2020, 1362–1377

are to be justified and verified. Descriptive considerations (or such that aim at a reconstruction of a model of jurisprudence within one of the two approaches) often intertwine with strictly normative observations, and in this respect, the methodological reflection on legal sciences shows no advance on the debates that were going on in twentieth-century general philosophy of science outlined above.

In the first, 1913 edition of the work that laid the foundations for the sociology of law, Eugen Ehrlich, one of the founders of the new field, observes:

> In jurisprudence… the distinction between the theoretical science of law (*Rechtswissenschaft*) and the practical science of law (*Rechtslehre*), i.e. practical juristic science, is being made only just now… This distinction… is the basis of an independent science of law, whose purpose is not to subserve practical ends but to serve pure knowledge, which is concerned not with words but with facts.[2]

Ehrlich strives to demonstrate that it is only through the emancipation of research-oriented studies of law and dissociation from the so far dominant dogmatic legal model of knowledge, accumulated for its immediate practical usability, that jurisprudence can finally rest on truly scientific foundations. This is the requirement that legal sciences must meet to recover from a methodological setback. Ehrlich argues, quoting Anton Menger, that compared to other sciences, the condition of jurisprudence resembles

> an out-of-the-way town in the provinces, where the discarded fashions of the metropolis are being worn as novelties.[3]

Limiting jurisprudence to practical knowledge of the content of applicable law produces deplorable results. It turns legal sciences into a field comparable to medicine without biological foundations or materials engineering focused on concrete problems but not equipped with appropriate materials science knowledge. The greatest advance legal dogmatics had ever made, Ehrlich argues, fell on the time when it turned to history, because the history of law was the only juristic discipline concerned with the scientific study of fragments of legal reality. However, the central discipline, legal dogmatics, remains predominantly practical and investigates law with a view to passing sentences, counselling, winning lawsuits, or preparing documents indispensable in legal transactions.

---

2 E. Ehrlich, *Fundamental Principles of the Sociology of Law*, trans. W. L. Moll (Cambridge, MA: Harvard University Press, 1936), pp. 3–4.

3 Ibid.

This deplorable condition of jurisprudence, Ehrlich continues, results from the fact that it is not based on a separate, autonomous science of law, a science whose objective is not immediate practical usability in legal practice but juristic basic research, aiming at understanding and explaining law as a special type of social phenomenon, together with its mechanisms and perceivable regularities. On this understanding, the main task of the science of law is not acquiring practical skills related to current legal practice but developing the knowledge of law as a value in itself, just as in any other basic science.[4] This is not to say that such knowledge cannot ultimately become a useful tool for improving reality, helping to solve specific problems more effectively. Still, its application remains an indirect, secondary result of an activity whose main objective – accumulating knowledge – stems primarily from the disinterested cognitive curiosity of scholars who study a particular field.

Limiting legal studies to practically oriented jurisprudence results in the lack of a clearly delimited scientific concept of law and, in consequence, of appropriate methods of its study. From the perspective of jurists in their social roles and their practice, what counts is the norm to which they refer in argumentation as judges, solicitors, or prosecutors. However, this kind of "lawyers' law" (*Juristenrecht*) not only does not do justice to the complexity of the matter but also misses its essence. The kernel of legal reality, Ehrlich claims, lies somewhere else. It rests in those social rules which actually give shape to specific legal relations, such as transactions of exchange, compensations, undertaking and continuing cooperation, and family relations.

According to Ehrlich, what is crucial for a scientifically appropriate understanding of the legal order is the concept of "living law" (*Lebendesrecht*), that is, a set of rules which shape human behaviour, develop naturally and spontaneously, and are obeyed. Living law should be distinguished from "decision norms" (*Entscheidungsnormen*), that is, rules of adjudication and processing of claims by state organs, which come into play when the natural operation of living law fails and appropriate institutions must interfere. Decision norms are indirect emanations of living law; however, their content is transformed into general, abstract laws expressed in linguistic formulas, which are then used in processing other cases. In this way, decision norms fossilise the ever-evolving rules of living law, inhibiting rather than facilitating the development of legal order.

For Ehrlich, the distinction between the social reality of living law, on the one hand, and abstract decision norms which were the focus of lawyers' law, on

4 Ibid., p. 7.

the other, was the starting point for a sociology of law. Only a sociology of law was able to provide a solid basis for applied knowledge about the ways in which legislation and legal practice can effectively influence social life and solve problems that arise there. However, distinguishing dogmatic studies of the content of law and its normative consequences from the more basic, knowledge-generating science of law as a social phenomenon appears much more fundamental and universal in nature, and indeed independent of the concept of living law or the sociologically oriented science of law that Ehrlich proposed. It points to a difference which should be acknowledged, as it influences the way in which the significance, objectives, and methods of the study of law are understood in various approaches to legal sciences.

Many of these approaches understand juristic knowledge as knowledge of the content of legal norms, which is prerequisite to ensuring that they are properly applied and obeyed and, hence, to ensuring that the legal order functions appropriately. Other approaches rest on the assumption that it is the task of a legal scholar to describe the way a legal order functions "from outside," that is, as seen by an observer who does not participate in or share the responsibility for the phenomena that he or she investigates. On this view, the science of law as a set of facts that comprise a particular legal order is external in relation to that order. This kind of description is made from a standpoint that might be poetically referred to as "with a cold apple in one's hand on a narrow chair with a view of the ant-hill and the clock's dial."[5]

The perspective assumed by this external *science of law* is radically different from that of *legal science*, which is itself part of a legal order, prepares the content of binding norms, and helps remove doubts concerning their interpretation and application. Statements of legal science are inherently aimed at influencing the operation of a legal order. They indicate how the currently binding norms are to be interpreted and in what way they are to determine the content of legal decisions that refer to them. By contrast, the perspective assumed by the science of law can be compared to an approach taken by a scholar who describes laws that are no longer in force (which may be the reason why, for Ehrlich, the model branch of scientific jurisprudence was the history of law) or laws of another country. Thus, in this case, the scholar is not a participant whose statements offer both a description of law and an indication of how it should be understood and applied within this system.

5 Z. Herbert, "Elegy of Fortinbras," trans. C. Miłosz, in E. George (ed.), *Contemporary East European Poetry: An Anthology* (Oxford: Oxford University Press, 1993), pp. 134–135.

The idea of distinguishing practical legal science from the knowledge-oriented science of law, introduced by Ehrlich, was taken up in a variety of forms by twentieth-century legal sciences.[6] Its principal variation was the development of the sociology and general theory of law, pursued as investigations into the very nature of the phenomenon and the key concepts which describe the legal order (e.g., norms, interpretation, sources, force, or legal system), irrespective of the concrete models of behaviour which it comprises at a particular place and time. In the analytic theory of law, the conceptual tool which may help capture this difference is the distinction between external and internal legal statements, proposed several decades after Ehrlich's death by Herbert L. A. Hart.

In one of the best-known passages of *The Concept of Law*, Hart points out that a social rule "affords an opportunity" for two very different types of assertions, made from the "external" or "internal" points of view. Hart explains the difference in the following way:

> it is possible to be concerned with the rules, either merely as an observer who does not accept them, or as a member of the group which accepts and uses them as guides to conduct.[7]

From the perspective of the participants in the legal order, that is, those who actually use the rules on an everyday basis as "guides to the conduct of social life, as the basis for claims, demands, admissions, criticism, or punishment," the description of the rules they accept does not have a purely cognitive value but establishes the reasons for their conduct (including the reason for "a hostile reaction" in situations when others violate the rules).

Seen from the external perspective, statements concerning social rules may be of two different kinds. Firstly, they may record certain behavioural regularities, that is, the behaviour of members of a group in response to a particular situation (e.g., stopping the car at a red light). This "extreme external point of view" allows for correlating reactions with particular circumstances. A social rule is here understood as a "regular" behaviour of members of a group in response to certain circumstances. However, this perspective

---

6 I do not refer here to Ehrlich's sociological legal thought in its entirety, in particular to his concept of *Lebendesrecht*, but to ideas which appeared in the twentieth century and proposed a scientific study of law as an empirical phenomenon, carried out from a non-dogmatic perspective. For more details on the vitality of Ehrlich's sociological legal thought, see in particular D. Nelken, "Ehrlich's Legacies: Back to the Future in the Sociology of Law?" in *Living Law. Reconsidering Eugen Ehrlich*, ed. M. Hertogh (Oxford: Hart Publishing, 2009), p. 237f.

7 H. L. A. Hart, *The Concept of Law*, 2nd ed. (Oxford: Clarendon Press, 1994), p. 86.

> does not give any account of the manner in which members of the group who accept the rules view their own regular behaviour … [the] description of their life cannot be in terms of rules at all, and so not in the terms of the rule-dependent notions of obligation and duty.[8]

The fact that the behaviour of members of a group coincides with a particular set of circumstances does not imply that there is any commonly accepted model of conduct which is the reason for this coincidence. Thus, an observer who adopts the extreme external point of view, limited to observable behaviour patterns, will necessarily miss an important dimension of the social life of the studied group.

> His view will be like the view of one who, having observed the working of a traffic signal in a busy street for some time, limits himself to saying that when the light turns red there is a high probability that the traffic will stop. He treats the light merely as a natural sign that people will behave in certain ways, as clouds are a sign that rain will come. In so doing he will miss out a whole dimension of the social life of those whom he is watching, since for them the red light is not merely a sign that others will stop: they look upon it as a signal for them to stop, and so a reason for stopping in conformity to rules which make stopping when the light is red a standard of behaviour and an obligation.[9]

Taking into account the internal aspect of social rules, then, requires going beyond the empirically observable correlations between certain circumstances and the occurrence of particular types of behaviour. It must also include the reasons for the recorded behaviour pattern, which may involve a rule that members of the group consider binding. If this is the case, the presence of a model of behaviour becomes the reason for the conduct of a member of the group and the basis for expectations towards and evaluation of other group members, who are also subject to the rule. At the same time, Hart observes that adopting the non-extreme external point of view should not be confused with the internal perspective. An external description is not made from the vantage point of a person who considers the rule binding (that is, for whom it is the reason for a particular type of behaviour); however, it is not limited to recoding observable behaviour regularities, since it "bring[s] into account the way in which the group regards its own behaviour" and "refer[s] to the internal aspect of rules seen from their internal point of view." According to Hart,

> the observer may, without accepting the rules himself, assert that the group accepts the rules, and thus may from outside refer to the way in which they are concerned with them from their internal point of view.[10]

---

8 Ibid.
9 Ibid.
10 Ibid.

The distinction introduced by Hart is indispensable and it continues to be regarded as one of the fundamental methodological assumptions of modern legal sciences. Nevertheless, the discussion that followed the publication of *The Concept of Law* suggests that it is not as clear-cut or obvious as it might seem at first glance. One of the first critical discussions of Hart's concept of the external and internal points of view appeared in a volume devoted to the juristic thought of H. L. A. Hart by Neil MacCormick.[11]

MacCormick notices, among others, that the internal point of view may take more than one form. On the one hand, it may imply complete internal acceptance of a rule. On the other, however, it may merely be limited to acknowledging that in view of the fact that other group members accept it, the rule is the binding model of behaviour for all the members, irrespective of the extent to which a particular individual respects the reasons why it is commonly accepted.[12] At the same time, MacCormick makes several pertinent comments on Hart's notion of the external point of view. In fact, what he considers as one of the most serious weaknesses of *The Concept of Law* is the rather cursory and superficial treatment of this concept.[13]

There is no doubt that the non-extreme external point of view is crucial for the approach to legal order that Hart himself referred to as "descriptive sociology." It requires that patterns of behaviour should be described in terms of social rules; hence, it must take into account the internal perspective participants in a legal order adopt towards them (that is, members of the group that accepts the rules as binding models of behaviour). As a result, a description of a legal order must involve "understanding" how its participants treat models of behaviour manifest in particular behavioural regularities. This approach implies a "hermeneutic" perspective. According to it, a description of behaviour patterns of social group members must include some cognitive elements of their own internal point of view (corresponding to what a given rule "means") and reconstruct (but not adopt) its volitional elements.[14]

MacCormick compares statements made from a hermeneutic point of view to statements about somebody's religious duties made by a person who knows and understands the duties imposed by the religion but is a non-believer.[15] The

11 N. MacCormick, *H. L. A. Hart* (London: Edward Arnold, 1981).
12 Ibid., pp. 34–35.
13 Ibid., p. 37.
14 Ibid., p. 38.
15 Ibid., p. 39.

statement "you ought to go to Mass today" is ambiguous, because it may be uttered from an internal or hermeneutic point of view. The difference consists in accepting this duty as the reason for one's own behaviour or, conversely, merely understanding why it is a valid reason for someone whose perspective is internal.

MacCormick observes that the non-extreme external point of view enables statements about both the fact that others accept certain rules and the fact that they have particular duties arising from this acceptance. In the latter case, the fact that the group members accept the rule is not explicitly stated, but remains a presupposition, like in statements uttered from the internal point of view by people who accept the rules as binding.[16]

The need to distinguish assertions which, in Hart's system, are neither typically internal nor external and have the form of normative statements made from the perspective of a set of rules not necessarily adopted by the speaker is also recognised by Joseph Raz. In his view, they form a category of "detached legal statements."[17] Detached legal statements state that in particular circumstances, a certain rule applies. At the same time, Raz emphasises that they do not state that anybody accepts the law or considers it valid. Such statements can be made regardless of whether or not such a person exists in real life.

Thus, detached normative statements are not empirical statements about psychosocial reality. At the same time, they are not internal statements in the sense of Hart, because they do not involve accepting the rules which are the source of rights and obligations as valid. Instead, they express certain normative consequences that, according to the speaker, follow from accepting particular norms as reasons for conduct (respecting them as binding). Hence, they are made from the point of view of a given system of norms, from the hypothetical perspective of a person who would accept them as reasons for his or her behaviour. For instance, an expert in a religious doctrine may utter a statement concerning the appropriate (in his or her view) understanding of duties that follow from the rules of this doctrine, without being its follower, that is, without accepting them as reasons for his or her conduct.

As a result, Raz distinguishes between three types of normative statements. Internal statements, asserting who and in what way should behave, are, in a sense, cases of using the rule one accepts as a criterion to evaluate and a tool to influence the behaviour of the addressee. External statements (including non-extreme external statements) refer to a person's behaviour, attitude, and

16 Ibid., p. 40.
17 J. Raz, *The Authority of Law* (Oxford: Clarendon Press, 1983).

normative beliefs. They describe psychosocial facts which form the empirical substratum for the practice of formulating and applying norms. Detached statements, in turn, do not belong to either of these categories, as they do not describe anybody's beliefs and do not refer to one's own commitment to a particular normative social practice which involves the use of norms (in order to establish that particular rights and duties apply).[18]

Raz observes that detached legal statements are typical tools of legal scholars (as long as they act as scholars, since if they act as judges, solicitors, or simply citizens who are subject to a given legal order, they make primarily internal statements). In this way, even anarchists may describe rights and obligations arising from a legal order that they do not accept. Moreover, such an account need not be confined to a description of the actual normative beliefs shared by their fellow citizens (that is, those who accept this order and who make internal statements based on it).

Also Hart, influenced by Raz and MacCormick, acknowledges the need to distinguish between statements about rules (or obligations that arise from them) made from the internal point of view and statements expressing a hermeneutic perspective, that is, normative statements that refer to rules in a detached way, made by a speaker who does not accept them as the reason for his or her behaviour. In a self-critical commentary on his (indeed misguided) polemic against Alf Ross's views, Hart observes that his argument rested on the assumption that internal statements about duties, obligations, or rights could only be juxtaposed with external statements, and that the latter could only be understood as pertaining to external facts, which would preclude any reference to concepts that express normative qualifications.

Hart corrects this simplification, introduced in an essay where he criticised Ross (published before *The Concept of Law* and the discussion that ensued), in the following way:

> But I wrongly wrote as if the normative vocabulary of 'ought,' 'must,' 'obligation,' 'duty' were only properly used in such internal statements. This is a mistake, because, of

---

18 For instance, a specialist in the Christian doctrine may claim (rightly or wrongly) that the obligation to accept refugees from Arab countries, irrespective of their faith, follows from the norms of the doctrine. In doing so, he or she does not claim that Christians indeed have such normative beliefs (in fact, he or she may criticise the unanimous beliefs of all the followers of the doctrine, who, in his or her opinion, are in error). Nor does he or she express acceptance of this norm, which would turn him or her into a believer and thus a participant in the religious social practice based on the norms of the Christian doctrine.

> course, such terms are quite properly used in other forms of statement, and particularly in lawyers' statements of legal obligations or duties describing the contents of a legal system (whether it be their own or an alien system) whose rules they themselves in no way endorse or accept as standards of behaviour.[19]

Although Hart noticed this problem in *The Concept of Law*, he admits ex post that the solution he proposed there, that is, the concepts of internal and external statements, was not fully satisfactory, in particular with regard to the non-extreme external point of view. From this perspective, Hart writes,

> lawyers report in normative form the contents of a law from the point of view of those who do accept its rules without themselves sharing that point of view. In terms of Raz's distinction, already mentioned, such statements of legal obligation: or duties are 'detached,' whereas the same statements made by those who accept the relevant rule are 'committed.' Of course those who make such 'detached' statements must understand the point of view of one who accepts the rule, and so their point of view might well be called 'hermeneutic.'[20]

To sum up, following Raz, MacCormick, and Hart, who sympathises with their arguments, it is possible to distinguish three main types of statements about rules: external, internal, and hermeneutic, which express obligation in a detached way. It is the last-mentioned category that serves as the basic tool for the description of norms of behaviour (which is, as Hart observes, one of the key methodological elements in Kelsen's pure theory of law).[21]

An interesting comment on Hart's concept of the internal point of view is made by Scott Shapiro.[22] While he regards it as Hart's greatest contribution to the theory of law, in his opinion, the concept is not understood properly. According to Shapiro, Hart's idea that the description of law should take into account the internal point of view of those who accept the rules as the reason for their behaviour actually opposes the theories that aim at establishing a close connection between the concept of law and legal sanctions (e.g., those proposed by John Austin or Hans Kelsen). In fact, Hart's intention is to demonstrate that the very functioning of law does not depend on the fear of predictable punishment but on the attitude that enables the internalisation of certain rules (in particular, those which come from legitimate sources). This is why a full recognition of the

19 H. L. A. Hart, *Essays in Jurisprudence and Philosophy* (Oxford: Clarendon Press, 1983), p. 14.

20 Ibid.

21 Ibid.

22 S. Shapiro, "What Is the Internal Point of View?," *Fordham Law Review* 75 (2004), pp. 1157f.

complexity of the relations between social rules and their internalisation, as well as between the internal point of view and the hermeneutic (and non-extreme external) description of these rules, is prerequisite to any scientifically acceptable semantics that could enable an undistorted description of a legal order.[23]

It is also worth pointing out that Hart's views to a large extent coincide with the views of Alf Ross, the foremost representative of Scandinavian legal realism, a similarity that Hart himself apparently underestimated. However, in contrast to Hart, Ross puts emphasis on the distinction between two approaches to the study of law which resemble the juxtaposition introduced half a century earlier by Eugen Ehrlich. Ross refers to them as the doctrinal study of law and the general science of law, respectively.

The doctrinal study of law consists of statements which reconstruct normative models of behaviour expressed in directives of a given legal system. Thus, according to Ross, it is in principle idiographic. It aims at a detailed and faithful description of the content of statements of duty which follow from the sources of law recognised in a given legal system (in accordance with the normative doctrine of the sources of law accepted in, or co-constituting, this system). Although Ross includes historical and comparative considerations into the broadly understood doctrinal study of law, its core is the reconstruction of desired patterns of behaviour which comprise the current legal system (for Ross, the doctrinal study of law in the strict sense of the term).

This approach to the study of law should be distinguished from the general science of law. Ross argues that, historically speaking, the general science of law comprises three main perspectives on its nature and the way in which it should be pursued. The first one identifies it principally with conceptual considerations on the very nature (or concept) of law. For Ross, a classical representative of this position is his first master and teacher Hans Kelsen. Another perspective on the general science of law is that of classical systems of natural law, which aimed at pointing out the objectives of law and the norms thanks to which these objectives were to be attained. Considerations conducted in this spirit can be referred to as the philosophy of law, or the search for the general idea of law. The third perspective comprises ideas proposed by sociology-oriented theories of law, which perceive it as a historically dynamic socio-cultural phenomenon. Ross includes here both the German historical school and pioneers of anthropology and sociology of law. However, he points out that in many cases, these proposals are not empirically based scientific theories of legal phenomena but "a political philosophy in

23 Ibid., pp. 1168–1169.

disguise." An empirically based and methodologically mature general science of law is still a research programme for the future; according to Ross, his version of the realistic theory of law has provided foundations for this programme.

A major difference between statements of the doctrinal study of law and the general science of law consists in that doctrinal statements assume, or, as Ross apparently believes, implicitly "include" statements about the validity of norms of a given legal system. By contrast, the aim of the general science of law is to explain the nature of this validity and to propose a general theory of the sources of law which are recognised in various legal systems (thus providing normative doctrines of the sources of law). Its object of study is then, to a large extent, whatever forms the basis for the doctrinal study of law and whatever the doctrinal study of law assumes as self-evident without scientific reflection.

A scientific explanation of the validity of law must be based on the description and analysis of facts. This is why the general science of law must assume a realistic perspective. It is interested in these norms of a legal order which in fact apply in practice, that is, which are manifest in the behaviour patterns of its participants (in particular, in courts' decisions). However, as Ross repeatedly emphasises, no legal studies can be limited to recording external, observable behaviour. Behaviour patterns are part of the practical operation of a legal order in that they result from particular inner experiences of its participants (that is, from taking into consideration in one's actions whatever one perceives as a legal obligation).

Only in this way is it possible to distinguish between behaviour patterns which are part of the reality of a legal order and patterns of behaviour which are only superficially similar to them (but are not subjectively related to mental representation of legal norms or the obligations that follow from them). A study of any rule-based practice must take into account, on the one hand, "the actual effectiveness of the rule which can be established by outside observation" and, on the other, "the way in which the rule is felt to be motivating, that is, socially binding."[24] This observation holds true both for legal norms and for all other systems or practices based on rules (e.g., the game of chess).

> A behaviouristic interpretation... achieves nothing. The changing behaviour of the judge can only be comprehended and predicted through ideological interpretation, that is, by means of the hypothesis of a certain ideology which animates the judge and motivates his actions.[25]

---

24 A. Ross, *On Law and Justice* (Clark, NJ: The Lawbook Exchange, 2004), p. 16.
25 Ibid., p. 37.

For Ross, the actual effectiveness of rules and their motivating psychological effects (the fact that they are experienced as binding) are "different sides of the same thing." The legal order is made of rules which are observed because, according to ideological assumptions of participants in the legal order (in particular, the judges), they are binding and should be obeyed and applied. Contrary to Hart's criticism, Ross does not reduce the internal aspect of rules to a purely emotional impulse. Actually, referring to the attitude of judges, which forms the basis for the social effectiveness of law, he points to a shared normative ideology motivating them to treat as binding rules that come from the sources of law recognised in a given legal order. The normative ideology is a coherent whole and involves both treating certain rules as "legally binding" and experiencing a relevant emotional reaction that motivates the subject to apply the rules in his or her actions. This is what makes decisions of judges and other law-applying officials consistent and predictable enough to function as the basis for a relatively coherent legal order (at least with regard to validation decisions and their consequences).

The normative doctrine of the sources of law varies according to a legal system (and changes throughout history). Thus, its reconstruction is a matter of facts, that is, establishing what kind of norms (of what origin) are actually perceived as binding and applied in the practice of a given legal system. Ross's views are in fact very similar to Hart's "rule of recognition." According to Hart, the rule of recognition also refers to a complex set of facts, namely, to a systematic practice by law-applying officials to rely on a certain set of criteria in order to establish whether a given rule is valid and, as a result, to look upon it from the internal point of view. Although Hart apparently ignored, or at least underestimated, this similarity, a direct comparison of his views with those expressed (somewhat earlier) by Ross leaves no room for doubt. The differences between them are of secondary importance in view of their general affinity in terms of what constitutes the core of the real legal order: the attitude of people who play a crucial role in the actual operation of law, which Ross refers to as "normative ideology" and Hart calls "the rule of recognition" (connected with his concept of the internal point of view).

In both cases, the attitudes comprise beliefs about the criteria a norm must satisfy to be considered as valid and the willingness to accept the norms that pass the criteria as valid and applicable. The beliefs about what characteristics make norms valid (in particular, their origin) are determined by the catalogue of the sources of law of a given system. Naturally, they are deeply entangled with various axiological and ethical-normative views as well as other metalegal assumptions that legitimise and give significance to the way law is construed and this particular understanding of law is applied.

At the same time, both for Hart and for Ross, the reconstruction of the rule of recognition or normative ideology (including, in particular, the doctrine of the sources of law) is an empirical issue. As Ross puts it, it must be established "how courts do in fact proceed to find norms on which their decisions are based."[26] Hart, in turn, points out that the rule of recognition manifests itself in the way in which courts, officials, citizens, and their legal advisors identify valid rules.[27] The two perspectives appear even more similar if one takes into consideration the reservations the authors make. Hart observes that it is crucial for the legal order that the rule of recognition be used by a relatively small group of "officials." At the same time, in his view, it is of secondary importance whether other participants in the legal order conform to legal norms because they accept the rule of recognition or merely out of fear of legal sanctions or other consequences of the violation of norms introduced by the officials as binding on the basis of adopted validation criteria. Ross, in turn, remarks that although for him the key element is normative ideology accepted by courts, he uses the term "court" as

> a comprehensive term for the authorities which combine to administer criminal prosecutions: police, prosecuting authority and courts.[28]

Thus, both for Ross and for Hart, empirical findings must refer to observable, relatively consistent patterns of behaviour of individuals who play crucial roles in the legal order. Legal order is constituted and organised in a particular way because of the beliefs and attitudes that underlie their actions. These beliefs and attitudes influence the way in which they identify and apply legal rules, so that they implement in practice accepted normative models. Interestingly, Ross and Hart (at least at a later stage, when he added the famous postscript to *The Concept of Law*) do not exclude the possibility of moral criteria interfering in those beliefs and attitudes. However, they both emphasise the need to keep apart legal validation criteria and subjective moral views of judges or other officials. Ross refers to this problem when he discusses the concept of legal consciousness, connected with the willingness to accept rules as binding because of their legal status rather

---

26 Ibid., p. 77.

27 Hart, *The Concept of Law*..., p. 116.

28 Ross, *On Law and Justice*..., p. 35, note 1. A major difference between the two approaches is, of course, the fact that for Ross, the sanction for breaking a law is of paramount importance, while Hart criticises and rejects this view of law.

than a moral imperative related to the models of behaviour than follow from them. This legalistic attitude is thus in principle formal and

> directed toward the institutions with recognition of their validity as such, irrespective of whether the demands in which they manifest themselves can be approved of morally right or just. Law is law, and law must be kept, people say, and they apply this maxim even to those cases where the demands of the law are in conflict with their ideas of right and justice.[29]

Moreover, and most importantly in the context of the present discussion, Hart was also wrong in his basic criticism of Alf Ross's views. Hart claimed that Ross ignored the difference between predictive statements concerning the validity of rules and other uses of language by the judge, who, in stating that the rule applies, does not express predictions about his or her own behaviour.[30]

Not every statement about the validity of norms, Hart argues, is a description of expected facts. For a judge, such statements point to the reason that justifies his or her decision in a given case. However, from Ross's discussion, it does not follow that each statement about the validity of rules must at the same time form a predictive hypothesis concerning future actions of the judge. Only statements formulated within the general science of law must meet this requirement, but it does not apply to legal practice (which is the object rather than an element of theories that explain the operation of law).

Also, it does not seem – although this remains a matter of controversy – that Ross's position necessarily leads to the conclusion that the only reasonable interpretation of statements about the validity of rules, formulated by the doctrinal study of law, must be treating them as empirical-predictive statements.[31] It appears that apart from predictions, this category of statements may also include expressions that merely attempt to describe the content of norms which apply in a given legal system. This description does not have to reconstruct the way in which such norms are understood in adjudicatory practice, but to *aim at* its development, criticism, and improvement. The decisions of judges are central to the description of a legal order from the perspective of the empirical science of law, but the doctrinal study of law may to a large extent influence these decisions (and hence the real shape of the legal order). To some degree, then, doctrinal

29 Ibid., p. 55.

30 Hart, *Essays in Jurisprudence…*, p. 165.

31 Nevertheless, Ross apparently endorsed this model of the doctrinal study of law; cf. K. Eliasz, *Realistyczna koncepcja prawa Alfa Rossa* [A Realistic Concept of Alf Ross's Law] (Warszawa: Wolters Kluwer, 2016), p. 51.

interpretative and validation findings may "mediate" between the activity of the lawmaker and the law-applying institutions (and this is what, in fact, happens).

Referring to Hart's terminology, one might argue that it is only within the general science of law that, to count as meaningful, statements about validity of rules must be treated as predictive-empirical external statement (although Ross explicitly rejects the extreme external point of view in favour of statements which take into account the subjective, psychological underpinnings of legal behaviour patterns). On this understanding, for legal science to develop, there must exist and function a legal order, with judges (and, perhaps, representatives of the legal doctrine) assuming the internal point of view on its rules and formulating relevant statements based on the acceptance of the rules as valid. The validity of these rules, in turn, follows from the criteria defined by the doctrine of the sources of law adopted in the particular legal system.

Ross's and Hart's approaches differ not so much in the essence as in the terminology and in radically different philosophical inspirations. Ross drew primarily from the logical positivism of the Vienna Circle and from Axel Hägerström, who developed similar ideas in Scandinavia. Hart, by contrast, was influenced by the Oxford philosophy of ordinary language and John L. Austin.[32] These differences, however, had no major impact on the very nature of the solutions proposed by the scholars with regard to some of the main problems they discussed. This conclusion stands in contrast to Hart's view that there were fundamental discrepancies between his positivist ideas and the version of Scandinavian legal realism developed by Ross.

On the basis of explorations by Ehrlich, Hart, Ross, and many other scholars, the following thesis can be proposed. Legal research can in principle be approached in two ways. The first aims at establishing the content of norms which are applicable in a legal system and, hence, at describing the obligations, rights, and other normative consequences which follow from them. This is the task of legal sciences which investigate particular branches of law and which comprise the doctrine, or dogmatics, of current law. In practice, there is no doubt that such investigations address a broader range of problems than establishing a set

32 For more detail, see N. Lacey, *A Life of H.L.A. Hart. The Nightmare and the Noble Dream* (Oxford: Oxford University Press, 2004), p. 142f, and J. Evald, *Alf Ross. A Life* (Copenhagen: DJØF Publishing, 2014), p. 89f. On Ross's positive and negative inspirations, see a comprehensive discussion in Eliasz, *Realistyczna koncepcja prawa…*, p. 14f.

of behaviour patterns which are prohibited, obligatory, or permitted in the light of valid legal norms.

Investigations of this kind address historical problems connected with specific regulations and legal institutions, conduct comparative analyses, and are involved in critical and postulative reflection on the content of rules. They consider various sociotechnical factors, problems of correctness, clarity, or legislative precision, consistency with other norms of the system, and the axiology that underlies them. These are, however, secondary issues, auxiliary with respect to the core of such investigations, which involve validation, interpretative, and systematising efforts, serving knowledge generation and providing a direct foundation for legal practice (in terms of both education of lawyers and support in dealing with practical legal problems within a given branch of law).

The intellectual activities of scholars who analyse legal material in dogmatic legal terms are governed by certain methodological criteria which limit the randomness of the results and allow for their relatively objective verification by the community of specialists in a particular branch of law. Thanks to this procedure, such activities can legitimately be called scientific (which is not to say that the criteria are satisfied, or even respected, in every individual case; this reservation, however, seems to apply to all scientific disciplines). For the sake of clarity, we will refer to this approach to the study of law as *legal science*.

As a rule, legal science is practiced within a particular normative doctrine of the sources of law adopted in a given legal order, together with the rules of exegesis (that is, the "fully developed" conception of the sources of law, as Ziembiński calls it). Seen in this light, its findings, in principle, have the status of internal statements sensu Hart, or detached normative statements, which point out that in view of the content of particular norms, certain behaviour patterns should be regarded as prohibited, obligatory, or permitted. Their task is to *describe* the content of valid norms or to formulate directives or judgements relativised to this content.

Focused on dogmatic legal issues (but not limited to them), legal science addresses a variety of questions and problems connected with establishing what behaviour patterns are obligatory, prohibited, or permitted by the applicable law. These comprise validation considerations, including problems of mutual relations between legal regulations, diverse rules, and other than positive models of behaviour, if they are regarded as normatively relevant in a given legal order (usually this is the case with various basic legal rules, general intertemporal rules, etc.).

Apart from validation problems, central to legal science are interpretative issues, both related to the exegesis of phrases and words used in a legal text and to the conclusions drawn from it by reasoning *per analogiam*, hence, by referring to instrumental relations (a process often referred to as *Rechtsfortbildung*).[33]

Closely related to these problems are studies into various circumstances (e.g., legislation materials) which may be indicative of the "real intention" of the lawmaker and into their role in the validation and interpretative processes. There is also a close association with *de lege ferenda* considerations, related both to the axiological evaluation of this intention and to the choice of measures to ensure that it is carried out in an optimum way. Thus, although legal science seeks answers to questions about the *understanding* of legal texts and the effects their understanding has on the evaluation of actions undertaken by participants in the legal order, it is – like the science of law – to an important extent empirical in nature.[34]

In fact, addressing the question "What does law say?" consists in the search for the best possible explanation of facts (empirical data), which comprise, first and foremost, actions (especially statements) by the lawmaker. To a large extent, it involves an attempt to explain the meaning of actions undertaken by subjects who are the source of texts that contain legal norms, that is, to establish *why* the lawmakers acted in the way they did, *why* they used these words and not others, *why* at this point in the text and not elsewhere, etc. From this perspective, one cannot but agree with the view that the interpretation of laws – which is at the heart of legal science – ultimately consists in uncovering the intention of the lawmakers (in other words, it aims to explain why, or with what goal in mind, they made particular statements or acted in a particular way).[35]

Thus understood, legal science can be juxtaposed with studies of a very different nature, which focus on the legal order construed as a real phenomenon. From this perspective, what must be described and understood are behaviour patterns of participants in this order (both officials and other addressees and users of law), together with the beliefs that underlie their behaviour, decisions

---

33 For the role that may and should be played in such exegesis by a reference to a broader theoretical, in particular – conceptual, framework produced by a doctrine of a given domain of a law see A. Somek, *The indelible science of law*, International Journal of Constitutional Law, 7 (2009), 424–41;

34 That is why a normative approach to legal science seems to require much broader interdisciplinarity than the approach limited to reporting the content of valid legal rules to ascertain legal reasons for action (on that see A. Stark, Interdisziplinarität der Rechtsdogmatik, Mohr Siebeck, Tübingen 2020).

35 For more detail, see a comprehensive discussion in Z. Tobor, *W poszukiwaniu intencji prawodawcy* [The Search for the Legislator's Intentions] (Warszawa: Lex a Wolters Kluwer, 2013).

made as a result of these beliefs, communicative acts, and the ways in which they make use of the whole array of relevant cultural artifacts. What is at stake is not (or, perhaps, not only) idiographic description of these patterns but an attempt to identify and explain the psychological and social regularities which determine the ways in which they are formed, their evolution, and their mutual relations. On this understanding, the reality of a legal order is a fragment of the social life. To understand it, one must take into account complex sets of facts and processes which are at play both at the social level and at the level of individual psychology, together with the underlying evolutionary and biological resources of the human mind as well as cultural and historical contexts of particular situations and social systems.

To distinguish between the two approaches to legal research, the efforts to explain the interdependencies and mechanisms that together comprise an empirical legal phenomenon can be seen as the province of the *science of law* rather than legal science. In contrast to legal dogmatics, which focuses on the interpretation of texts and actions in relation to certain norms and goals, the science of law seeks to explain the mechanisms that underlie the formation and operation of law as a certain complex set of facts. For the science of law, legal science is an element of the real legal order, since the shape of the legal order is influenced by what is said, written, and done by legal science researchers who participate in the practical legal discourse by formulating views concerning how law should be understood by those who apply it.

The goal of the science of law is to describe and explain empirical aspects of the operation of a legal order in their entirety. It seeks to give a possibly complete account of the factors that make participants in the legal order behave – in legal contexts – in the way they do. This includes both the effect law has on human behaviour, that is, the reactions and decisions of those to whom a legal statement is addressed, and mechanisms underlying the actions of those who evaluate and apply law, that is, mechanisms which are constitutive of law and its operation.

Thus, ultimately, the science of law also aims at an explanation of behaviour patterns, but it looks into them primarily in terms of their causes and effects, not in terms of objectives, intentions, or meanings. Still, a considerable proportion of such patterns involve intentional behaviour (they aim to express a will) and elicit reactions from others who recognise the meaning they express. This is why subjective aspects of actions undertaken by participants in the legal order are also an object of immediate interest for the empirically oriented science of law. They are, however, merely elements of the whole, offering a better insight into how certain beliefs and views lead to behaviours which, because of the way people interpret them, evoke particular reactions from others. These complex relations form a real picture of the operating legal order.

Hence, the science of law comprises both sociolegal issues and problems of the psychology of law: creation, interpretation, application, and observance of legal norms. It also addresses issues connected with the genealogy of law as a special type of social practice, including the biological-evolutionary and cultural-historical mechanisms that predispose the human mind to create and apply normative categories in a way that leads to the formation of a social legal reality and its diversification.[36] At its core lie phenomena and processes that form the social ontology of the legal order, endowing "raw" natural facts with additional conventional or institutional meanings. It is thanks to them that the legal reality becomes a domain of symbolic thought and communication, making it possible for individuals to be creative and to move around in a maze of complicated and interdependent norms.

Thus understood, the science of law is necessarily interdisciplinary in nature, combining reflection and instruments characteristic of such fields as sociology, psychology, neurobiology, anthropology, cultural studies, history, etc. Its elements originate from (at least apparently) very different disciplines and areas of research. It comprises such diverse lines of thought as research by sociologists of law into the behaviour of judges,[37] legal awareness,[38] or Ehrlich's living law,[39] psychological-legal models proposed by Petrażycki,[40] Wojciech Załuski's evolutionary philosophy of law,[41] the theory of institutional facts as the structure of social reality developed by John Searle,[42] and

---

36 For more detail, see, e.g., W. Załuski, *Ewolucyjna filozofia prawa* [The Evolutionary Philosophy of Law] (Kraków: Wolters Kluwer, 2009); B. Brożek *Normatywność prawa* [Normativity of the Law] (Warszawa: Wolters Kluwer, 2012); J. Stelmach, B. Brożek, and A. Brożek *Fenomen normatywności* [The Phenomenon of Normativity] (Kraków: Copernicus Center Press, 2013).

37 E.g., L. Baum, *The Puzzle of Judicial Behavior* (Ann Arbor: University of Michigan Press, 1998).

38 M. Borucka-Arctowa, *Świadomość prawna a planowe zmiany społeczne* [Legal Awareness and Planned Social Change] (Wrocław: Zakład Narodowy im. Ossolińskich, 1981).

39 E. Ehrlich, "Die Erforschung das Lebendes Rechts," in Ehrlich, *Recht und Leben. Gesammelte Schriften zur Rechtstatsachenforschung und zur Freirechtslehre*, ed. M. Rehbinder (Berlin: Duncker & Humblot, 1967).

40 L. Petrażycki, *O pobudkach postępowania i istocie moralności i prawa* [On the Motives of Conduct and the Nature of Morality and Law] (Warszawa: Oficyna Naukowa, 2002).

41 Załuski, *Ewolucyjna filozofia prawa…*, passim.

42 J. Searle, *Making the Social World. The Structure of Human Civilisation* (Oxford: Oxford University Press, 2010; see also N. MacCormick, *Institutions of Law* (Oxford: Oxford

investigations into the legal order of the Trobriand tribes carried out by Bronisław Malinowski.[43]

Such a broad scope of reflection on law – both within legal science and within the science of law – is certainly an idealisation. A complete description of the legal order – a reconstruction of all behaviour patterns which are obligatory, prohibited, and permitted – is virtually impossible to achieve. What is possible to produce (and assimilate) are only more or less temporary and accurate reconstructions of parts of the valid legal system. In view of that, it seems more than unlikely that a complete empirical theory of the legal order as a social practice will ever be proposed. A theory of this kind can only comprise a more or less developed network of fragmentary hypotheses, concepts, and explanations offered by particular subdisciplines investigating selected aspects of the legal phenomenon.[44] Although these fragments are parts of the same complex whole, and it should be possible, in theory at least, to put them all together, one cannot expect that they will, in fact, ever be combined to form what could be dubbed a "legal version of a theory of everything." As in any other discipline, the "chain of truths" that Jean d'Alembert referred to two centuries ago is "broken in a thousand places" and will remain so for a long time, perhaps forever.

***

From the methodological point of view, it is therefore crucial to distinguish between two basic models of jurisprudence: legal science and the science of law. Each of them is further diversified, with individual disciplines differing in the object of study and in the research methods used for its study. In the study of law, external statements are of fundamental importance. They concern external behaviours and specific cause-effect regularities between them, together with the underlying experiences and psychological processes (which demand the non-extreme external point of view).

University Press, 2007); K. Lagerspetz, *The Opposite Mirrors. An Essay on the Conventionalist Theory of Institutions* (Dordrecht: Kluwer Academic Publishers, 1995).

43 B. Malinowski, *Zwyczaj i zbrodnia w społeczności dzikich. Życie seksualne dzikich* [Crime and Custom in Savage Society. The Sexual Life of Savages] (Warszawa: PWN,1984).

44 Examples of such considerations include my hypotheses concerning the place, role, and mechanisms of intuitive psychological processes in law application decisions, in particular, partial interpretive decisions, evidence decisions, etc.; for more detail, see T. Pietrzykowski, *Intuicja prawnicza. W stronę zewnętrznej integracji teorii prawa* [Legal Intuition. Toward an External Integration of Legal Theory] (Warszawa: Difin, 2012).

Such external statements may also lead to directives which, referring to the established cause-effect regularities, indicate what course of action (e.g., with respect to law-making or the application of law) will be effective or ineffective in view of the planned goals. However, as a result of the complexity of the processes involved and of the fact that human behaviour and decision-making patterns are of necessity statistically generalised, this "scientific policy of law" remains a remote theoretical construct rather than a practically useful area of applied knowledge.

By contrast, in legal science, of primary importance are detached hermeneutic statements and internal statements about the validity and content of norms of a legal system, as well as the normative consequences that follow from them. Apart from such statements, legal science offers a wide variety of proposals, in particular with reference to desirable changes in the content or formulation of norms of a given system and to the amendment or removal of particular regulations.

Moreover, legal science and the science of law differ in their social function. The former, in fact, co-constitutes the legal order it describes. Its cognitive goals serve other goals as well, so that law can be made, understood, and applied in the way in should be according to a particular scholar. Describing the content of law often involves a search for the optimum way of reading it, that is, one which makes it as consistent and orderly as possible and best suited to furthering the values to which it is committed. At least some peculiarities of the methodology of legal science are directly connected to this double role of decisions that are made within its framework.[45] The "doctrinal resolutions" concerning instances of vagueness, doubts, or problems not explicitly regulated by laws frequently become elements of the *corpus iuris*, on a par with regulations introduced directly by the lawmaker (a prime example being the role of constitutional adjudication and doctrine in relation to the "bare" laws of constitution). In this sense, dogmatic analysis of law contributes to the positivisation of law.[46] Thus understood, the practical role of legal science is not less important than the cognitive goals it achieves.[47]

The science of law, in turn, has purely cognitive goals and does not aspire to influence the ways in which law is interpreted and applied. It is not part of the

---

45 Cf. L. Nowak, *Próba metodologicznej charakterystyki prawoznawstwa* [An Attempt at a Methodological Characterization of Jurisprudence] (Poznań: Uniwersytet im. Adama Mickiewicza, 1968), pp. 180–182.

46 For more detail, see J. Leszczyński, *Pozytywizacja prawa w dyskursie dogmatycznym* [Positivization of Law in Dogmatic Discourse] (Kraków: Universitas, 2010), passim.

47 See, e.g., F. Bydlinski, *Grundzüge der juristischen Methodenlehre* (Wien: UTB GmbH, 2012), p. 17.

legal order; rather, it offers its external description from the point of view of an observer. Unlike legal science, it is not expected to provide support in everyday legal practice. Instead, it aims to understand why the legal order exists, how it operates, what functions it fulfils, and what facts it comprises.

A possible practical application of these findings (in the construction of what Petrażycki, Ross, and other scholars referred to as the "scientific policy of law") is not the main objective of the science of law. It is a basic science, whose results may serve as the basis for adaptation by applied science. However, to make this kind of transfer possible, we need sufficiently developed, consolidated, and accurate knowledge of the processes that shape legal reality and of the cause-effect relations that it comprises. Otherwise, any attempts to translate its findings into practical directives will be premature and, hence, ineffective, or will produce unplanned effects.[48]

The mutual relations between legal science and the science of law seem complementary rather than competitive. The approaches also have much to offer to each other. Legal science co-constitutes the actual shape of the legal order and, hence, is part of the object of study of the science of law. The science of law, in turn, is the source of knowledge of the mechanisms and conditions that underlie the legal order, which may play a role in the validation and interpretative decisions made by legal science. In this way, each type of legal reflection complements the other, without aspiring to replace or eliminate it as a "dispensable" or "unscientific" form of jurisprudence.[49]

---

48 As an example, one may invoke research into the role and mechanisms of intuition in legal decision-making; in this case, an attempt to draw practical conclusions for the conditions and ways in which such decisions are made would seem premature. For more detail, see T. Pietrzykowski, *Intuicja...*, pp. 277–278.

49 A. Ross, *On Law...*, p. 20.

3 Legal science

On the basic level, the nature and tasks of legal science no longer seem to be a matter of major controversy. The long-term discussion on the character and status of legal dogmatics has produced a certain degree of consensus; however, it has not put an end to methodological disputes which are still pending and which concern the object, role, and methods of legal science.

The core of the contemporary model of legal dogmatics dates back to the nineteenth-century processes of codification of western legal orders and philosophical-legal developments that accompanied them (such as positivism and formal-dogmatic approach). They underwent a thorough revision in the twentieth century as a result of the turn towards the fundamental legal principles and basic rights of individuals, whose status and role were brought back into focus (if not necessarily directly or fully positivised). This has led to the emergence of a modestly positivist (or, at least, text-centred) paradigm of dogmatics, concerned primarily with the analysis and systematisation of the rules of statutory and adjudicatory law. Dogmatics elaborates the concepts of particular branches of law, defines their institutions and major types of legal constructions that they adopt, and identifies their basic principles and the interpretative consequences that follow from them. Moreover, in the course of time, it increasingly often addresses problems of the operation of law and undertakes criticism of solutions adopted by the lawmaker, combined with considerations *de lege ferenda*.[1]

The findings of legal science are based on the idea of law as a system consisting of norms which are expressed or implicitly present in legal texts and in legal practice that develops on their basis (specifically, in judicial practice). Such norms may vary in nature, but they form a system which is *ex hypothesi* non-contradictory and complete and which provides a footing for decisions concerning the legal consequences (or lack thereof) of each possible state of affairs (or any possible act). A reconstruction of this system requires validation and interpretative data in order to make the legally binding norms more precise, as well as systematisation in order to bring to light the relations obtaining between various norms of the system.

---

1 J. Wróblewski, "Paradygmat dogmatyki prawa a prawoznawstwo" [The Paradigm of Legal Dogma and Jurisprudence], in Wróblewski, *Pisma wybrane* [Selected Works], ed. M. Zirk-Sadowski and T. Bekrycht (Warszawa: Wolters Kluwer, 2005), pp. 43–44.

As noticed by Jerzy Wróblewski, according to the present paradigm of legal dogmatics, all these efforts are cognitive rather than creative in nature. Legal science is to aim at a reconstruction of the actual organisation and content of the legal system, which is treated as an entity independent of the research activities of which it is an object.[2] This does not mean, of course, that such activities can be described by an algorithm. On the contrary, they are deeply entangled with axiological, ideological, and situational factors, as a result of which the same legal problems can be resolved in different ways by different scholars, who may propose mutually exclusive "scientific" descriptions of the same fragments of a legal system.

In spite of the general consensus regarding the fundamentals of legal science as it is construed and practiced by legal scholars today, the details of its methodology provoke serious controversies, giving rise to various models of scientific study of law. The differences between these models refer to both tasks and methods regarded as appropriate to solve properly formulated problems of legal science.

3.1 The descriptive model

Perhaps the most classic and consistent model of jurisprudence in this understanding of the term is Kelsen's "pure theory of law" (*Reine Rechtslehre*). It takes as the point of departure the need to "purify" legal science of whatever, according to Kelsen, is "alien" to it. The claim of purity applies both to the object and method of legal science and to non-scientific ideological elements, which should be eliminated. Thus, for Kelsen, purification refers to the scientific nature of jurisprudence ("pure" science) and to its exclusive focus on the appropriate object of study (science investigating "pure" law).

Thus understood, legal science is to study the system of laws which comprises valid norms. The validity of a norm is determined by the norm-setting competence underlying its institution, which follows from another norm that is already part of the system (hence, it is valid). This refers both to abstract general norms (laws which follow from the constitution and secondary legislation based on the laws) and to individual concrete norms (judgements in individual cases, based on general norms).

2 Ibid., pp. 47–48.

Thus, the only object of legal science is norms that fulfil the so-defined criterion of validity. They belong to a legal system whose validity (and social effectiveness) depends ultimately on the "basic norm," a metalegal (transcendental) assumption without which it is impossible to treat legal material as a system of valid norms (hence, a system of norms which give rise to legal obligations). Norms which are not legally valid (that is, have not been introduced on the basis of the norm-setting competence that follows from other legal norms) are outside the scope of legal science.

According to Kelsen, a legal norm consists in *imputation* (*Zurechnung*) of effects to a particular situation. It is the task of legal science to reconstruct the content of legal norms, that is, to establish what consequences are imputed to what circumstances. Imputation combines events that should occur with circumstances in which their occurrence is a matter of legal obligation. Thus, in the domain of obligation (*Sollen*), it is a normative counterpart of what is referred to as cause-effect relationships in the domain of being (*Sein*). The latter are studied by empirical sciences, which aim at establishing relations between facts: causes and effects. By contrast, legal science is concerned with relations that occur as a result of regulation. They follow from norms whose validity turns effects into obligatory consequences of particular circumstances.

Thus, in Kelsen's view, there is a fundamental difference between legal science and sciences which describe actual behaviour (including a sociological description of the legal order). The findings of legal science do not depend on whether or not individuals behave in accordance with the obligation that follows from the norm. Their actual behaviour is important for the practical operation of the legal order (it gives rise to specific obligations imputed to particular behaviours). However, it is meaningless for legal science, which seeks to explain in what circumstances what kinds of behaviour *ought to* occur, irrespective of whether or not they actually take place. In other words, the findings of legal science comprise statements about relations obtaining as a result of imputation. The practical operation of a particular norm, in turn, falls within the scope of other disciplines (e.g., sociology of law, criminology, psychology, etc.), which study cause-effect relations between facts rather than relations arising as a result of obligation.

For legal scholars, the object of study (the legal system) comprises a set of legally binding imputations. It is their task to provide its thorough and detailed description, reconstructing the relations between hypothetical facts on the one hand, and facts which *ought to* arise as their consequence. As a result, the claims of legal science (rules of law, or *Rechtssätze*) are, as Kelsen puts it, "hypothetical judgments,"[3] as they determine what, according to valid legal norms, ought to follow if a given hypothetical fact did take place.

Most importantly, however, a jurisprudential description is limited to existing imputations, that is, to the links actually established between facts and circumstances by valid norms. It is not its task to argue what facts *ought to* be linked with what circumstances. In this sense, legal science merely describes the obligations imposed by the lawmaker; it does not formulate recommendations, suggestions, or demands, which fall within the scope of the policy of law and ultimately depend on subjective judgements of those who make a case for or against particular imputations. This is why, such recommendations cannot be treated as objective, scientifically verifiable cognitive statements, but as preferences rooted in accepted values. It is these preferences that enable making choices and undertaking decisions, which are acts of will and not acts of knowledge. By contrast, for jurisprudence to be scientific, it must remain a "pure science." Thus, it must be descriptive and objective (independent of the individual preferences of the scholar), even though the object of its description are norms (that is, obligations) rather than cause-effect relations between facts.

For Kelsen, the idea of the purely descriptive nature of legal science (as a prerequisite for its objectivity) has interesting consequences. He is aware of the fact that, in principle, a general legal norm (e.g., a statutory norm) does not fully determine the content of an individual norm that is based on it (e.g., a judgement or decision). It merely provides a certain framework which admits different specifications as to what should follow from it in a given set of circumstances. This leads Kelsen to the conclusion that the interpretation of a norm by legal science is in important respects different from that by the law-applying institution. The latter must not only reconstruct the range of possible meanings of the norm and decisions that fall within this range. It must also make a decision regarding the individual norm, which is *eo ipso* a concrete manifestation of the general norm applied and a result of choosing one solution from those it admits as possible. This is not the case with the interpretation by legal science.

> Jurisprudential interpretation can do no more than exhibit all possible meanings of a legal norm. Jurisprudence as cognition of law cannot decide between the possibilities exhibited by it, but must leave the decision to the legal organ who, according to the legal order, is authorized to apply the law.[4]

---

3 H. Kelsen, *Pure Theory of Law*, trans. M. Knight (Berkeley: University of California, 1967), p. 71.

4 Ibid., p. 355.

The choice of an appropriate decision is an act of will determined by evaluation of possible solutions. Yet legal science must remain an objective description of law also in those (very common) cases when it does not identify one applicable solution but leaves some range of discretion to the law-applying institution. The choice of a particular meaning of a norm and the way in which it is to be applied from among the options allowed by the objective content of the norm is a political-legal decision rather than a scientific-cognitive act. Legal policy of this kind is the province of law-applying institutions, which interpret law with a view to choosing "the most appropriate" or "accurate" understanding of a norm; however, their judgement cannot be presented as "scientific truth."[5] In this case, the lawyer is involved in the creation of law based on his or her individual assessments and axiological, ideological, or political preferences. In no way can this practice be regarded as scientific or having any objective cognitive value.

In methodological terms, Kelsen's ideal of pure jurisprudence is perhaps the most consistent model of legal science understood as an objective study of the content of legal norms. It proposes a clear definition and delimitation of its object and its tasks. At the same time, it calls for maintaining a clear-cut distinction between legal science and, on the one hand, whatever concerns law but does not aim at its scientific study (e.g., policy or ideology) and, on the other, whatever is a science but does not concern the content of law (focusing on actual behaviours or relations between observable facts rather than ought-facts). Thus, Kelsen's model of pure legal science leaves out a considerable portion of what legal scholars (including dogmatists) are in fact concerned with and what they consider part and parcel of their discipline and problems it addresses.

This refers in particular to statements about the appropriate interpretation of law. They are considered by legal disciplines not only as a valid result of legal dogmatics but also as its major task and role. Doctrinal considerations to a large extent comprise arguments in favour of one particular way of understanding the regulations under analysis. As an example, one may invoke the following discussion of the institution of the falsus procurator in the Polish civil code. Ewa Rott-Pietrzyk observes that "there appears doubt within the doctrine" as to whether the so-called tacit attorney can be regarded as the *falsus procurator*, in accordance with Article 103 of the Civil Code. The author addresses the problem as follows:

> I think one should assume that if an attorney-in-fact conceals the fact that he or she acts on behalf of the represented party, he or she ought to be treated as an indirect

5 Ibid., p. 356.

> representative. Thus, his or her legal actions have effects for him or her and not for the represented party, as it is the case with a direct representative (e.g., an attorney-in-fact). Therefore, a tacit attorney cannot be regarded as an alleged attorney-in-fact. Hence, it is impossible to evaluate the actions of a tacit attorney on the basis of Article 103 §3 of the Civil Code.[6]

As a result of the fundamental discrepancy between Kelsen's model of descriptive jurisprudence and the practice and self-awareness of legal dogmatics, some scholars attempt to reconcile the descriptive approach to the study of law with the actual situation of legal dogmatics as well as with expectations and tasks it faces in legal practice. One such attempt has been undertaken by Ann Ruth Mackor, who proposes another understanding of the "descriptive" approach to legal science, broader than that advocated by Kelsen.[7]

According to Mackor, the distinction between norm-descriptions, on the one hand, and norm-contentions and norm-recommendations, on the other, is of fundamental importance. Norm-descriptions describe the actual content of norms (that is, they are close to Kelsen's descriptions). They are true in as much as they correspond to the content of norms in their actual form, as a social fact. If the content is ambiguous, unclear, or vague, its description must be limited to pointing out the ambiguity, lack of clarity, or vagueness. Thus, a norm-description should not go beyond what can be indisputably established on the basis of the particular linguistic shape of a norm as formulated by the lawmaker and its content as known in legal practice (where it functions as a social fact).

Apart from norm-descriptions, Mackor distinguishes two other types of statements. Norm-recommendations propose a normative content for extra-legal reasons (such as personal moral preferences of an author, his or her beliefs about what is just, right, or appropriate, etc.). They comprise statements *de lege ferenda* as well as some statements *de sententia ferenda*, if they propose an interpretation or reinterpretation of a norm on extra-legal grounds. Finally, of special

6 The author adds that "a converse opinion is also expressed, according to which a tacit attorney ought to be treated in the same way as an unauthorised representative. As a result, supporters of this position express the view that the effects of actions by a tacit attorney can be evaluated on the basis of Article 103 §3 of the Civil Code;" E. Rott-Pietrzyk, "Agent jako rzekomy pełnomocnik" [The Agent as Alleged Representative], *Przegląd Prawa Handlowego* [Commercial Law Review] 9 (2005), p. 53.

7 A.R. Mackor, "Explanatory Non-Normative Legal Doctrine. Taking the Distinction Between Theoretical and Practical Reason Seriously," in *Methodologies of Legal Research. Which Kind of Method for What Kind of Discipline?*, ed. M. Van Hoecke (Oxford: Hart Publishing, 2013), pp. 45f.

importance to Mackor is the distinction between norm-recommendations and norm-descriptions, on the one hand, and between norm-recommendations and norm-contentions, on the other. The author explains the difference as follows:

> In cases where the formulations of norms are vague or ambiguous, where the norms turn out to be inconsistent or incoherent, or where there are gaps in the law, the only norm-description that legal scholars can offer is the statement that the formulations are vague or ambiguous, or that the law contains a gap, etc. In order to remove the vagueness, ambiguity, inconsistency or incoherency, legal scholars have to make proposals on how law as a social fact has to be changed in order to deal with these deficiencies.[8]

According to Mackor, the crucial difference between norm-contentions and norm-recommendations is that the former do not make personal appeals based on extra-legal considerations (such as personal beliefs about what is just, right, moral, appropriate, etc.). They express opinions concerning how a norm should be understood taking into consideration *internal legal* criteria (such as consistence with other norms, concepts, or legal principles which are accepted in the dogmatic discourse of a given branch of law in a particular legal order). The author illustrates this point with the Dutch Supreme Court sentence, where the "no punishment without guilt" principle of Dutch criminal law is interpreted as not only prohibiting punishment if no guilt can be attributed to the offender, but also prohibiting punishment disproportionate to the guilt.

In Mackor's view, norm-contentions can be regarded as prescriptive or descriptive statements. On the first understanding, they do not aim at expressing the content of norms as specified by the lawmaker; rather, they express

> claims about what a court or the lawgiver should do and what they would do if they were thinking rationally or at least reasonably, ie normatively coherently, about positive law.[9]

However, they can also be treated as descriptive statements not about law "as a social fact" but about law "as *an optimal, internally coherent normative system*."[10] Seen in this light, a norm-contention provides a description of a legal norm as a construct, an idealisation based on the criterion of coherence with other norms and on other internal legal reasons. On this understanding, norm-contentions describe law not as a real-life entity, but as its possible optimised reconstruction. In the systematisation of law, they comprise the part which is non-equivalent to

---

8 Ibid., p. 64.

9 Ibid., p. 65. At this point, Mackor's views are very close to the approach to legal dogmatics proposed by Leszek Nowak, who refers to the construct of rational lawmaker (discussed in more detail in Section 3.4).

10 Ibid., p. 66.

its actual content but refers to a possible optimal way of its understanding. An equivalent systematisation would have to be limited to the description of norms in the particular form in which they exist as a social fact. A non-equivalent account of law in this sense of the term comprises both norm-descriptions and norm-contentions.

A preliminary condition for the acceptance of norm-contentions is that they are not contradictory to norm-descriptions. Mackor refers here to the concept of "hard core" of a research programme (scientific theory) in the understanding of Lakatos. Norm-contentions form a modifiable protective belt around the hard core, which consists of descriptions of norms of a particular system (together with the fundamental values of a given legal culture). The hard core cannot be changed by norm-contentions (this can only be achieved by the lawmaker's intervention). By contrast, norm-contentions are hypothetical and alterable; they are manifestations of the need to optimise law in the face of unavoidable inconsistencies, lack of clarity, and other imperfections inherent in the content of the hard core.

Mackor attempts to provide methodological foundations for legal science that would reflect the way in which it is actually practiced. The aim of this approach is to enable treating legal science as a descriptive discipline and, at the same time, to avoid the criticism that, while its conclusions aspire to scientific "truths" of "discoveries," they are in fact emanations of personal axiological, ideological, or political-legal preferences of a scholar. Interesting as this attempt is, it does not seem entirely successful. In practice, it is extremely difficult (if possible at all) to distinguish between norm-contentions, referring to internal legal system reasons, and interpretive proposals based on personal, extra-legal preferences of the interpreter but presented as if, in one way or another, they "followed" from the values, principles, or norms of the legal system. This difficulty is particularly well visible in discussions about the constitutional judiciary and the differences in the content of (and in the way of making) normative statements by particular judges and other participants in the constitutional discourse.

Thus, it would seem that the flaw of Mackor's proposal lies in the lack of clear distinction between norm-contentions and norm-recommendations and between norm-contentions and "pure" descriptions of norms. Moreover, the criteria of acceptability (truth?) of norm-contentions are not clearly defined. It would be difficult to assume, at least prima facie, that both the truth and the ways of proving it are only a matter of an arbitrary consensus of the community of legal scholars. If this were the case, legal science would be radically conventionalist in nature, regarding as true all and only these statements about law which are accepted by a sufficiently large majority of experts in a given legal discipline, who would make decisions on the "anything goes" basis (or who would apply this principle to decide which methods of establishing the truth of norm-contentions are acceptable).

3.2 The normative model

A very different view of legal science and its methodology has been proposed by scholars who understand jurisprudence as a study of law whose character and tasks are normative rather than descriptive. One of the most interesting and coherent concepts within this model of legal science is the one proposed by Jaap Hage.[11] Hage assumes that scientific activity consists in collaborative effort to obtain, accumulate, and systematise knowledge. However, for this activity to be scientific, a number of conditions must be satisfied; in particular, there must exist a method that enables obtaining cognitively credible results in a given scientific discipline. In the case of law, these results refer, of course, to the content of legal norms (obligations).

At the same time, Hage adopts what he calls "the normative view of the law." On this view, law is a response to a strictly normative question: what to do. Strictly speaking, it embraces this part of the normative discourse which is concerned with what ought to be achieved by collective enforcement of rules. In other words, it is an answer to the question about the content of rules which should be collectively enforced by appropriate institutions.

According to J. Hage, it is also important to distinguish between positive law (rules that exist as a matter of social fact) and "real" law. The latter consists in rules that ought to be collectively enforced in particular circumstances. It does not need to overlap with positive law. The aim of legal science is to establish the content of real law, which is a strictly normative task. In Hage's view, a scientific reflection on real law is possible because we have at our disposal an objective standard of such evaluation: a utilitarian calculus of happiness (which Hage refers to as H-standard). Rules should be enforced collectively if their enforcement promotes and maximises the long-term happiness of sentient beings.

It is also important to note that there are methods which make it possible to determine to what extent this condition is satisfied in a particular set of circumstances. They are not, strictly speaking, legal, but refer to such areas of knowledge as biology, psychology, sociology, economics, etc. They enable a credible

---

11 J Hage, "The Method of a Truly Normative Legal Science," in *Methodologies of Legal Research. Which Kind of Method for What Kind of Discipline?*, ed. M. Van Hoecke (Oxford: Hart Publishing, 2013), p. 19.

assessment of the level of subjectively experienced happiness and of measures which are more or less conducive to maximising it. This, in turn, makes a normative legal science possible, a *science* which looks for objective *knowledge* about "real law," that is, the content of rules which should be collectively enforced. It has access to both the *standard* to determine what ought to be achieved by the rules and *reliable methods of assessment* of the rules' effectiveness with respect to the planned results.

What is the role of positive law in this view of jurisprudence? At first glance, it is significant only insofar as it overlaps with real law, that is, as long as its rules satisfy the H-standard and, hence, ought to be enforced. In order to ascertain that, legal science must first establish the content of real law. Only then is it possible to compare it with the content of positive law (although, at this stage, this comparison seems redundant from the perspective of the tasks of legal science). However, according to Hage, the relation between positive law and real law is more complex. The author observes that positive law plays an important role in coordinating human behaviour, which depends on positivised rules of relatively accessible content. As a result, apart from the content itself, also the confidence that such rules exist and are respected contributes significantly to the way in which the H-standard is satisfied. As Hage puts it,

> [p]ositive law, that consists of the rules contained in the traditional legal sources, makes 'real' law, law in the sense of rules that should be enforced by collective means, if and to the extent that it contributes to legal certainty.[12]

This is why methods of interpretation, which aim at establishing the content of positive law, are part of normative legal science. Although they do not directly advance its main goal (that is, the study of the content of real law), they contribute to it indirectly by determining the content of rules whose collective enforcement plays a significant role in satisfying the H-standard. Their special role follows from the certainty and predictability of the effects of one's actions and the ability to coordinate one's actions with expected actions of others. Moreover, the rules of positive law may have democratic legitimation, which is an additional reason why enforcing them contributes to the H-standard. As Hage observes,

> to the extent that democracy matters, the intention of the democratic legislator may also be relevant for the interpretation of legislation.[13]

12 Ibid., p. 42.
13 Ibid., p. 43.

Thus, legal science is normative in nature, its main task being to determine the objective content of the norms of "real law." Although, in principle, methods used to establish which rules should be enforced to maximise the H-standard must refer to natural and social sciences, they also contain interpretive elements related to positive law (especially to democratically established law).

Hage argues that this scientific activity should be distinguished from another function of legal writing which he refers to as the maintenance of the legal system.[14] Its goal is to describe and systematise the content of law and adjudication that accompanies it, to criticise solutions which fail to yield expected results, and to propose amendments. Although these tasks require the highest professional qualifications and are commonly called legal science, they only partially overlap with true legal science, aiming at establishing the content of norms that should be collectively enforced.

Hage's proposal is prospective in nature in that the model of legal science he advocates is fundamentally different from the one that has so far been adopted. At the same time, the assumptions of the model and the conclusions drawn from them are rational, fit well with empirical knowledge of the world, and coincide with appeals for external integration of jurisprudence. Nevertheless, this kind of scientific endeavour seems to be a scientifically grounded version of legal policy rather than legal science understood as a description of valid positive law (which is closer to what Hage calls maintenance of the existing legal system).

This difference is blurred by the terminology used by Hage, where real law does not refer to any set of existing (established or accepted) rules of behaviour. Instead, it refers to norms which, if enforced, maximise the H-standard and which, in consequence, should be collectively enforced. These norms emerge from a rational scientific reflection and need not overlap with the content of any existing legal regulations. So understood, the concept of real law is reminiscent of Daniel Dennett's jocular account of magic. He argued that real magic is the magic that is not real, while the magic that is real is not real magic.[15] Similarly, real law (sensu Hage) refers to law that does not exist in reality, while the law that is real is not, in Hage's terms, real law (at least, it seems very unlikely that there should be any set of positive legal rules entirely overlapping with a set of regulations that, if enforced, would maximise the H-standard).

14 Ibid., p. 24.

15 D. Dennett, Explaining the 'Magic' of Consciousness, *Journal of Cultural and Evolutionary Psychology* 1/8 (2003), p. 8.

Hage's proposal is regarded as a model of legal policy rather than of positive legal science (focused on positive rather than real law); it also manages to avoid the problem of the fundamental heterogeneity of methods. The task of establishing the content of existing legal norms (that is, norms of positive law) is essentially different from that of proposing the content of regulations which, if enforced, would maximise the H-standard. However, as a model of legal policy, Hage's approach would be a target of the same philosophical criticism which is levelled against ethical utilitarianism.[16] It does have to mean (and, in my view, it does not mean) that such criticism cannot be defeated, but a detailed discussion of the strong points and weaknesses of utilitarianism and its criticism is beyond the scope of this chapter.[17] I will only note that Hage's proposal, understood as a model of rational legal policy, seems well justified and much more promising than any other possible solution.

3.3. The integral model

One of the best known and most frequently discussed models of jurisprudence as legal science has been proposed and developed over the past decades by Ronald Dworkin. Thanks to the amount of attention it has attracted, its main points are relatively well assimilated into legal discourse (which does not mean that they are properly understood) and will not be reiterated here. Instead, we will focus on these elements which are crucial for the reconstruction of his original view of the nature and specific features of legal science.

From this standpoint, of paramount importance is the interpretive nature of law emphasised by Dworkin. Law is a social practice that is not morally indifferent and whose effects include decisions concerning the circumstances in which the use of violence is justified. Modern states have a monopoly of legal coercive force, and law specifies the conditions and limits of the acceptable use of force by the state against its citizens. Decisions concerning what is legally permissible and, consequently, what ways of making and verifying such decisions are acceptable are thus not only intellectual-cognitive in nature. They are necessarily connected with the acceptance or disapproval of concrete acts of violence,

---

16 For a short discussion of the main arguments raised in the debate, see, e.g., T. Pietrzykowski, *Etyczne problemy prawa* [Ethical Problems of the Law] (Warszawa: LexisNexis, 2011) and bibliography there.

17 For most up-to-date literature, see, e.g., P. Singer and K. de Lazari-Radek, *The Point of View of the Universe. Sidgwick and Contemporary Ethics* (Oxford: Oxford University Press, 2014), passim.

which are seen as, respectively, legitimate acts of law enforcement or reprehensible infringement calling for appropriate reaction.[18]

The view of law as a social practice that constrains the use of force implies that: (i) the concept of law is – like that of medicine or art – interpretive in nature, its understanding depending on the interpretation of the underlying social practice in the light of the goals and values it pursues; (ii) decisions concerning what law is, what it recommends, and how this is to be established are inseparable from decisions concerning which way of understanding a particular social practice is preferable, what law should recommend, and how this ought to be determined; and (iii) the theory of law, legal science, and adjudication are in fact part of the same enterprise, but they operate on a different level of abstraction, basic theoretical legal arguments being, in Dworkin's famous phrase, a "silent prologue to any decision at law."[19]

Because law and legal practice are interpretive in nature, law cannot be studied in a neutral, purely descriptive way (unless one aims at a strictly sociological description of the legal phenomenon). Every view on what law is (and, as a result, on what forms its content and how this content should be established) imposes its own criteria for distinguishing between true and false statements concerning what is lawful and what is not. This, in turn, leads to different conclusions regarding the uses of violence that are to be considered as justified. There is no impartial way of describing law; each attempt at a description implicitly involves approval or disapproval of decisions related to its content. This is why Dworkin doubts whether it is possible to provide a theory of law (or a description of its dogmatic content) that would offer a metalinguistic, neutral explanation of what valid law is and what it comprises. Each such description is at the same time an act of stancetaking – conscious or not – towards political-normative issues, that is, towards the ways and principles of legitimating organised violence.[20]

Thus, the theory of law implies politically and axiologically involved participation in the decision-making process regarding the best possible justification of coercion applied by the state to the citizen (as well as the monopoly the state claims in this respect). This is why Dworkin argues for understanding law as positive rules integrated with fundamental principles, valid because of their moral

---

18 See R. Dworkin, *Law's Empire* (Cambridge, MA: Harvard University Press, 1986), p. 93ff.

19 Ibid., p. 90.

20 See R. Dworkin, *Justice in Robes* (Cambridge, MA: Harvard University Press, 2006), p. 140f.

significance and not because of any formal acts of lawmaking. Looking for solutions to individual cases (in particular, hard cases), the interpreter should aim at a reconstruction of principles which would provide the best possible justification for legal practice so far (including rules of statutory law) relevant to the problem at hand, showing this practice in the best possible light.

The principles must meet two criteria. First, they must fit as closely as possible with the "material" of lawmaking and court decisions that constitute the current practice of making and applying law in a particular domain (the dimension of fit). Second, they must provide the best possible justification for this practice (the dimension of justification).

Referring to the often-quoted metaphor of law as a chain novel written by various authors, Dworkin argues that each next author (interpreter of law) must be true to the ongoing project in which he or she participates. This means that his or her interpretation must fit the characters, the plot, and the motives, at the same time providing a continuation in the light of which their actual form and shape appear best justified.[21]

Thus, interpretation of law consists in revealing the moral principles (which may but do not have to be positivised in legal rules) underlying specific lawmaking and court decisions as well as the arguments and justifications that are invoked to support them. These principles integrate positive law material dispersed across various judgements, decisions, or statements, shaping it into a consistent and coherent set of basic rules, at the same time providing them with a moral justification. It is only when such principles are taken into consideration that the true profundity and complexity of "law's empire" can be appreciated, heavily oversimplified by treating law as a one-dimensional set of regulations based in positivist sources of law.

Because the reconstruction of such legal rules is a complex process, Dworkin introduces the figure of Judge Hercules, whose cognitive capacities and patience are unlimited, and who does not work under time pressure. This is why he is able to thoroughly analyse the entirety of legal material and, in this context, to consider all moral principles that potentially justify it. In this way, Judge Hercules

---

21 A perfect illustration of Dworkin's chain novel idea is provided by Cass Sunstein, who refers to the Star Wars series, where authors had to make their episodes fit those that had been produced earlier in a way that made them seem a natural and almost necessary result of the earlier parts, thus providing the best possible explanation and justification for the entire story (and hence presenting it in the best possible light); see C. Sunstein, "How Star Wars Illuminates Constitutional Law;" available at http://papers.ssrn.com/sol3/papers.cfm?abstract_id=2604998.

is able to identify the principle or principles which optimally satisfy the dimensions of fit and justification throughout the legal history relevant to the case at hand. In the light of these principles, in turn, it is possible to identify the best (and, as a result, the only legally appropriate) solution to every legal case, even "a hard case" (the so-called one-right-answer thesis).

Thus, Dworkin rejects the view, commonly shared by jurists (in particular, by legal theorists), that in hard cases, there are usually several possible – and legally acceptable – solutions, and that the choice between them is determined not by law as such but by non-legal values, preferences, or subjective beliefs of interpreters. Dworkin does not dispute the fact that this is what actually takes place in legal practice. However, he believes that this does not mean that there is no just one objectively correct solution to a difficult legal case, namely, one that is determined by the reconstructed rules relevant to the case at hand. Rather, it demonstrates that legal practitioners, misunderstanding the nature of law and guided by a wrong theory of interpretation, do not engage properly in the search for one right answer (although it is only the idealised Judge Hercules that is fully able to discover it).

For the past decades, both advantages and weaknesses of Dworkin's model have been the topic of intense philosophical-legal debate.[22] Without going into details, it is useful to point out a major problem that this theory poses if we treat it as a vision of the way in which legal science (understood by Dworkin as a theory of solving legal problems and adjudicating individual cases) should be practiced. The point is that this model is to a considerable extent based on metaphysical speculations concerning the possibility of reconstructing real legal material as a coherent, tangible set of principles that would identify one objectively best solution to each possible case.

However, it is equally plausible that legal material can be "explained" by various competing and mutually exclusive sets of moral principles, leading to contradictory decisions, all of them equally fitting with the history of law so far (e.g., two conflicting lines of adjudication) and morally controversial. Thus, the construct of Judge Hercules requires very strong ontological and

22 See, e.g., *Dworkin and His Critics*, ed. J. Burley (Oxford–Malden, MA: Blackwell 2004); The *Legacy of Ronald Dworkin*, ed. W. Waluchow and S. Sciaraffa (Oxford: Oxford University Press, 2016); S. Guest, *Ronald Dworkin* (Stanford: *Stanford* University Press, 1991); S. Guest, "How to Criticize Ronald Dworkin's Theory of Law," *Analysis* 69/2 (2009), pp. 352 ff.

epistemological assumptions (in particular, a strong version of ethical objectivism and cognitivism).

At the same time, the method of interpretation used by the ideal Judge Hercules, if reduced to what is possible for real judges in the practice of applying law, may produce highly disputable results. It poses the threat of combining subjective judgements and moral values with the unshaken faith in discovering "the objectively best way" of interpreting the content of legal principles that determine decisions in particular cases. In other words, the transformation of the Herculean method into a practicable approach to the interpretation of law by real people who act as judges may easily turn the former into its moralistic caricature, with objectivist rhetoric disguising huge amounts of arbitrariness and the tendency to engage in decision-making processes biased towards specific outcomes (motivated reasoning).[23]

3.4 The derivational model

This original and interesting model of legal science originated in contemporary Polish legal theory. Its main founders were Leszek Nowak, Zygmunt Ziembiński, and Maciej Zieliński. It takes as its starting point the concept of the rational lawmaker, proposed by Nowak. On this approach, jurisprudence – understood as legal science – "falls within the scope of a particular methodological model of the humanities" which assume that the behaviours they strive to interpret (explain) are rational in nature.[24] Economics, history, literary studies, and legal science – all these disciplines assume that the behaviours they study (or their products) proceed from goal-orientation and develop according to the knowledge (and beliefs) of the agents. A historian explains the actions of historical figures through the prism of the preferences and beliefs ascribed to them, assuming that they acted rationally, that is, in a way that, according to the knowledge they had, was possibly most effective in attaining their goals. Economic theories and interpretations of literary works or other cultural artefacts rest on similar assumptions.

Jurisprudence also adopts the assumption of rationality of behaviours it seeks to interpret. However, in this case, the assumption is modified in an important respect. Rather than refer to the rationality of individuals who participate in lawmaking processes, it assumes the rationality of a construct called "the lawmaker."

23 On motivated reasoning and research into its role in legal thought, see T. Pietrzykowski, *Intuicja prawnicza. W stronę zewnętrznej integracji teorii prawa* [Legal Intuition. Toward an External Integration of Legal Theory] (Warszawa: Difin, 2012).

24 L. Nowak, *Próba metodologicznej charakterystyki prawoznawstwa* [An Attempt at a Methodological Characterization of Jurisprudence] (Poznań: Uniwersytet im. Adama Mickiewicza, 1968).

Thus, according to Nowak, legal science rests on the assumption of the rationality of the lawmaker understood as a collective, institutional author of legal texts. In the process of legal interpretation, these texts are treated as products of a rational author, who aims at creating a coherent and consistent system of norms that embody particular values.

The assumption of the rationality of the lawmaker is part of the "deep structure" of jurisprudence.[25] It does not contribute directly to the interpretation of law, but rather explains the reasoning and arguments used in legal theory and interpretive practice. As an example, one may invoke directives according to which it is unacceptable to propose that the lawmaker who used the same word in one normative act several times did so with different meanings in mind or, conversely, that the lawmaker used different terms to express exactly the same idea. The directives which ban synonymic and homonymic interpretations are, in fact, emanations of the assumption that the lawmaker acts rationally and hence uses linguistic resources consistently and purposefully (even though the jurist who refers to them may be unaware of that).

A radical rejection of this assumption would make interpretation of any legal text impossible. In the case of an author who acts irrationally, it would be difficult to find any connection between the linguistic expressions used and the intention or will to regulate a problem in a particular way (the use of terms which the author may expect to be understood in the intended way is, in fact, a manifestation of some elementary instrumental rationality).

In contrast to the deformed and inaccurate account of the concept of the rationality of the lawmaker in legal practice (and even in legal literature, including legal theory publications), this assumption does not involve the belief that individuals who actually take part in the creation of law (actual lawmakers) always act fully rationally. Moreover, it does not rest on the belief that the regulations introduced by the lawmaker are always wise and sound (and hence that any unwise or absurd regulation automatically refutes the assumption of the rationality of the lawmaker). Nowak makes this point quite clear:

> Lawyers cannot act as if they assumed that the actual lawmaker was an irrational legislator. This is not to say that they cannot personally believe a given lawmaker to be irrational, or that they cannot express their personal views to question the rationality of the actual lawmaker.[26]

25 L. Nowak, *Interpretacja prawnicza. Studium z metodologii prawoznawstwa* [Legal Interpretation. A Study in the Methodology of Jurisprudence] (Warszawa: PWN, 1973), pp. 11, 35f.

26 L. Nowak, *Próba…*, p. 73.

The point is that, acting in their social roles, lawyers interpret law in a way which de facto respects this assumption, even though they may personally see no solid evidence that concrete individuals involved in the actual creation of law are fully rational (or, for that matter, wise). As a result, interpretation is often at the same time an act of optimisation of law. It is frequently the case that the actual lawmaker – out of ignorance, haste, etc. – regulates a legal matter in a way which is far from perfection, clarity, or coherence. In such situations, legal scholars aim at an interpretation which presents the regulation, as far as it is possible, as a product of a rational author (they eliminate contradictions, gaps, and inconsistencies that can be removed by interpretation). In this way, legal interpretation to some extent perfects law and makes it internally consistent, but its ascribes the effects of this process to the will of the rational lawmaker rather than the skill of the interpreter. Thus, the assumption is not only not counterfactual, but necessary and useful, the more so, the less the actual lawmaker fits the models of rationality adopted in the practice of legal interpretation.[27]

The theory of legal interpretation as the implementation of the concept of the lawmaker's rationality, proposed by Nowak, is in fact a thorough reconstruction of assumptions that underlie the construct of the rational lawmaker, consolidating the established interpretive practices of jurists. Nowak includes here assumptions concerning the language used (the lawmaker is never wrong but chooses words and phrases which express exactly what the lawmaker intends to express), the knowledge of law (the lawmaker does not establish new rules without knowing what follows from other valid norms, and if they seem contradictory, one should assume that the lawmaker's intention was to introduce an exception from a more general rule, etc.), the knowledge of facts, a coherent and consistent system of values which underlies the actions, etc.[28]

The reconstruction of the assumption of the lawmaker's rationality introduced by Nowak was, in principle, descriptive in nature, as was the methodological view of legal science and interpretive practice based on it. It was not designed as a tool to guide jurists in how to do legal science. Its aim was to reveal the deep-structure methodological assumptions which had given jurisprudence its actual shape. Thus, it was to explain how and on what basis legal scholars in

27 Nowak believes that, in contrast to other branches of science, for jurisprudence, the assumption of the rationality of the lawmaker is non-verifiable; legal scholars accept it dogmatically, without checking its truth value, as the basis for statements about the content of law; ibid., pp. 170f.

28 For more detail on the distinction between the rational lawmaker and the ideal lawmaker, proposed later by Nowak, see ibid., pp. 43ff.

fact solved legal problems and what course of action was actually adopted in legal science in this respect. Moreover, it indicated the methodological features of jurisprudence which identified it as part of the humanities. However, in the course of time, the theory became the basis for perhaps the most comprehensive and advanced normative approach to the methodology of legal science that has emerged in the Polish legal theory: the derivational model of legal interpretation.

A connection between Nowak's proposals and the derivational model of legal interpretation was established by the understanding of the relation between rules and legal norms introduced by Ziembiński in the 1960s.[29] The starting point for this approach was the definition of legal norm as a statement which explicitly and unambiguously states what kind of behaviour is prescribed or prohibited, to whom, and in what circumstances. Elements of so defined unambiguous legal norms may be (and usually are) scattered across a variety of rules. It is only when all such rules are taken into consideration that a fully developed legal norm can be constructed, indicating clearly the addressee, the circumstances, and the prescribed or prohibited behaviour.

These assumptions form the basis for the derivational model of legal interpretation, proposed and developed by Maciej Zieliński. According to this model, the interpretive practice of legal scholars consists in transforming rules into sufficiently explicit and clear norms of behaviour.[30] Thus understood, the process of legal interpretation is highly complicated, since fragments of a particular legal norm scattered across various rules must be found and put together to form a whole. In many cases, the relevant rules belong to several normative acts, established at different points in time. This stage (called the reconstruction stage in the derivational model)[31] produces a norm-shaped form of expression, which contains all components of the norm. Next, other directives of interpretation are applied in sequence (the perceptual stage of interpretation), but it is not until all directives are applied that a sufficiently explicit and clear norm of behaviour can be reconstructed.

---

29 Z. Ziembiński, "Przepis prawny a norma prawna" [Legal Provisions and Legal Norms], *Ruch Prawniczy, Ekonomiczny i Socjologiczny* [The Legal, Economic and Sociological Movement] 1 (1960), p. 105ff.

30 Zieliński develops this idea in subsequent editions of his work published for the first time in 2002. The present discussion is based on its fifth edition; see M. Zieliński, *Wykładnia prawa. Zasady, reguły, wskazówki* [Interpreting Law. Principles, rules, guidelines] (Warszawa: LexisNexis, 2012).

31 This stage is preceded by the ordering stage, in which the up-to-date forms of all relevant rules are established, to be taken into consideration in further stages of interpretation; see Zieliński, *Wykładnia...*, pp. 318ff.

The derivational model differs from the classical model of interpretation (the so-called clarification theory of legal interpretation) in three important respects. First, in order to perceive the meaning of a norm, one must reconstruct it from rules, which are only "semi-finished legal material."[32] Thus, law consists not of rules, but of norms encoded by the lawmaker in legal text. Although legal text is divided into regulations, they are only technical, editorial units. Only when its components are found and the norm is recreated on the basis of all relevant fragments of legal text, is it possible to establish who and in what circumstances should act in what way. This, in turn, usually requires taking into consideration a large number of rules which contain fragments of a single legal norm. As Zieliński observes:

> in a vast majority of cases, legal rules are not at the same time norms, because their syntactic structure is different or their content is not sufficiently unambiguous.[33]

Norms can be fragmented – when elements of one norm can be found in more than one rule – or condensed, if the same rule is a component of more than one norm. The interpreter must identify the core rule which expresses (usually partially) a particular obligation, and then find all elements of the same norm in rules contained in the entire legal text.[34] These are mainly supplementary and amending regulations. As an example of the core rule, one may invoke Article 415 of the Polish Civil Code, according to which anyone who by his or her fault causes damage to another person is obliged to remedy it. However, the content of this obligation (or the norm that expresses it) is modified, for instance, by Article 423, which states that this obligation does not apply if the damage was caused by self-defence. Another rule modifying the content is Article 426, according to which a minor under thirteen is not liable for damage caused. Finding and taking into account all the rules that contain elements identifying the addressee, the circumstances, and the type of prescribed or prohibited behaviour allow for the reconstruction of the norm-shaped form of expression, which is the object of the next, perceptual stage of interpretation, when its meaning is determined (the meaning expressed in the legal norm).

The second major difference between the standard approach to interpretation and the derivational model consists in the analysis of the reconstructed norm-shaped form of expression in the perceptual stage, where the meaning of the norm (that is, the content of the norm-shaped form of expression) is understood.

32 Ibid., p. 18.
33 Ibid., p. 25.
34 Ibid., p. 257.

Zieliński argues that in each case, the process of understanding law necessarily involves the application of linguistic, systemic, and functional directives of interpretation.[35] They are applied successively, in the form of a detailed sequence of interpretive steps (which Zieliński understands as a set of principles, rules, and guidelines governing the process of interpretation at every stage).

The third important difference between the derivational model and the classical approach to interpretation concerns the *clara non sunt interpretanda* principle, which Zieliński rejects in favour of the opposite *omnia sunt interpretanda* principle.[36] In his view, each case of establishing the meaning of a legal text (at least for the first time) requires both reconstructing the complete norm-shaped form of expression on the basis of all relevant rules (its elements rarely belong to a single rule) and applying sequentially all directives of interpretation: linguistic and non-linguistic ones. Only at later, post-interpretation stages is it possible to restrict the process – albeit with appropriate caution – to the application of norms which have already been subject to interpretation and whose accurate meanings have been established.[37] Of course, this model is normative rather than descriptive. Applying a complete sequence of interpretation stages in each case of the application of law (or doctrinal interpretation) is a precondition for the correct interpretation procedure and not a description of actual actions undertaken in legal practice by courts or other interpreters.[38]

---

35 If the use of linguistic directives results in lack of ambiguity, systemic directives need not (or even cannot) be applied, but functional directives should be applied in all cases; ibid., pp. 337, 342.

36 For a detailed discussion of this juxtaposition, see A. Grabowski, "*Clara non sunt interpretanda* vs. *omnia sunt interpretanda*. A Never-Ending Controversy in Polish Legal Theory?" *Revus. Journal for Constitutional Theory and Philosophy of Law* 26 (2015), pp. 67f.

37 Zieliński emphasises that this applies to decision cases rather than interpretation cases.

38 Although in court adjudication the *omnia sunt interpretanda* principle is occasionally declared, in practice, interpretation is carried out only in cases when the content of particular rules or their fragments is the subject of dispute between the parties or raises some preliminary doubts for the court concerning the (range of) meanings of the words used. Also in rulings where the courts refer to the *omnia sunt interpretanda* maxim, the principle is, in fact, applied only to the rule or its fragment which is the subject of dispute in the particular case, while the part of the normative basis for the decision which remains uncontroversial (usually the main part) is understood directly. As an example, one may invoke the judgement of the Polish Supreme Administrative Court of 17 January 2013 (VII SA/Wa 2336/12), in which, referring to the *omnia sunt interpretanda* principle, the court considers the content of Article 28 of the Code of Administrative Law (in a way which is, incidentally, quite remote from the guidelines

The derivational model of interpretation may be treated not only as a perspective on how legal interpretation should be performed but also as a comprehensive and sophisticated methodological theory of legal science. Based on the assumption of the rational lawmaker, it offers a coherent and inclusive view of the appropriate course of action of a legal scholar who aims to establish the content of valid legal norms. The concept of the lawmaker's rationality makes it possible to assume (counterfactually) that complex, complicated, and unambiguous norms were "encoded" in legal text directly by the lawmaker but that their elements were scattered. It is the task of the jurist to identify them and to reconstruct the norm in the original shape, that is, as "conceived" by the lawmaker before it was fragmented and placed in various points of legal text (in rules).

Since law is the product of a rational (and not actual) lawmaker, it may be assumed that, "in reality," it does not consist of rules but of unambiguous and complete norms of behaviour, whose fragments were "distributed" by the (rational but not necessarily actual) lawmaker across a variety of rules, often established at a different time and of different origin and status. Even if the actual lawmaker was not aware of the fact that a newly introduced regulation modified the content of the norm – composed of rules of many other normative acts – there is no reason why such awareness and intention (will) should not be attributed to the rational lawmaker (who has a thorough knowledge of the entire legal environment and its internal interdependencies and does not introduce changes whose effects are unexpected or unintended).

The derivational model rests on a particular view of law (to my mind, a noticeably metaphysical view) developed on the basis of the works of Nowak. Law is here understood as a system of norms (rather than rules), and it is norms (not rules) that are identified as valid. The task of legal science is to reconstruct a system of coherent and unambiguous norms, valid in a particular legal system, on the basis of legal text, where legal text acts as a medium through which the rational lawmaker communicates (usually indirectly) the norms of behaviour. It is only at the level of norms that the will of the rational lawmaker can be fully appreciated, with changes introduced in the rules actually modifying the models of behaviour encoded in regulations scattered across the legal system.

This view of law, and the consequences that follow from it, can be criticised on various grounds, and such critical remarks appear in particular in the literature

---

of the derivational model of interpretation), but, referring to Article 82 section 2 of the Construction Law, does not see it fit to interpret it and is satisfied with direct understanding.

on legal interpretation.[39] While I generally share this criticism, here, I would like to focus on three elements of the model which have received relatively little attention in the discussion so far. Firstly, the view of law as a set of fully developed norms "encoded" by the lawmaker in rules established at different points in time and in various normative acts (often by different institutions) is openly counterfactual. Constructing the norm on the basis of a number of rules, the interpreter usually does not "recreate" any entity that was earlier fragmented by the actual lawmaker, but produces a certain normative construct that could not have been thought of beforehand by anybody (certainly not by the actual lawmaker). Thus, the activity of the interpreter consists in the construction and creation of norms rather than in their re-construction and re-creation. This is why understanding norms constructed by the interpreter as "real law" – as entities that were "encoded" in legal text by the lawmaker and of which it can be predicated that they are valid "in reality" (in contrast to rules of normative acts) – appears dangerously close to hypostasising.

Secondly, the derivational model as a method of interpretation ignores empirical data concerning human cognitive and decision processes, which often do not take place on the conscious level. They give rise to various impressions of the intuitively obvious, of immediate clarity and "direct understanding" (not necessarily identifiable with the strictly linguistic meaning of a text), and of the subjective acceptability of alternative solutions to cognitive problems. They are not fully controlled by conscious reasoning, which is only partially capable of counteracting the influence of extra-conscious processes on the decision-making process.[40] Despite the indisputable merits of the Herculean and derivational approaches to each act of application (or, indeed, understanding) of law, the fundamental obstacle to adopting them as methodological guidelines lies in the fact that they are impossible to implement in practice, and *impossibilium nulla obligatio.*

This objection is strengthened by Zieliński's rejection of "easy cases" (a stance that echoes Dworkin's view) which do not require a complete process of conscious interpretive actions. The argument is as follows: only after this process is completed can one be sure that treating the case as easy (and hence not requiring

---

39 See, e.g., Grabowski, "*Clara…*," pp. 67f; K. Płeszka, *Wykładnia rozszerzająca* [Extensive Interpretation] (Warszawa: Wolters Kluwer, 2010), pp. 197f; B. Brożek, "Derywacyjna koncepcja wykładni z perspektywy logicznej" [Derivative Concept of Interpretation from a Logical Perspective], *Ruch Prawniczy, Ekonomiczny i Socjologiczny* [The Legal, Economic and Sociological Movement] 1 (2006), pp. 81f.

40 For more detail, see Pietrzykowski, *Intuicja…*, pp. 135f.

a complete interpretive procedure) is not premature and does not proceed from ignoring some important aspects that must not be omitted in the solution – a solution that, at first glance, seems obvious and indisputable. In other words, easy cases are, at best, a type of hard cases where it finally turns out that the results of conscious interpretive procedures overlap with the initial, intuitive impression of "direct understanding" of the rules.

The third remark concerns the controversy around the principles *clara non sunt interpretanda* and *omnia sunt interpretanda.* I am in complete agreement with Zieliński's rejection of the *clara non sunt interpretanda* principle in at least two contexts in which it is often invoked in adjudication. In the first one, interpretation of rules is prohibited or redundant whenever they appear subjectively clear to the interpreter who holds institutional power – even if the parties or other subjects raise interpretive arguments that challenge the understanding accepted as intuitively obvious. This leads to glaring arbitrariness based in the ill-founded belief in the accuracy of one's own intuitive judgements or subjective sense of the obvious. At the same time, it makes it possible to avoid considering arguments in favour of one or another understanding of a rule by referring to one's own perception of the clarity or indisputability of its sense. In the second context, the principle prohibits non-linguistic interpretation of rules which appear linguistically clear. Also in this case, the subjective impression of clarity, based in one's linguistic competence, may (and often does) become a tool for imposing one's own understanding, a priori dismissing arguments and reasons which, if taken into consideration, could effectively challenge this reading. Exposing this function of the *clara non sunt interpretanda* principle and subjecting it to criticism is undoubtedly a major achievement of the derivational model of interpretation and its founder Maciej Zieliński.

However, it is neither justified nor realistic to expect that *omnia sunt interpretanda* may replace *clara non sunt interpretanda* in the third sense in which this principle is used. According to it, it is unnecessary to perform a complete interpretive procedure with respect to a rule whose meaning in given circumstances does not raise doubts of the court or any other participant in the case (because the dispute concerns other matters and the parties agree on the understanding of the relevant rule), or indeed any other jurist. Of course, applying the comprehensive, detailed procedure of interpretation to every rule relevant for the case would reduce the risk of implementing a regulation – with the active or silent approval of the parties – in a different meaning than the "correct" one (especially when this departure from the correct understanding has no impact on who wins the case). Still, a risk of this kind seems to be the unavoidable (and, at the same time, acceptable) price to pay for the practicability and efficiency of the process of applying law and decision-making in real-life disputes.

3.5 The hermeneutic model

Understood as a reflection on the meaning of texts and other forms of communication (Gr. ἑρμηνεύειν, *hermęneúein* 'to clarify, to explain'), hermeneutics has roots in philological traditions of antiquity and Christian Biblical studies. Its beginnings are connected with the search for an appropriate reading of poems and myths. In the first philosophical account of hermeneutics, Aristotle defines it as a general analysis of the way in which language becomes the carrier of meaning.[41] The strongest impulse for its further development came from Christianity and the discussions underway in the first centuries of our era that concerned the appropriate method of interpretation of the Holy Scripture, and later, from the next wave of debates connected with the divisions caused by the Reformation.

In modern philosophical thought, hermeneutics as a reflection on the methods and role of understanding was studied, in particular, by Friedrich Schleiermacher, Wilhelm Dilthey, Martin Heidegger, and Hans Georg Gadamer. Rather than discuss the views of individual scholars who shaped philosophical hermeneutics in the past two centuries, I will assume, after Jerzy Stelmach and Bartosz Brożek, that it is possible to distinguish two slightly different approaches.[42] In the first one, hermeneutics is treated as a method of understanding language (in particular, written language) and regarded mainly as epistemology. The most prominent representatives of this direction include Schleiermacher, Dilthey, and the so-called school of analytical hermeneutics. The co-founders of its adaptations for law are Friedrich Karl von Savigny, Helmut Coing, Emilio Betti, Josef Esser, and Karl Larenz.[43]

The second approach to hermeneutics comprises views which construe it as a general "philosophy of being" of subjects capable of comprehending reality. On this understanding, hermeneutics is no longer confined to epistemology, but becomes at the same time an ontological stance. Viewing understanding as a particular form of being has roots in the concept of *Lebenswelt* (living world) introduced by Edmund Husserl and *Dasein* (being-in-the-world), the central concept in the philosophy of Heidegger, which refers to a specific type of

41 Aristotle, *On Interpretation*, trans. E. M. Edghill; available at http://classics.mit.edu/Aristotle/interpretation.html; accessed 6.05.2019.

42 See J. Stelmach and B. Brożek, *Metody prawnicze* [Legal Methods] (Kraków: Zakamycze, 2004), pp. 235f.

43 Ibid., pp. 245f.

presence characteristic of a conscious individual. Indeed, it is to Heidegger that the greatest contribution to the "ontological turn" in philosophical hermeneutics is attributed.[44] According to Stelmach and Brożek, representatives of this approach include Hans Georg Gadamer and Paul Ricoeur. It was introduced to legal studies by Adolf Reinach, Walter Meihoffer, and, in particular, Artur Kaufmann.

Some scholars identified with the philosophical tradition of hermeneutics and interested in legal studies treat legal interpretation as an exemplary case of hermeneutic understanding; Stelmach, in turn, argues that law should be considered not as an exemplary case but as a special case (*Sonderfallthese*).[45] Regardless of these differences, there is no doubt that the properties of the act of understanding which are the focus of philosophical hermeneutics apply to a large extent to the interpretation and understanding of law. These properties include, in particular, the linguistic character of the act of understanding, its historicity, the circularity of its structure, and the role of the so-called pre-understanding.

One of the properties attributed by hermeneutics to the act of understanding is its dependence on language. Language is regarded not only as a neutral tool, but as a factor which to a considerable extent constitutes both the object and the result of each act of understanding. This applies a fortiori to the interpretation of statutory law, which, in principle, has the form of authoritative texts. Understanding them requires "translating" the lawmaker's text into the language of a concrete decision in an individual case (i.e., "adapting" general text to facts and circumstances to which the text is to refer in this particular case of law-application). Moreover, legal language is uniquely performative: it creates entities (such as, e.g., legal persons, rights, legal relations, etc.) which exist by virtue of the "binding force" conventionally attributed to statements made by the lawmaker. The entities constituted by legal language are at the same time an important element of the meanings of legal texts; in this sense, legal language is strongly self-referential in nature. Such properties as normativity, authoritativeness, and performativity are, to some extent, characteristic also of other, non-legal languages (e.g., the language of ethics or religion) and hence of other types of interpretation or understanding processes, but in the case of legal texts, their

44 T. Botts, "Legal Hermeneutics," IEP; available at http://www.iep.utm.edu/leg-herm/.

45 J. Stelmach, *Współczesna filozofia interpretacji prawniczej* [Modern Philosophy of Legal Intepretation] (Kraków: Wydawnictwo Uniwersytetu Jagiellońskiego, 1999), pp. 73–74; see also T. Gizbert-Studnicki, "Das hermeneutische Bewußtsein der Juristen," *Rechtstheorie* 18 (1987), p. 366.

unique configuration determines the processes of interpretation and gives them their specifically legal hue.

From the hermeneutic standpoint, each act of understanding is perceived as a historical act. Anchored in concrete circumstances of time and place, it is necessarily situated. At the same time, it continues a particular "tradition" comprising the origins of the text which is to be understood (and which has its own historical context), the history of its later readings, contingent situational context of the act of understanding, and, last but not least, all earlier experiences of the interpreter. All these contexts coincide in one historical act of understanding a legal text.

Interpretation of law is thus rooted in historical circumstances and in the so far accepted understanding of the interpreted text – or, at least, in the so far adopted standards of legal interpretation. The juristic understanding of a text emerges in a dialogue between the meaning and history, that is, between the interpreter's own beliefs concerning the semantic content of the text on the one hand, and, on the other, the historical circumstances in which it originates, the history of its readings by other interpreters, the interpreter's own situation, and the expected effects of his or her interpretive decisions.

However, understanding a text is not only oriented towards the past (that is, towards the circumstances connected with its origins and its former interpretations); it is also a projection of its future readings. Thus, the act of understanding cannot be separated from a certain vision of the future and the way in which the established meaning will "fit" with the present and future historical circumstances to which the text is to refer. It is in this sense that hermeneutics speaks of both "opening" interpretation to tradition and relating it to a certain subjectively defined (and definable) "horizon" of the future.

This planning of meaning with the future in mind is well visible in legal interpretation, where understanding usually supports the decision-making process in a particular case (that is, where it is to serve a concrete practical purpose in the nearest future, which provides the immediate time horizon for the act of understanding). So understood, the historicity of the act of understanding in legal interpretation is tightly connected with its adaptive nature. The aim of legal interpretation is understanding oriented towards the *present* circumstances that need a legal decision, but the decision is to be based on a text that comes from the past (often more or less remote). In this sense, legal interpretation is an act of making the interpreted text not only concrete and definite but also up to date, with the processes of understanding combined with adaptation to new circumstances.

However, what should distinguish legal interpretation from other types of interpretation is the need for the interpreter to preserve a certain degree of "dogmatic distance."[46] The aim to adapt and concretise so as to achieve an "appropriate" resolution of the case (that is, a resolution consistent with the axiological and pragmatic expectations of the interpreter) is counterbalanced and constrained by the canon of legal interpretation accepted in a particular legal culture and the so far adopted readings.

One of the principal hermeneutical claims is that the act of understanding is a circular process. Understanding emerges as a result of "wandering perception," which moves between the whole text and its parts, between the normative text and facts of the case, between the aim of the norm and its linguistic shape, etc. Individual words make it possible to understand the rule they form, and, conversely, their meanings can be determined on the basis of the sense of the whole. To make the meaning of a norm concrete and definite, one must refer to relevant circumstances of the case; deciding whether and which circumstances are relevant requires understanding the text in the light of which they become normatively significant. All elements of the act of understanding are interconnected, making it possible to arrive at a picture of the case through a sequence of approximations that emerge as a result of perception wandering between its elements.

Thus, hermeneutics rejects the syllogistic-deductive model of understanding law, where a decision is identified with the conclusion drawn from premises comprising the general legal norm and the actual circumstances of the case.[47] The process of understanding is much more complex and proceeds through a series of gradual concretisations which emerge from a spiral movement between the perception of the whole case and its individual elements. The target for wandering perception is the ultimate act of understanding law, that is, finding the correspondence between the norm and the actual state of affairs.

Interestingly, hermeneutic intuitions concerning the structure of the act of understanding now receive strong support from theories of cognition and decision-making processes, based on advances in modern neurocognitive research. Far-reaching similarities to the concept of hermeneutic circle can be found, in particular, in the connectionist model, according to which the mind forms a coherent image of the problem and its solution through mutual

---

46 Stelmach, *Współczesna...*, p. 78.

47 Cf. M. Zirk-Sadowski, *Wprowadzenie do filozofii prawa* [Introduction to Philosophy of Law] (Warszawa: Wolters Kluwer, 2011), p. 91.

strengthening of perceptions of elements which fit together and reducing the weight of elements which do not.[48] It is not impossible that further research into the neuropsychological mechanisms of solving cognitive and decision-making problems will provide additional, solid empirical support for the hermeneutic concept of circularity of legal interpretation processes, on the basis of which concrete legal cases are resolved.

It is also worth noticing that the circularity of the process of understanding need not exclude the syllogistic structure of legal reasoning. Constructing the premises for syllogistic reasoning may be treated as the final result of the processes of perception and decision-making, indispensable in the structure of reasoning in which a general norm must be applied to actual circumstances. This does not mean, however, that the form and content of the premises are accessible for the interpreter "in advance." On the contrary, the path leads through very complex acts of perception, associating, understanding, choice-making, etc., which only partially take place on the conscious level. Thus, legal hermeneutics seems to be incompatible only with a very simplistic and crude view of legal syllogism, understood as an exhaustive description of the actual process of reasoning of the jurist, covering the entirety of mental operations which are involved in the process of law-application.[49]

Equally important to hermeneutics is the concept of pre-understanding (*Vorverständnis*), regarded as both a condition and an inherent element of each act of interpretation. Although pre-understanding, like other similar concepts employed in hermeneutic approaches (such as prejudice – *Vorurteil*), is defined in a variety of ways, it can be said to refer to whatever the interpreter brings to the act of understanding, whatever he or she "contributes." This concerns, in particular, prior knowledge, expectations regarding the text under interpretation and its possible meaning, values, aims, and aspirations which influence the act of understanding.

Pre-understanding not only takes part in every act of understanding by the interpreter, but also is a necessary condition of its success. The knowledge of the language of the interpreted text, at least rudimentary awareness of its cultural context, and a certain level of general knowledge of the world are indispensable for any act of understanding to take place. Moreover, pre-understanding is to some extent individual, and thus, it can diversify both the process and the

48 For more detail, see Pietrzykowski, *Intuicja…*, pp. 248f.
49 Ibid., pp. 216f.

result of the interpretation of the same text by various interpreters.[50] Such differences may concern the intellectual component of pre-understanding (beliefs about the interpreted text, its immediate context, and general knowledge of the world), the emotional component (values, judgements, and the affective attitude of the interpreter), and the volitional component (subjectively assumed goals or aspirations connected with the circumstances accompanying the process of interpretation).[51]

Pre-understanding determines the preliminary expectation of sense, thus directing the process of understanding towards the initially adopted interpretive hypotheses. In this way, it defines a certain decision area for the interpreter.[52] This is not to say that this area is fixed and stable; rather, it is part of a "game" going on between the text (or the way in which it is perceived), the interpreter's pre-understanding, and external circumstances and conditions of the process of interpretation, where all elements mutually interact.

Pre-understanding is involved not only in the actual understanding and decision-making processes but also in the justification of decisions already made. As noticed by Tomasz Gizbert-Studnicki, for any argumentation to take place – including legal argumentation – there must exist a shared common ground of knowledge and axiological or normative beliefs. This substratum constitutes an interpretive community; without it, justifying anything would be impossible.[53] Any justification must have a certain point of departure, a foundation which needs no justification; it must refer to some "common points," which function as indisputable premises for the conclusions drawn by the interpreter. Seen in this light, pre-understanding is part of any justification of a legal decision, usually not expressed *expressis verbis*, providing the unique cultural foundation that makes interpretive discourse possible.

The act of understanding a legal text may be direct (intuitive) or indirect in nature, that is, it may proceed through conscious interpretive efforts and follow various methods of legal interpretation (directives or canons).[54] Still, even in the

50 T. Gizbert-Studnicki draws attention to the difference between pre-understanding understood globally (as shared knowledge which constitutes a particular interpretive community) and pre-understanding in the individual sense of the term, that is, the knowledge, expectations, and aims of particular interpreters; see Gizbert-Studnicki, "Vorverständnisbegriff in der juristischen Hermeneutik," *Archiv für Rechts- und Sozialphilosophie* 73 (1987), p. 480.

51 Ibid.

52 Stelmach, *Współczesna filozofia…*, p. 84.

53 Gizbert-Studnicki, "Vorverständnisbegriff…," p. 489.

54 Stelmach, Brożek, *Metody…*, pp. 266–268.

so-called immediate cognition, where it is not an effect of intentional interpretive activity, hermeneutic experience (the experience of understanding a text) does occur as a result of complex extra-conscious cognitive and decision-making processes.[55] Consciously undertaken interpretive activities, in turn, as part of the act of indirect, or mediated, understanding, are necessarily immersed in a large number of parallel, extra-conscious associative processes, which, in principle, escape any intentional control.

Thus, the distinction between immediate intuitive and conscious mediated understanding in intentional interpretive activity forms a certain continuum rather than a simple dichotomy of two opposite modes of action. Spontaneous, automatised associative processes and conscious mental states continually interact, turning any mediated cognition (including the act of understanding a text) into an activity that is deeply entrenched in a variety of intuitive perceptual-associative processes. For this reason, suggestions that direct understanding should be totally rejected from legal interpretation are psychologically unrealistic.[56]

Legal applications of ontological proposals formulated within the other hermeneutic approach are also very interesting and valuable. From this perspective, the act of understanding is central not only for the knowledge of law but also for the very existence of law. This approach to the ontology of law is founded on the refutation of the Cartesian division between the subject and object of cognition, which in the tradition of philosophical hermeneutics should be attributed primarily to Gadamer.[57] The Cartesian view of the relation between the subject and object of cognition is, in his opinion, impossible to sustain because the faith in the existence of pure judgements about facts (independent of any theoretical assumptions) is illusory, as is the belief in the independence of reason from contingent cultural and historical circumstances of the act of cognition and in the neutrality of the conceptual apparatus, supposedly reflecting objective reality without influencing it in any way.[58]

The most well-known ideas within the ontology of law are those proposed by Kaufmann. In his version of legal hermeneutics, the act of understanding, which

55 Pietrzykowski, *Intuicja…*, pp. 257f.

56 Ibid., p. 264.

57 See Zirk-Sadowski, *Wprowadzenie…*, p. 86; for more detail, see also Zirk-Sadowski, "Pozytywizm prawniczy a filozoficzna opozycja podmiotu i przedmiotu poznania" [Legal Positivism and the Philosophical Opposition of the Cognitive Subject and Object], in *Studia z filozofii prawa* [Studies in Philosophy of Law], ed. J. Stelmach (Kraków: Wydawnictwo Uniwersytetu Jagiellońskiego, 2001), pp. 83ff.

58 Zirk-Sadowski, *Wprowadzenie…*, p. 87.

consists in achieving "a correspondence between norm and fact," is at the same time an act of realisation of law (*Rechtsverwirklichung*).[59] It is only in the process of understanding that law acquires its final shape. Otherwise, it exists merely as a certain potentiality, actualised in the hermeneutic act of understanding.

According to Kaufmann, the process of realisation of law proceeds in three stages: from general principles of justice, predating positive law, through abstract and general norms of acts of law, to situated decisions. It is only in the act of understanding that norm and fact are combined, that obligation and a real-life entity are assimilated.[60] The creativity of the act of understanding does not merely consist in the fact that it is not limited to recreating the meaning of a norm which exists "out there." It means, first and foremost, that it is only in the act of understanding that a norm can be associated with a particular state of affairs, thus constituting the final, concrete shape of law.

Hermeneutic theories of law offer an original and very promising perspective on jurisprudence as legal science (focused on the study of the content of norms that comprise the legal order and the legal consequences that follow from them). At the same time, they are typically descriptive in nature. They propose a thorough analysis of the characteristics of the act of understanding as the basic tool for gaining knowledge about law (and, in some sense, also for creating law) by its interpreters. In doing so, they do not formulate any prescriptions as to how to overcome the situational and subjective entanglement of legal interpretation.[61] Thus, they expose the illusory nature of many prejudices (or pre-judgements) dominating the methodological self-awareness of legal science, without striving to provide any recommendations that could make legal acts of understanding more objective.[62]

The indisputable advantage of hermeneutic inquiries into the nature of understanding and interpretation of law is thus connected, first and foremost, with raising the critical self-awareness of legal science with regard to the dependence of the course and results of these processes on a variety of factors, often contingent ones. These factors make it impossible to treat the products of understanding and interpretation as objective truths, formulated "from no particular

59 Ibid., p. 91.

60 See Stelmach, Brożek, *Metody…*, p. 261.

61 Gizbert-Studnicki, "Das hermeneutische," p. 366.

62 As noticed by Leyh, "[h]ermeneutics neither supplies a method for correctly reading texts nor underwrites an authoritative interpretation of any given text, legal or otherwise;" *Legal Hermeneutics: History, Theory, and Practice*, ed. G. Leyh (Berkley: University of California Press, 1992), p. xvii.

point of view." In sum, the contribution that hermeneutics has made to the development of the methodological foundations of legal science is primarily that of criticism and unmasking:

> the activity of questioning and adopting a suspicious attitude toward authority is at the heart of hermeneutical discourse. Hermeneutics involves confronting the aporias that face us, and it attempts to undermine, at least in partial ways, the calm assurances transmitted by the received views and legal orthodoxies.[63]

At the same time, the hermeneutic perspective points to the similarity between the act of understanding in legal science (with its inseparable historical-subjective entanglements) and that in any other field of the humanities that relies on interpretation. Therefore, it does not attack specifically the unfounded methodological claims of legal science, but rather draws attention to the nature of cognition and understanding in general, regardless of their object. In this way, it helps reduce the methodological inferiority complex that legal science has experienced in relation to other fields of cognition.[64] In other words, it demonstrates that the problems connected with the objectivity of legal cognition are in fact common not only to all humanities but also to all other forms of understanding the world.

3.6 The realistic model

Both American and Scandinavian versions of legal realism to a large extent aim at transforming jurisprudence from legal science to the science of law. For this reason, they will be discussed in more detail in the chapter devoted to this second line of legal reflection. Nevertheless, also within approaches that construe jurisprudence as legal science, attempts have been made to apply realistic models. Riccardo Guastini's methodological proposal may serve as an example of such attempts.[65]

Guastini's version of analytical realism is a conjunction of three theses: ontological, interpretive, and epistemological. According to the ontological thesis, law denotes a set of normative formulations. In systems of statutory law, normative formulations take the form of legal rules. However, normative formulations are not, strictly speaking, law. Law consists of norms which are the content of the

---

63 Ibid.

64 Gizbert-Studnicki, "Das hermeneutische...," p. 367.

65 R. Guastini, "A Realistic View on Law and Legal Cognition," *Revus. Journal for Constitutional Theory and Philosophy of Law* 27 (2015), pp. 45ff.

formulations rather than of formulations as such. Thus, law refers to the meanings attributed to normative formulations by their interpreters.[66] At the same time, the ontological thesis assumes that norms are linguistic entities (that is, in contrast to the majority of realistic approaches, it adopts a linguistic view of the norm) which can only become part of law as a result of appropriate legislation processes (in other words, there is no norm without a norm-giver).

The ontological thesis is complemented by the interpretive thesis, which introduces a distinction between cognitive interpretation and adjudicative interpretation. Cognitive interpretation takes place when the interpreter identifies the range of possible meanings of a particular expression; it is also applied in cases where, as a result of ambiguity or vagueness, it is possible to interpret a text in more than one way. By contrast, adjudicative interpretation is not limited to identifying the range of possible meanings of an expression but chooses one of the options as the definite one. This choice is not cognitive in nature; it is an act of decision-making that is determined by the interpreter's judgements and aims (influenced by his or her practical interests, beliefs about what is just and right, and the adopted conceptual framework of legal dogmatics).[67] Thus, interpretive statements of this type are not descriptions that can be assigned a truth-value; rather, they ascribe a concrete meaning to an expression and hence cannot be true or false.

Jurists not only carry out adjudicative interpretation of legal norms (both in adjudication and in dogmatic reflection on the content of law) but also engage in legal construction. Guastini includes here, among others, the creation of normative and axiological gaps (which are, in principle, products of the interpreter's activity rather than objective features of law),[68] the creation of an axiological hierarchy of norms, the specification and weighing of legal rules, and the construction of norms which are implicit in the normative formulations by the lawmaker.[69] Like ascriptions, statements which are effects of legal construction cannot be assigned a truth-value. According to Guastini,

> if interpretation properly understood is not a cognitive activity, legal construction is a fortiori the output not of cognition, but of decision. In fact, legal construction amounts to genuine juristic and/or juridical law-creation.[70]

---

66 Ibid., pp. 48–49.

67 Ibid., pp. 46–47.

68 In Polish literature, this view was propagated by J. Nowacki in e.g. "Luki w prawie. Ideologia" [Gaps in the Law. Ideology], in *Studia z teorii prawa* [Studies in Legal Theory]. (Kraków: Zakamycze, 2003), pp. 349ff.

69 Guastini, "A Realistic View…," p. 47.

70 Ibid., p. 48.

Legal constructions are not ascriptions but rather concealed prescriptions. They are "secretly prescriptive" in that, although they appear to be existential propositions, claiming that such and such norms exist in the legal system, they in fact aim at creating and introducing new norms into this system.[71]

The ontological and interpretive theses form the basis for the epistemological thesis, which is the core of the realistic model of legal science proposed by Guastini. According to the epistemological thesis, the traditional approach to the tasks and practice of the doctrinal study of law cannot be considered truly scientific, because its supposedly cognitive statements about law are in fact ascriptions or prescriptions. They have no cognitive value (they are neither true nor false), and so they cannot be treated as genuinely scientific. Rather, they are elements of legal policy, that is, the operation and development of the legal system, and hence should be part of the object of description.

Guastini believes that jurisprudence may have a scientific value provided that it is realistic. On this view, it would have to comprise three types of statements. The first type corresponds to cognitive (and not adjudicative) interpretation of normative formulations by the lawmaker. The second type includes descriptions of adjudicative interpretation and legal construction decisions which are actually made in legal practice. The third involves descriptions of the meanings of normative formulations which are most likely to be applied in practice (without providing further justification for such decisions or comments regarding the "appropriate" understanding of a norm in cases where a variety of existing interpretations precludes effective predictions about actual application).[72]

Thus transformed, legal science would only make statements that have a truth-value and that refer to the content of normative formulations by the lawmaker,

---

71 Ibid., p. 51, note 20.

72 It is interesting to note that in this respect Guastini's views may be conceived as specifying and to some extent – correcting the idea of rational jurisprudence proposed by H. Albert. According to Albert the scientific jurisprudence modelled after Popper's hypothetical-deductive method should treat norms and their interpretations are hypotheses of what will be the most effective mean to achieve the presupposed social ends (H. Albert, Rechtswissenschaft als Realwissenschaft. Das Rechts als Soziale Tatsache und die Aufgabe der Jurisprudenz, Nomos, Baden Baden 1993, 24ff.). Guastini, however, emphasizes that the practically relevant norms and their interpretations are produced by legal decision-makers rather than a legal doctrine aiming to accurately report the content of the law. Thus, norms and their interpretations are subject-matter of descriptive endavour of legal science instead of the scientific theories or hypotheses themselves.

to their understanding by courts and other interpreters, or to predictions about their future understanding by courts (that is, to legal norms that are "in force" in the realistic sense of the term).

Guastini's methodological proposal is an interesting attempt to combine elements of Kelsen's normativism, legal realism, and analytical philosophy of law. It is an original view of legal science that aims at providing a realistic description of the content of law and offering predictions based on this description. Still, it seems to form a certain superstructure built on the foundation of interpreters' "normal" activity, which, in the model proposed by Guastini, has no scientific value. This activity consists in formulating ascriptions and prescriptions with no truth-value, that is, products of adjudicative interpretation and legal construction. Thus, descriptive legal science (that is, one that meets Guastini's criteria and so is a "genuine" science) does not replace but rather tacitly assumes "non-scientific" dogmatic-legal activity, whose statements and findings are then the object of legal science in the realistic model proposed by Guastini.

In sum, Guastini's model cannot, in fact, replace legal science in the present understanding of the term; rather, it offers its meta-description (thus being, to some extent, a science of legal science). The author himself clearly juxtaposes legal science and what he calls legal scholarship, which comprises:

> the usual academic investigation into the law, namely into the normative texts which are regarded as the official sources of law.[73]

At the same time, as he observes elsewhere, direct interpretation (in legal practice and legal dogmatics) is an inseparable and indispensable element of the legal order.

> One cannot even imagine the law without interpreters (namely, jurists) as well as one cannot imagine a religion without priests or theologians.[74]

With this in mind, one may doubt whether Guastini's proposal can be treated as a model of jurisprudence as legal science (in the here-adopted understanding of legal science, as opposed to the science of law). Instead, it appears to be an attempt at a description and reconstruction of the decisions and claims made by the dogmatically (rather than realistically) oriented legal science, which is construed as an activity that co-creates the content of positive law. On this view, legal science remains an indispensable component of legal scholarship, even though,

73 Ibid., p. 51.
74 Ibid., p. 50.

according to Guastini, it has no cognitive value as such and cannot be treated as a source of any scientific knowledge about law.

***

The practical value and importance of legal science understood as a reflection oriented towards the interpretation, validation, and systematisation of the content of positive law is beyond doubt. Its basic task is to produce statements concerning who and how should behave in particular circumstances so as to act in accordance with law. What remains disputable is its status as a science, in particular, if science is understood as an activity that aims at formulating true and intersubjectively verifiable statements about its object, in this case, about the content of law. There is no doubt that systematic efforts of legal dogmatics produce vast amounts of knowledge whose practical and educational merits cannot be denied (including knowledge of historical facts, views held by other dogmatists, theories and concepts they propose, their arguments and problems involved, etc). What may raise doubts is whether this is knowledge about law or, perhaps, about legal dogmatics itself, as it identifies the conventional consensus of the learned with the knowledge of the existing content of law.

In fact, all directions in the modern methodological reflection on legal science are unanimous that in its present shape, it does not describe the content of law (or, at least, it is not limited to its description) but co-creates it. In most cases, the creative function of legal science takes the form of the optimisation of the content of legal norms. By formulating statements in such a way that they appear to merely reconstruct the existing "real content" of a given regulation, it often manages to achieve this effect. As the belief becomes established among interpreters that a particular doctrinal description reflects the real content of the norm, it is accepted in this particular form and so applied.

Recognition of the Janus face of legal science – as a description which performatively shapes its object to fit the description – is to a large extent unrelated to whether or not it is treated as a normative activity and whether or not it is regarded as scientific. This perspective, however, is quite remote from the image of legal science that dominates the self-awareness of scholars, who usually treat their findings as a mere description of the objective content of norms of the legal system. Arguments that refer to optimisation (for instance, that point to better or worse effects of a particular interpretation) are commonly accepted as sound reasons for determining the "real" content of a given norm. This, in turn, leads to gross simplification and identification of the scientific merit of legal dogmatics with providing a true description of its object, which in this case would be the real content of legal norms.

This view of legal dogmatics is not only simplified and anachronistic; first and foremost, it ignores its important, and perhaps fundamental, value, that is, its essential contribution to the development, improvement, and practical functionality of the legal order. It comprises, but at the same time extends far beyond, what Hage calls the maintenance of the legal system, connected with such major tasks as systematising law and enabling assimilation of changes and amendments. This contribution is largely independent of whether or not – and to what extent – this activity deserves the name of a "scientific" study of law.

4 The science of law

In parallel to the evolution of modern concepts of jurisprudence as legal science, other models have also been proposed that view it as a science of law. They treat the legal phenomenon as a set of empirically studied facts which must be explained and described, together with the regularities that govern them. This is viewed as the condition for the rise of genuinely scientific jurisprudence. On this understanding, the science of law does not aim at the systematisation, clarification, or optimisation of legal content; rather, it seeks to explain the way in which the legal order is constituted by the behaviour and experiences of people who contribute to the formation, application, and observance of law.

Precursors of this approach include pioneers of the sociology of law, in particular, Eugen Ehrlich, and modern anthropology of law, such as Bronisław Malinowski, as well as Leon Petrażycki, the founder of the psychological theory of law.

In the context of the sociology of law, Ehrlich usually appears together with two other co-founders of this discipline; nevertheless, his contribution deserves special mention for at least three reasons. Firstly, as noted in Chapter 2, it was Ehrlich who as early as at the beginning of the twentieth century argued that, apart from the legal-dogmatic study of law, there was a need for an empirically oriented science of law (although he expressed this idea in different terms). Secondly, while for Emil Durkheim and Max Weber, the co-founders of general sociology, law was merely a fragment of their research interests, Ehrlich focused specifically on the sociological description of the operation of legal norms. Thirdly, the famous dispute between Ehrlich and Kelsen occasioned a direct confrontation and further development of two radically different views on law and on the tasks and methods of science that should study it.

At the heart of Ehrlich's views is the belief that it is only possible to describe law "as it is in reality" by analysing social practice, that is, the rules that are observed and that shape the actual behaviour of people. This is what constitutes the "living law," which may – but does not have to – overlap with statutory or adjudicatory regulations. Living law emerges spontaneously at the grass-roots as socially accepted and respected models of behaviour that ought to be applied in concrete circumstances. Ehrlich puts it in the following way:

> Zweifellos entsteht ein grosser Teil des Rechts unmittelbar in der Gesellschaft: das ist die innere Ordnung der gesellschaftlichen Verhältnisse, der Ehe, der Familie, der sonstigen gesellschaftlichen Verbände, die Bodenverfassung, die Verträge, die Erbgange.[1]

In western legal culture, this kind of "living law" was initially the only form of law. In the course of time, solutions to concrete cases were gradually worked out by specially prepared lawyers (as in Roman praetorian law or English common law). This has given rise to "lawyers' law" (*Juristenrecht*), which to a large extent co-determines the ways of settling disputes before appropriate authorised institutions. Still, in practice, the entirety of social relations is primarily regulated by living law, irrespective of whether or not – and to what extent – it actually contributed to the formation of rules of lawyers' law.

Apart from living law and lawyers' law, another type of legal rules developed rapidly, influenced mainly by the Enlightenment ideals of codification: statutory law (*Gesetzesrecht*). Here, law has the form of norms which are relatively general and remote from concrete circumstances of real-life cases.[2] Statutory law does not replace living law, which continues to function in social relations and everyday interactions. Although it may influence living law to various degrees, it should not be identified with it.[3] Norms that in practice shape the content of social relations and determine the patterns of behaviour of their participants always prove much more complex and numerous than any written codes or acts. Any attempt to reduce the inherent diversity and dynamics of law – with its vast array of models of behaviour and mutual normative expectations accepted in a given community (e.g., family, economic relations, societies, companies, etc.) – to a closed register of rules may be compared to the following situation:

> wenn man einen Strom in einen Teich sperren wollte: was davon hineinkommt, ist kein lebender Strom mehr, sondern Totes Gewasser, und viel kommt überhaupt nicht hinein.[4]

An appropriate and faithful description of the entirety of law requires a broader approach than a dogmatic focus on the texts of statutory law, which are neither the point of departure nor the target of the legal order. On the contrary, it is living law that is its essence and its core. This is why a scientific study of

---

1 E. Ehrlich, "Gesetz und Lebendes Recht," in Ehrlich, *Gesetz und Lebendes Recht*, ed. M. Rehbinder (Berlin: Duncker & Humblot, 1986), p. 229.

2 Ibid., p. 231.

3 As an example of a mismatch between living law and statutory law, one may invoke, in the Polish legal context, the practice of the so-called trade credit, which does not exactly follow legal regulations preventing payment gridlocks.

4 Ibid., p. 232.

law must focus on the rules that actually shape people's behaviour in situations which Ehrlich refers to as "facts of law" (*Tatsachen des Rechts*), such as the relations of domination and possession, the declaration and realisation of will, etc.

Ehrlich's views triggered a famous polemic with Hans Kelsen, initiated by Kelsen's frontal attack on Ehrlich's main work.[5] Kelsen criticised his proposals for, among others, a failure to distinguish between norms of living law and other social norms (morality, custom, habit, religious duties, etc.). Law, in Ehrilch's view, "dissolves" in the variety of factors that influence actual behaviour patterns. While Kelsen did not reject the possibility or need to carry out empirical analyses of the social effects of law, he did not consider them as falling within the true scope of jurisprudence. According to Kelsen, jurisprudence should be a normative science with a clearly defined object: the content of obligations in the legal sense of the term.[6]

For the general public, the discussion demonstrated that Ehrlich could not provide a satisfactory answer to Kelsen's critical remarks. He regarded the problem of distinguishing legal norms from other socially accepted models of behaviour as an insignificant and peripheral terminological issue, or argued that this distinction could be based on the type of feelings produced by the violation of a norm.[7] Nevertheless, he conceded that it was impossible to provide a sharp, scientifically justified distinction between law and morality without imposing

5 The polemic continued in the years 1915–1917 in the journal *Archiv für Sozialwissenschaft und Sozialpolitik*. In his later years, Kelsen apparently regretted his too radical and aggressive criticism of Ehrilch's ideas; for more detail, see M. Garcia-Salmones, "On Kelsen's Sein: An Approach to Kelsenian Sociological Themes," *No Foundations. An Interdisciplinary Journal on Law and Justice* 8 (2011), p. 43.

6 In fact, Kelsen's criticism went further and referred to Ehrlich's failure to distinguish between laws in the normative sense of the term and laws understood as observed regularities (as in the case of "laws of nature"). This point was already at that time, and continued to be, one of Kelsen's *idées fixes*. Ehrlich was noticeably resentful about it and replied that "to accuse someone of confusing an ought rule with a law of nature… comes close to calling him a fool;" see B. von Klink, "Facts and Norms. The Unfinished Debate Between Eugen Ehrlich and Hans Kelsen," *Tilburg Working Paper Series on Jurisprudence and Legal History* 06-03 (28 August 2006), p. 9. Still, van Klink also observes that the approach to law proposed by Ehrlich does not provide a tool to distinguish between rules and types of behaviour that some are *de facto* able to extort from others (ibid., pp. 17–18).

7 Indignation in the case of legal norms, condemnation in the case of moral norms, disgust in the case of norms of custom, etc.

some arbitrary definition and thus ignoring the complexity of norms which actually function in society.[8]

Parallel to the development of sociological approaches to law, the foundations of the modern anthropology of law were being formed, with the works of Bronisław Malinowski making the most significant contribution to the development of the methodological basis for the study of law in so-called primaeval communities. Although first anthropological-legal theories appeared earlier (e.g., proposed by Henry Maine or Savigny), it was Malinowski's theoretical concepts and empirical observations that marked the beginning of anthropology in its modern shape. The following century of research into various forms of law in non-state societies, carried out within world anthropology, can in fact be seen as "the pursuit of Malinowski's agenda."[9]

Malinowski not only introduced new methodological concepts, developed during his expeditions and stays in the communities of the islands of the South Pacific. With regard to law, the most important innovation was his rejection of the then dominant notion of law as an institutionalised system of formally established rules enforced by specially authorised organs. This view of law led to the conclusion that, in "primitive communities," law did not exist at all or that its form was heavily reduced. Moreover, it was commonly believed that "savage societies" either were incapable of developing legal rules (because their level of civilisation was too low) or did not need them, because actions of their members were governed exclusively by rules of custom, which ensured harmony and eliminated potential conflicts (following the myth of the Noble Savage, propagated in the West by Jean-Jacques Rousseau).[10]

Malinowski, in turn, argues that legal rules are social norms whose function in a given community is

---

8 B. von Klink, "Facts...," pp. 11f. Since then, sociological reflection on law has repeatedly addressed the problem of distinguishing law from other socially accepted models of behaviour. Some attempts to solve it refer to functional criteria, an organised system of coercion, or, as in the case of Brian Tamanaha's proposal, the conventional understanding of "law" and its limits accepted in a given society.

9 J. Conley and W. O'Barr, "Legal Anthropology Comes Home: A Brief History of the Ethnographic Study of Law," *Loyola of Los Angeles Law Review* 27/1 (1993), pp. 46–47; available at http://digitalcommons.lmu.edu/llr/vol27/iss1/4.

10 For a very interesting discussion of these illusions of anthropology and attempts to overcome them, see S. Pinker, *The Blank Slate: The Modern Denial of Human Nature* (New York: Viking, 2002).

> to curb certain natural propensities, to hem in and control human instincts and to impose a non-spontaneous, compulsory behaviour – in other words, to ensure a type of co-operation which is based on mutual concessions and sacrifices for a common end.[11]

In contrast to "more developed" legal systems, in primaeval communities, the rules are not formally codified or safeguarded by highly organised professional institutions. Nevertheless, functionally, they play the same role as norms of legal acts or norms of precedent in Western countries. They are based on the principle of reciprocity (*do ut des*), according to which rights and benefits are balanced by corresponding obligations and liabilities. Legal rules are thus perceived as mutual rights and duties, although this reciprocity need not be direct. They often form complex chains, give rise to normative institutions which ensure social order, and are enforced on the basis of the principle of solidarity, with various forms of coercion and social pressure. In Malinowski's view, it is possible to distinguish legal norms, so understood, from other types of social rules (religious rules or rules of customs), although primaeval law is by no means isolated from the entirety of norms that regulate the behaviour of community members.[12]

Legal rules are invariably a manifestation of "biological, mental and social needs of human nature,"[13] a product of a natural human inclination to cooperate within a social group, to establish a family, and to look after the offspring. Ignoring the elementary relationship between the effectiveness of law and its compatibility with such natural inclinations leads to the naive belief in the lawmaker's omnipotence. Malinowski observed, not without a touch of irony, that Western societies' interest in primaeval communities had been marked by

> the over-emphasis of criminal justice … the attention devoted to the breaches of the law and their punishment … cases of blood-curdling crime, followed by tribal vendetta … accounts of criminal sorcery with retaliation, of incest, adultery, breach of taboo or murder … [to the exclusion of] the description of the ordinary; … of the law obeyed and not the law broken; of the permanent currents and tides in their social life and not its adventitious storms.[14]

Malinowski's anthropological-legal research opened new vistas for the twentieth-century study of law as an element of culture and contributed to the evolution of various versions of legal pluralism (which often referred to Ehrlich's sociological

---

11 B. Malinowski, *Crime and Custom in Savage Society* (1959), p. 64.

12 For more detail, see B. Olszewska-Dyoniziak, *Bronisław Malinowski* (Zielona Góra: WSP, 1996), pp. 111–123.

13 Malinowski, *Crime…*, p. 2.

14 Ibid., pp. 72–73.

concepts).[15] Important for their later development was the emphasis on the role of language in the shaping, perception, and understanding of social practices constituted by and in the use of language. Awareness of the role of language helped avoid the risk of producing their warped description resulting from a hasty translation and imposition of the conceptual apparatus of the scholar's own legal culture.[16]

The third line of development which blazed a trail for jurisprudence as the science of law comprises the ideas of legal psychologism formulated by Leon Petrażycki at the beginning of the twentieth century. Petrażycki's ideas were in many respects ahead of his time, although the shortcomings of empirical psychology, then a new and evolving field, heavily limited the possibilities of further development and application of his theory of law.[17]

Petrażycki's psychological theory of law was based on his own innovative methodological concepts. Among them, of particular importance was the notion of adequacy of a scientific theory. According to Petrażycki, for a theory to be well-built, its claims not only must be true, but they must also refer to an entire uniform class of objects. In other words, they must state that a certain property occurs in all objects that have this property, and only in these objects. Theories that correctly describe properties of objects but define their class too narrowly are called "limping theories," while theories that define the class too broadly are dubbed "jumping theories."

In Petrażycki's view, the starting point for the science of law is defining the class of phenomena to which its statements will refer. The class must be so defined that it is possible to propose an adequate scientific theory which correctly identifies important properties occurring in all its members, and only in its members. Theories referring to law in the "popular legal" understanding of the term fail to meet this criterion because, so understood, law does not refer to any uniform class of phenomena. The term was established in response to concrete practical needs and in this respect resembles such terms as "vegetables" or "game." They may be useful in everyday life (which is why they were coined), but

15 See, e.g., S. Jørgensen, *Pluralis Juris. Towards a Relativistic Theory of Law* (Aarhus: Det Laerde Selskab, 1982); G. Teubner, "Global Bukowina. Legal Pluralism in the World-Society," in *Global Law Without a State*, ed. G. Teubner (Aldershot: Dartmouth 1997), pp. 3ff.; M. Chiba, "Other Phases of Legal Pluralism in the Contemporary World," *Ratio Juris* 11/3 (1998), pp. 225ff.; B. Dupret, *Droit et sciences sociales* (Paris: Armand Colin, 2006).

16 See Conley and O'Barr, "Legal...," pp. 202f.

17 For more detail, see T. Pietrzykowski, "Wielkość i błąd teorii Leona Petrażyckiego," in Pietrzykowski, *Intuicja prawnicza. W stronę zewnętrznej integracji teorii prawa* [Legal Intuition. Toward an External Integration of Legal Theory] (Warszawa: Difin, 2012), pp. 278f.

an attempt to propose a botanical theory of vegetables or zoological theory of game would be a gross misconception.

The situation is similar in the case of theories referring to law in the sense in which the term is used by jurists. A legal scholar attempting to build a scientific theory of law, so understood, would be like a chemist who strives to propose a scientific theory of water, treating it not as a chemical compound but applying the common, everyday sense of the term (which, again, reflects concrete practical needs rather than denotes a uniform class of objects that can serve as a starting point for the construction of scientific theories).

Thus, a preliminary condition for any adequate theory of law is a precise definition of the concept, that is, replacing the popular understanding of the term with one that refers to an objectively defined fragment of reality (by analogy to a chemist who, before embarking on the research, must replace the popular understanding of water with its precise definition, enabling construction of adequate scientific theories).

Petrażycki believed that the class of phenomena that could serve as a foundation for a scientific theory of law comprises a special kind of mental experience, namely, the emotion of obligation of a bilateral imperative-attributive nature. By contrast, he referred to unilateral imperative emotions (emotions of obligation which are not accompanied by the sense of "claim" on any part) as moral emotions.

On this understanding, as the entirety of imperative-attributive emotions of obligation (that is, as defined by science), law differs widely from what is commonly understood by this term. In Petrażycki's view, it refers to the totality of bilateral imperative-attributive emotions of obligation. The actual class of legal phenomena is thus very different from what is meant by the "popular legal" use of the term law.[18]

Irrespective of the merits and flaws of its individual concepts, Petrażycki's theory is a methodologically sound attempt to lay solid foundations for jurisprudence, based on a radically different model than that of dogmatically oriented legal science.[19] It was not meant to replace legal dogmatics, whose task Petrażycki

18 Petrażycki distinguishes a subclass of legal phenomena which comprises "official law," that is, a set of rules "applied and supported by representatives of state authorities by virtue of the social duty they perform." It seems that a thorough description of the way in which law as individual mental experience transforms into "official law," and of the relation between the two, is the most important missing link in Petrażycki's account of the legal phenomenon (Pietrzykowski, "Wielkość...," p. 289).

19 This is not to say that Petrażycki was a "lonely giant;" rather, he was one of the most significant and outstanding representatives of his times, which were conducive to

defined as "additional elaboration and unification of positive law." Legal dogmatics was to provide the basis for "a system of statements that would satisfy the need of consistency as well as objective definiteness and impartiality of legal relations in a better and more comprehensive way than law itself."[20] And conversely, dogmatics cannot replace a general scientific theory of law, whose tasks are very different, as are the principles of formulating methodologically correct descriptions of legal reality. This reality, in Petrażycki's view, should be construed

> as a fact, as a phenomenon that can be studied empirically, rather than as an ideal obligation (material or formal), which is the sense of the norm.[21]

Petrażycki's views immediately came under substantial criticism. Objections were raised in particular against the very idea of reducing law to the level of individual mental experience. Still, his proposals gave impetus to many other important directions in the development of jurisprudence as the science of law. His approach significantly influenced the work of some of the most prominent sociologists of law (such as, e.g., Adam Podgórecki, Nicholas Timasheff, and Peter Sorokin),[22] while the shortcomings of his "one-dimensional" understanding of law as a phenomenon limited to individual psychology gave rise to the concept of the multilevel nature of legal phenomena, developed in the next decades.[23] It transformed Petrażycki's psychologism into a theory focused on one specific level of law. Critics of the multilevel approach, in turn, such as Ziembiński,

---

such enquiries; see. K. Opałek, "Teoria Petrażyckiego a współczesna teoria prawa" [Petrażycki's Theory and Modern Legal Theory], in *Z zagadnień teorii prawa i teorii nauki Leona Petrażyckiego* [Elements From Leon Petrażycki's Theory of Law and Theory of Science], ed. K. Opałek (Warszawa: PWN, 1969), p. 119.

20 L. Petrażycki, *Teoria prawa i państwa w związku z teorią moralności* [The Theory of Law and the State in Relation to the Theory of Morality], Vol. I (Warszawa: PWN, 1959), p. 312. For more detail, see A. Peczenik, "Petrażycki o dogmatyce prawa - krytyka czy obrona?" [Petrażycki on the Dogma of Law - Critique or Defense?] in *Z zagadnień teorii prawa i teorii nauki Leona Petrażyckiego* [Elements From Leon Petrażycki's Theory of Law and Theory of Science], ed. K. Opałek (Warszawa: PWN, 1969), pp. 137f.

21 Opałek, "Teoria," p. 121.

22 On the relation between Petrażycki's ideas and the later sociology of law, see, e.g., A. Podgórecki, "Unrecognized Father of Sociology of Law," *Law and Society Review* 15 (1980–1981); and A. Kojder, "Leon Petrażycki," In *Socjologia prawa. Główne problemy i postacie* [Sociology of Law. Key Problems and Figures], ed. A. Kojder and Z. Cywiński (Warszawa: Wydawnictwo Uniwersytetu Warszawskiego, 2014), pp. 288ff.

23 For more detail, see K. Motyka, *Wpływ Leona Petrażyckiego na polską teorię i socjologię prawa* [Leon Petrażycki's Influence on Polish Theory and Sociology of Law] (Lublin: Redakcja Wydawnictw KUL, 1993), pp. 109f.

foregrounded the linguistic and factual (psychological and social) aspects of the legal phenomenon. This view is not remote from the juxtaposition of the study of law as the content of norms (that is, legal science) and the empirical study of legal reality, which focuses on behaviours and psychological and social processes that underlie them (that is, the science of law).

Looking ahead to establishing the science of law, Petrażycki's psychologism, early socio-legal concepts proposed by Ehrlich, and anthropological-legal ideas of Malinowski announced a much broader trend which appeared in the first half of the twentieth century and developed into American and Scandinavian lines of legal realism.

4.1 Legal realism

Two lines of legal realism have been of particular importance to the transformation of jurisprudence into the science of law. The difference between classical legal science and the legal realist approach to law and its study is additionally highlighted by the tendency of many of its representatives to consciously overemphasise the contrast between their own views and whatever they regarded as the dominating "legal orthodoxy." Although after the heyday of legal realism in the first half of the twentieth century, its ideas lost part of their original strength and meaning, for the past several decades, interest in them has been growing, coinciding with attempts to reinterpret them as "new" legal realism.

American legal realism developed in a very special intellectual context, that is, in the context of pragmatic philosophy, very popular in American culture. This is particularly well visible in the views on law expressed by Oliver Wendell Holmes, a pioneer of this model and one of the most influential figures in American legal thought.[24] He advanced the approach to law from the perspective of a bad man, which may be considered prototypical for one of the main concepts of legal realism: law is court decisions. If, for pragmatists, true beliefs are those whose practical consequences work in reality, for Holmes, legal statements are true if they correctly predict decisions of the court. According to Holmes:

---

24 "Holmes would never have called himself a pragmatist; he associated the term with a desire to smuggle religion back into modern thought under a pseudo-scientific cover;" still, he believed that "life is an experiment and… since we can never be certain we must tolerate dissent is consistent with everything James, Pierce and Dewey wrote;" L. Menand, *The Metaphysical Club. The Story of Ideas in America* (New York: Farrar, Straus and Giroux, 2001), pp. 432–433. For more detail on the relation between Holmes and James as well as other pragmatists, see ibid., pp. 337f.

> you will find some text writers telling you that [law] is something different from what is decided by the courts of Massachusetts or England, that it is a system of reason, that it is a deduction from principles of ethics or admitted axioms or what not, which may or may not coincide with the decisions. But if we take the view of our friend the bad man we shall find that he does not care two straws for the axioms or deductions, but that he does want to know what the Massachusetts or English courts are likely to do in fact. I am much of his mind. The prophecies of what the courts will do in fact, and nothing more pretentious, are what I mean by the law.[25]

The mainstream of American realism defines law along these lines, that is, as referring to what is actually done in concrete cases by courts and other state institutions. As Karl Llewellyn puts it, "what the officials do about disputes is, to my mind, the law itself."[26] What is of practical significance, then, is not what the lawmaker includes in codes ("law in books"), but what is going on in reality ("law in action"). It is the task of the jurist to correctly predict what the court, or any other similar institution, will do in particular circumstances. Hence, the task for the scientific study of law is to explain the way in which legal decisions are made and the factors that influence them. Regardless of the differences between various realists, they were unanimous in the view that law in action could not be fully explained only on the basis of codes and other sources of general legal norms. To quote Holmes, "[g]eneral propositions do not decide concrete cases."[27]

According to realists, legal norms very often do not determine court decisions, because the same rules and legal doctrines surrounding them can, in fact, provide the basis for various decisions in the same case. It is not law in books that determines how rules are going to be selected, interpreted, and applied. These choices are made by judges, who invoke legal arguments to justify the decisions they have already made in view of various other factors and circumstances.

In order to correctly predict court decisions, the study of law must abandon the naive, mythologised view of law and its application, according to which it consists merely in drawing conclusions from general legal norms included in

---

25 O.W. Holmes, "The Path of the Law," *Harvard Law Review* 10 (1897), quoted in Holmes, *Collected Legal Papers* (New York: The Lawbook Exchange, 2006), p. 173. It is worth noting that the bad man perspective proposed by Holmes is in fact a kind of theory of rational action of human beings, who are concerned with maximising their gains and minimising the risk of loss. Individuals will orient themselves towards law, but only inasmuch as it provides them with real-life opportunities or, conversely, poses real threats.

26 K. Llewellyn, *The Bramble Bush* (New York: Oceana, 1951), p. 9.

27 O.W. Holmes in Lochner v. New York, 198 U.S. 45, 75 (1905).

legal acts. The main target of realists' attack is this naive model of "mechanical jurisprudence," "formalism," and "legal conceptualism," limiting the role of the court to syllogistic reasoning, where concrete decisions are made exclusively on the basis of objectively relevant and applicable legal acts or precedents.[28]

Apart from the lack of definitive connection between court decisions and legal norms, there are other (more important, perhaps) sources of problems in predicting court decisions: arbitrariness and randomness of fact-finding. As noticed by Jerome Frank, this influence is often underestimated, because legal scholars tend to focus on supreme courts. These, in turn, handle cases which are legally most controversial; facts established by courts of first instance are rarely verified. However, a closer look at the way in which these facts are established undermines all faith in objectivism and credibility of what is accepted as "the facts of the case." Indeed, as Frank concludes, it demonstrates that "facts are guesses."[29]

Thus, according to realists, jurisprudence should recover from the phase of infantile delusions and embark on a systematic study of the true nature of the legal order, which differs radically from the naive, idealised picture that underlies the "basic myth" of legal thinking. It has its sources in the childish, pre-scientific ideas about law preserved in the language which is conventionally used to describe its operation.[30] It presents judges as impartial arbiters who "apply" law, objectively establish "the facts of the case" and "reason" from them according to the rules of "legal logic," etc. A mature scientific perspective on law must acknowledge facts as they are, even if they demonstrate that legal decisions are made largely on the basis of subjective judgement, beliefs, and preferences of judges, who merely choose appropriate legal arguments to justify them.[31] Judges need not be aware of the role of these factors; still, their recognition is essential

28 In his famous article, K. Llewellyn compiled a list of "dueling" interpretive canons, which made it possible to decide each case in two opposite ways (e.g., by reasoning *per analogiam* or *a contrario*, by referring to a narrow linguistic interpretation or, conversely, to a broad teleological interpretation, etc.). According to Llewellyn, "in the field of statutory construction … there are 'correct,' unchallengeable rules of 'how to read' which lead in happily variant directions;" see K. Llewellyn, "Remarks on the Theory of Appellate Decisions and the Rules or Canons About How Statutes Are to Be Constructed," *Vanderbild Law Review* 3 (1950), p. 399.

29 J. Frank, *Courts on Trial. Myth and Reality in American Justice* (Princeton, NJ: Princeton University Press, 1954), pp. 14ff.

30 J. Frank, *Law and the Modern Mind* (New York: Anchor Books, 1963), pp. 69f, 87.

31 Ibid., p. 47.

for the understanding and explanation of the process of legal decision-making and its results.

The realist view of law has been criticised on various grounds (debates on its selected aspects were also going on between realists). Apart from the exaggerated indeterminacy of legal decisions, the most important criticism of "predictive theories of law" comes from Hart and his paradox. Hart points out that identifying law with the expected decision of the court ignores the point of view of the judge, for whom law is not, and cannot be, a prediction of his or her decisions. From the perspective of the judge, law is not a prediction but a rule which indicates how he or she *should* act in a given case (even if the rule itself is not completely determined and admits various interpretations). Because judges and other law-applying officials look at law from the internal point of view – as authoritative guidelines for deciding legal cases – the application of law is fundamentally different from whatever may be called "judge's whim game." This is why, in Hart's opinion, although realist models of law did shed new light on the difference between the reality of law application and its simplified, idealised image perpetuated in traditionally oriented legal sciences, they cannot be treated as a satisfactory theory explaining "what law is."[32]

However, Hart's critical remarks are based on a major misunderstanding. As noticed by Brian Leiter, realists' main aim was not to look for an answer to the conceptual-analytical question about the nature of law, but to demonstrate that what was needed was an empirical, descriptive theory of legal decision-making.[33] From this perspective, of major importance for understanding legal realism is the view shared by its followers that what influences the way of deciding individual cases is the judge's subjective sense of what is right rather than the content of legal norms. This sense, in turn, emerges primarily from the perception of facts and from the judge's own preferences concerning the appropriate solution in a given case.

Thus, for realist jurisprudence, the key to understanding legal reality is in the psychological processes of perception and decision-making that are going on in the minds of judges, together with a variety of social factors that co-determine them and make them consistent (such as legal education, participation in a particular environment, and even specific styles of decision-making prevailing in a given institution at a given time).

---

32 See H.L.A. Hart, *The Concept of Law*, 2nd ed. (Oxford: Clarendon Press, 1994).

33 B. Leiter, *Naturalizing Jurisprudence: Essays on American Legal Realism and Naturalism in Legal Philosophy* (Oxford-New York: Oxford University Press, 2007), pp. 18f.

To sum up, conceptual considerations concerning "what law is" were not, according to Leiter, the focus of the realist theory of law; rather, they were treated as a preliminary issue, important insofar as it demonstrated the need for and role of empirical research into the real causes and processes of decision-making by the courts. In fact, realists tacitly assumed a certain positivist understanding of law, and it is on this understanding that they based their main arguments regarding the lack of foundation for (at least some) court decisions in "law in books" (positivistically identified with a legal act or a precedent).[34]

In contrast to the American version of legal realism, its Scandinavian counterpart was based not on pragmatism but on the philosophical foundations of logical positivism and its agenda of fighting against the remnants of metaphysics that dimmed scientific thinking. According to the Vienna Circle ideal of true science, only statements which can be reduced to empirically verifiable protocol propositions or analytic truths of mathematics and logic can be considered scientific. Only such statements can be ascribed a truth value; statements with no truth value do not communicate any comprehensible content.[35] These views were introduced into Scandinavian legal thought by Axel Hägerström, a philosopher who turned opposition against metaphysics into his life motto (paraphrasing Cato's famous phrase as *Praeterea censeo metaphysicam esse delendam*).[36] Among his disciples and the continuators of his philosophical ideas, there were three most eminent representatives of Scandinavian realism in legal sciences: Alf Ross, Karl Olivecrona and Anders Vilhelm Lundstedt.

For Scandinavian realists, non-empirical concepts which form the basis for the reflection on law are the hotbed of pre-scientific, metaphysical reasoning in jurisprudence. Legal thinking commonly makes use of terms which do not

---

34 B. Leiter, "Legal Realism and Legal Positivism Reconsidered," *Ethics* 111(2001), pp. 278ff; for a criticism of Leiter's view, see D. Priel, "Were the Legal Realists Legal Positivists?"*Law and Philosophy* 27 (2008), pp. 309ff.; M. Green, "Legal Realism as Theory of Law," *William and Mary Law Review* 46 (2005), pp. 1915ff.

35 "The proposition is a picture of reality .... To understand a proposition means to know what is the case, if it is true .... The totality of true propositions is the total natural science (or the totality of the natural sciences)" (L. Wittgenstein, *Tractatus Logico-Philosophicus* (London: Kegan Paul, Trench, Trubner & Co., Ltd, 1922)), 4.021, 4.024, 4.11; available from Project Gutenberg at https://www.gutenberg.org/ebooks/5740.

36 A. Hägerström, *Philosophy and Religion* (London: Allen & Unwin, 1964), pp. 33f., 309f. For more detail, see also P. Mindus, *A Real Mind. The Life and Work of Axel Hägerström* (Dordrecht: Springer, 2009).

denote any real-life entities. Jurists propose theories referring to "rights," "claims," "duties," "binding force," "liabilities," "property," etc. These terms are, in fact, remnants of the magical-metaphysical thinking, which is where the roots of legal ideas and concepts lie. Turning jurisprudence into a science requires a radical reconstruction of both the language and the underlying ways of thinking, which in its current form cannot aspire to provide any sound description of reality.

Perhaps the most telling illustration of this need can be found in the famous article by Ross, where he describes an imaginary case of the anthropologist Mr. Ydobon, who studies the *Noît-cif* tribe inhabiting one of the isles in the South Pacific. The researcher discovers that its members believe in a mysterious phenomenon they call *tû-tû*.[37] Mr. Ydobon establishes that according to local beliefs, an infringement of certain taboos (such as eating food belonging to the chief) results in the person who has infringed them becoming *tû-tû*. However,

> [it] is very difficult to explain what is meant by this. Perhaps the nearest one can get to an explanation is to say that tû-tû is conceived of as a kind of dangerous force or infection which attaches to the guilty person and threatens the whole community with disaster.[38]

According to *Noît-cif* beliefs, a man who has become *tû-tû* must undergo special purification rituals, and the tribe's elders see to it that they are properly performed.

Ross' intention is to demonstrate that an anthropologist's enquiries into what *tû-tû* in fact *is* must be pointless, because it does not exist as any real-world entity. Rather, it is an object of beliefs shared by the tribe members, which motivate them to react to certain events in a particular way. Thus, explaining what *tû-tû* actually *is* does not consist in looking into the nature of the mysterious "state of impurity" characteristic of people who are treated by the tribe as *tû-tû*. It consists in accounting for the way in which – thanks to tribe members' shared beliefs – it manages to combine certain events with a particular type of reaction (the sense of obligation to behave in a particular way).

From the realist point of view, *tû-tû* merely provides a link between facts. Whoever is found guilty of a certain act becomes *tû-tû*, and if he or she is *tû-tû*, one is obliged to react in a particular way. This way of thinking gives rise to normative beliefs regarding the way in which one ought to behave, and these beliefs, in turn, are motivation to act. Ross' argumentation aims at demonstrating the purely inferential nature of the majority of legal concepts. A person who has acted in a particular way gains a "claim;" and once they have gained it, they can

---

37 A. Ross, "Tû-Tû," *Harvard Law Review*, Vol. 70 (1957), pp. 812ff.

38 Ibid., p. 812.

bring an action. A particular event triggers normative beliefs in judges and other participants in a legal order as to the way one should react to an action brought by a person whom they perceive as the claim holder. The belief that there exists something that *is* a claim does not substantially differ from Mr. Ydobon trying to find out what the phenomenon the *Noît-cif* tribe refer to as *tû-tû* "is in reality." Also in this case, a norm, properly passed and promulgated, becomes "valid," and because it has "binding force," its addressees ought to act accordingly.[39]

The realist perspective on law objects to treating such concepts as if they had denotation and opposes any attempts to identify the entities that they supposedly denote. In place of such hypostases, legal scholars should describe legal order in terms of causes and effects, mediated by the content of beliefs and other internal experiences of its participants. It is as a result of these beliefs that, when faced with certain events, the participants tend to act in this or that way. Such legal concepts must then be redefined so that they may refer to facts and may be used in statements that are empirically verifiable.

It is in this spirit that Ross formulates his behavioural definition of the validity of law. He argues that for an utterance "Norm X is valid" to be a scientific statement about law, it must be understood as referring to the probability of norm X being applied in particular circumstances. Ross refers here directly to the methodological assumptions of logical positivism:

> It is a principle of modern empirical science that a proposition about reality (in contrast to an analytical, logical-mathematical proposition) must imply that by following a certain mode of procedure, under certain conditions certain direct experiences will result.[40]

Thus, for the doctrinal study of law to be scientific,

> propositions about valid law must be interpreted as referring not to an unobservable validity or "binding force" derived from *a priori* principles or postulates but to social facts…[T]he real content of doctrinal propositions refers to the actions of the courts under certain conditions.[41]

From this perspective, scientifically acceptable statements about the validity of norms always concern the future and not the past (they predict future

---

39 Ross' approach has never ceased to raise interesting and heated discussions or provoke criticism. See, e.g., T. Gizbert-Studnicki and M. Klinowski, "Are Legal Concepts Embedded in Legal Rules?" *International Journal of Semiotics and Law* 25 (2012), pp. 553ff.; B. Brożek, "On *Tû-Tû*," *Revus. Journal for Constitutional Theory and Philosophy of Law* 27 (2015), pp. 15f.

40 A. Ross, *On Law and Justice* (London: Stevens & Sons, 1958), p. 39.

41 Ibid., p. 40.

behaviours). As a result, they are never entirely indisputable. They are merely more or less probable hypotheses based on various premises which justify a given prediction. Still, it is only the actual behaviour of addressees of a norm that, provided it tallies with what the norm prescribes, is the basis of its "validity." According to Ross,

> [i]t is merely empty words if legal writers insist on upholding a rule as "valid law," admitting that practice "wrongly" follows a different rule.[42]

Olivecrona explains law and the empirical nature of legal concepts in a similar way. Although he does not subscribe to the more radical views of Lundstedt, who argues for a complete elimination of terms with no real-life denotation from legal language (such as, e.g., right), he is of the opinion that:

> thinking in terms of rights, duties and legal qualities is inadequate from the scientific point of view. The object of study cannot be these supposed "moral entities" themselves. It can only be the ideas of rights, duties and legal qualities, their history, their import and their social functions.[43]

Empirical absence of entities which might serve as referents of legal concepts does not mean that there are no real mental experiences which are their content. Referring to such terms acts as an impulse, triggering certain ideas in the minds of the participants in a legal order, which, in turn, make them behave in particular ways. Olivecrona illustrates this relationship in the following way:

> when used according to certain legal rules, [the term] acts as an imperative sign for the debtor: he shall or must pay. The *idea* of his being obligated to pay is firmly connected with the *idea* of the lender's right. This will entail psychological pressure on him.[44]

For this reason, Olivecrona argues, a scientific study of law must refer to "psychological factors," thanks to which certain rules and other statements trigger in their addressees specific ideas concerning the appropriate course of action. It is these ideas that make them decide or act in one way or another. The cause-and-effect relationships between behaviour, specific uses of language, and mental experiences that underlie and are evoked by these uses are fundamental for the understanding and explanation of "law as fact."[45]

Legal realism is usually associated with exposing the indeterminacy of legal decisions and the role of psychological and social factors in accounting for the

---

42 Ibid., p. 50.
43 K. Olivecrona, *Law as Fact* (London: Stevens & Sons, 1971), p. 270.
44 Ibid., p. 191; emphases from the author of this book.
45 Ibid., pp. 177–185.

processes of legal thinking and decision-making ("judges are humans, too"). However, it can also be interpreted as a call for transforming jurisprudence from legal science into the science of law and shifting its focus from the analysis of legal texts to a description and explanation of the legal phenomenon understood as a set of causally interconnected facts. These facts comprise both the internal experiences of participants in a legal order (beliefs or ideas concerning what behaviour patterns are prescribed as rights or duties) and actual behaviour and its effects (such as lawmakers' and courts' decisions as well as practices of officials and other subjects of law).

On this understanding, a description and explanation of the processes shaping the legal order, undertaken from the external point of view, are very different tasks from the exegesis and systematisation of legal texts, which is the focus of legal science (the "orthodox" or "dogmatic" jurisprudence). It seems that realists were not quite aware of this fact; rather, they aimed at a "reform" of legal dogmatics to make it more empirical and scientifically "mature." However, a research project that is so radically different requires other methods and skills, with other criteria of scientific soundness than those which apply in the case of dogmatic systematisation of valid law. Moreover, if Leiter is correct in his observation that realists in fact assume a positivist view of law, whose operation needs to be studied and explained, then legal science is (or, at the very minimum, may and should be) an integral part of the object of such research. This is a consequence of the fact that doctrinal views are, at least *ex hypothesi*, among the factors that may significantly influence legal resolutions, even if they belong to what realists refer to as "law in books," unable (at least in a proportion of cases) to fully determine courts' decisions.

4.2 The critical model

As a perspective on the study and description of law, critical legal studies continue the tradition of American realism. This line of research combines realist ideas with European views of law as a historical phenomenon, part of culture, and a reflection of the current social, economic, and political situation. This way of thinking about law as a reflection of particular social factors (so-called social mirror thesis) has roots in the history of legal and social thought.[46] The same foundations served as the basis for the highly influential and powerful Marxist

---

46 For a comprehensive discussion and criticism of the social mirror thesis, see B. Tamanaha, *A General Jurisprudence of Law and Society* (Oxford: Oxford University Press, 1999), pp. 11f.

view of law, which is, next to legal realism, another major inspiration for critical legal studies.

According to classical Marxist historical materialism, the evolution of economic relations is the driving force behind the development of societies. In successive economic formations – slavery, feudalism, and capitalism – most groups in the society are exploited by the few that own the means of production and that expropriate a considerable part of the value produced by the exploited masses. Tough economic relations form the basis for the cultural and political superstructure, which is the site of both ideas that aim to maintain and legitimise the privileges of the owning classes and ideas that propel revolutionary aspirations of the exploited. Views that prevail in a given social class are an emanation of the socio-economic situation and interests of its members ("being determines consciousness").

Law, together with legal concepts and theories that justify it, is also part of this economically determined superstructure. This is why, in principle, the content and operation of law serve the status quo which furthers the interests of the privileged social strata, taking unfair advantage of the work of others. It is then a tool for enforcing obedience through an organised coercive apparatus of the state and legitimation of the existing socio-economic relations. Irrespective of the extent to which this true role of law is hidden behind ideology that justifies it, law is ultimately an instrument serving real economic and political interests of those who shape it.[47]

Marx and his followers believed that the laws of historical development they discovered would lead to a revolution, as a result of which all private property and class division would be abolished and, in consequence, state and law would wither away. The legal order is a tool for class control and economic oppression. If class division and private property are abolished, its *raison d'être* will disappear. Of course, nobody expected this process to be fast, although at the beginning, just after the October Revolution, Lenin apparently believed that the transformation into a non-state communist society would take less than two years. Even though this prediction proved wrong, throughout successive decades, communist regimes declared, at least officially, that the disappearance of state and law was only a matter of time.[48]

---

47 For more detail, see A. Walicki, *Marksizm i skok do królestwa wolności* [Marxism and the Leap into the Realm of Freedom] (Warszawa: PWN, 1996); H. Kelsen, *The Political Theory of Bolshevism. A Critical Analysis* (Clark, NJ: The Lawbook Exchange, 2007/1948).

48 J. Paszukanis, *Ogólna teoria prawa a marksizm* [The General Theory of Law and Marxism], trans. L. Lisiakiewicz (Warszawa: PWN, 1985), p. 47.

It was emphasised that the process of eliminating the relics of the capitalist formation required opening up "the narrow horizon of bourgeois law," and abandoning the principle of proportionality not only in relations of work and exchange but also in criminal law. Abandoning irrational concepts of offence, guilt, or proportional return was to lead to the replacement of punishment with social re-education programmes with a medical and pedagogical slant (mainly in the form of "corrective work").[49] Offences, or what might appear an offence, were to be replaced by symptoms of a socially dangerous state, with "the society" deciding when it was necessary to take appropriate protective actions against an individual. Naturally, court trials and judgements were in this case redundant; what was at stake was not "administering justice" but "an act of pure purposefulness" aimed at "correction or elimination of a dangerous member of the society."[50]

One cannot escape the irony that the author of these words, the foremost legal theorist of the early years of the post-revolutionary Soviet state, simply disappeared without a trace despite desperate attempts to adjust his theories to current shifts in the party line. He was probably arrested and shot for lack of loyalty, without a trial or sentence, or any other "bourgeois relic."[51]

As a result of the intellectual and moral fiasco of traditional Marxism, the genocide committed in its name, and the terror in the Soviet Union and other states governed by parties influenced by Marxist ideas, classical Marxism found itself in retreat on many fronts, including legal thought. This is not to say that the whole Marxist tradition withered away; many of its ideas have been adopted by influential and effective legal models developing in parallel to the fall of orthodox Marxist ideology (especially in its official, imposed version). Among the most important ones is the critical legal studies movement, developing since the 1970s, which combines certain elements of the Marxist tradition with the philosophical ideas of twentieth-century postmodernism.[52]

---

49 One of the relics of *bourgeois* law is, as Paszukanis puts it, "the indeed preposterous idea that each offense can be weighed on scales and expressed in months and years of imprisonment;" ibid., p. 201.

50 Ibid., pp. 201–204.

51 See M. Head, *Evgeny Pashukanis. A Critical Reappraisal* (Abingdon: Routledge-Cavendish, 2008), pp. 15f.

52 Another important post-Marxist tradition is the so-called Frankfurt School, developing its own version of social criticism. One of its best-known representatives is Jürgen Habermas, who, in the later years of his career, played an important role in the development of the twentieth-century philosophy of law. For a synthetic overview, see B. Dupret, *Droit…*, pp. 108f.

At the core of postmodernist philosophical thought is the belief that the modernist vision of the world has collapsed. This vision was based primarily on the Enlightenment's faith in the progress of humanity, warranted by Reason capable of discovering objective and universal truths, which were to free humans from errors and prejudice that hindered the process of improving the world and making it more rationally organised. According to François Lyotard, a classic of postmodernism, in the face of the catastrophic events of the twentieth century, such "grand narratives" fell apart like a house of cards. Their collapse exposed the particularism and contingency of all such fundamentalist (that is, universality-claiming) visions of the world. All religious, scientific, philosophical, and ideological views are merely contingent and ephemeral narratives, emerging in concrete cultural circumstances and competing with each other. The collapse of faith in the exclusive, timeless truth of any of them is what makes the fundamental difference between postmodernism and the modernist Reason, trapped in their bonds and hence dangerous.

It is the task of critical philosophy to practice "the hermeneutics of suspicion," that is, to unmask the groundless objectivist and universalist claims of particular narratives. This can be achieved by exposing their genealogy, cultural contingency, economic entanglements (noticed already by Marxism), and non-economic interests that they legitimise (and which Marxism overlooked). This process enables not only criticism but also emancipation of individuals or groups whose interests are marginalised in the name of supposedly objective, "reasoned" truths. The latter are, in fact, merely tools to further particular interests of groups dominant at a given place and time. This is the situation of weaker social classes but also of communities that are being victimised by various cultural narratives (e.g., women, placed by "tradition" in a position subordinate to men, sexual minorities perceived as "deviations," "primitive" cultures, etc.).

Modern society, as Michel Foucault argues, is a web of such narratives and institutions of disciplinary power that are based on them. Imposing normalising standards makes it possible to control whatever is defined as deviation, and to subject it to corrective action. In this way, modern society has become a panopticon, a perfect prison, where the prisoners are at the same time guards. Dispersed structures of power (such as schools, armies, companies, hospitals, etc.) have blended in the society, applying continuous but invisible disciplinary and corrective action to all symptoms of what they define as deviation.[53]

53 Cf. M. Foucault, *Discipline and Punish*, trans. A. Sheridan (New York: Pantheon Books, 1977).

These philosophical assumptions have given rise to the idea of critical legal studies, where the legal order is treated as a contingent emanation of interests and ideologies that support them. Legislation, application of law, and discourses that legitimise it are just some of the forms of political competition among individuals, groups, classes, and ideas, regardless of how hard they strive to pass as neutral embodiments of universal rationality, truth, or justice. Adam Sulikowski, a leading representative of critical reflection on law in Poland, emphasises that its main task is to penetrate under the surface of rhetorical structures that conceal real functions and interests furthered by legislation – invariably and unavoidably practiced from particularist positions – and the ideas that legitimise these interests.[54]

Thus, critical legal studies strive to continue the best traditions of Marxist analyses of the nature and role of bourgeois law and jurisprudence, at the same time rejecting the concept of the class identification of individuals, central to classical Marxism. Class identification is perceived as just another form of oppressive narrative, misusing the authority of science in the name of its own ideological assumptions, much like other trends of Enlightenment scientism. Law, in turn, is viewed as an emanation of interests of those who control legislation and are able to impose a narrative that legitimises them by referring to supposedly universal truths and values. It is the task of critical legal studies to keep an appropriate dose of "suspicion with regard to seemingly positive, that is, objective categories" and to aim at "revealing beliefs captured in rules, tracing the contingency of prevailing theories, unmasking the relationship between knowledge and power," and exposing political ideologies which are presented as objective and neutral scientific accounts of facts.[55]

Challenging ideological narratives that legitimise the legal order and exposing the economic and political reality they conceal not only provides knowledge but also turns critical legal studies into a powerful emancipation movement. It enables looking at law from the perspective of the Other: the left out, the marginalised, and the ignored by legal norms and relevant ideological narratives that foster the interests and preferences of socially or economically dominant groups. In this way, critical legal studies paved the way for the ideas developed

54 Cf. A. Sulikowski, "O możliwościach postmodernizacji nauki prawa konstytucyjnego" [On the Postmodernization Possibilities of Constitutional Law], *Państwo i Prawo* [State and Law] 12 (2010), p. 8; for more detail, see also Sulikowski, *Konstytucjonalizm a nowoczesność. Dyskurs konstytucyjny wobec tryumfu i kryzysu moderny* [Constitutionalism and Modernity. Constitutional Discourse in the face of the Triumph and Crisis of Modernism] (Wrocław: Wydawnictwo Uniwersytetu Wrocławskiego, 2012), in particular, p. 199f.

55 Ibid.

by feminist legal theory as well as for criticism of the residue of ethnocentric and racial prejudice entrenched in the seemingly objective view of the world that serves as the basis for various legal solutions. The movement also questions education practices, which are perceived as indoctrination, as a process of raising generations of jurists in the spirit of ideological narratives that legitimise and petrify the legal status quo.

Perhaps no other contemporary philosophical ideas have raised such controversies as postmodernism. Especially at the beginning, postmodernists and their work tended to evoke extreme reactions: from sheer delight to the heaviest criticism, including that of their pretentious jargon that covered up the shallowness and banality (if not meaninglessness) of the content.[56] In the course of time, however, more balanced opinions were being expressed, for instance, by Edward O. Wilson, one of the most outstanding proponents of modern scientism, whose views and entire intellectual framework is the exact opposite of the spirit of postmodernism.

For Wilson, Jacques Derrida's works exemplify "ornately obscurantist prose" which leaves the reader in doubt as to whether the author "himself knows what he means." He argues that Derrida's views on science demonstrate his absolute ignorance in this respect, marked as they are with "the incoherence of a dream, at once banal and fantastical." As a result, his argumentation resembles "the pronouncements of a faith healer unaware of the location of the pancreas." At the same time, however, Wilson adds that, apart from affording relief to "those who have chosen not to encumber themselves with a scientific education," postmodern ideas

> are like sparks from firework explosions that travel away in all directions, devoid of following energy, soon to wink out in the dimensionless dark. Yet a few will endure long enough to cast light on unexpected subjects.[57]

A similar discussion has been going on about critical legal studies. Also in this case, doubts have been voiced regarding the validity of deconstruction as a method or the grounds for the most radical claims identifying law with politics or proposing equal "contingency" of all legal ideas and models. Proponents of critical philosophy have been criticised for the lack of any positive programme

56 Possibly the best-known example of such criticism can be found in A. Sokal and J. Bricmont, *Fashionable Nonsense: Postmodern Intellectuals' Abuse of Science* (New York: Picador, 1998), preceded by the famous Sokal Hoax in *Social Text*.

57 E.O. Wilson, *Consilience: The Unity of Knowledge* (New York: Knopf, 1998), pp. 45–47.

that could provide an alternative to the ideas and solutions they "expose" as instruments of oppression, violence, and dominance.[58]

In our case, however, what is truly interesting is not the validity of particular claims of postmodern critical legal studies, or arguments raised against them, but the general research attitude and the tasks of jurisprudence identified by its supporters. Jurisprudence should aim at revealing the true origin, social function, and economic, political, and cultural entanglements of legal solutions, reasoning, and argumentation, as well as of legal theories and ideologies that legitimise them. Thus, the task of the legal scholar is to critically deconstruct them in order to expose their cultural and social origin as well as the function they actually play.

Also here, a scientifically valuable study of law is understood differently than in the case of legal science. Still, even in the critical model – much like in legal realism – certain beliefs concerning what law is are, in a way, taken for granted. It is the starting point for legal criticism that law can be delimited and that it has certain distinctive features that can become objects of critical reflection. Since objects of legal criticism include ideas, concepts, and legal theories that co-create the social reality of law and jurists' self-awareness, critical legal studies must also form a superstructure raised on legal science, which is part of the real legal order.

4.3. The economic model

Another line of research inspired by American legal realism and regarded as its continuation is the law and economics movement. It developed approximately at the same time as critical legal studies, but if the latter is understandably more popular among left-wing circles, the economic analysis of law is often perceived as a philosophical-legal ally of the free-market right wing.

The core of law and economics is the application of tools developed by modern economic theories to the description of the legal order and its operation. For this reason, it rests on the assumption of rationality of individuals, fundamental for the neoclassical theory of economics. According to it, human beings seek to maximise profits and minimise the costs they entail (*homo oeconomicus*).[59] This is why they choose a course of action which, considering the circumstances, is

---

58 See, e.g., S. Sinha, *Jurisprudence* (St. Paul, MN: West Publishing, 1993), p. 314.

59 See J. Stelmach, B. Brożek, and W. Załuski, *Dziesięć wykładów o ekonomii prawa* [Ten Lectures on the Economy of Law] (Warszawa: Wolters Kluwer, 2007), pp. 18–19. On the role of the assumption of rationality in classical and modern economic theories, see, e.g., M. Gorazda, *Filozofia ekonomii* [The Philosophy of Economy] (Kraków: Copernicus Center Press, 2014).

most conducive to their preferences and at the same time generates minimal "costs" (that is, takes into account their negative preferences). The assumption of rationality does not imply that individuals always consciously consider all possible decisions, selecting optimum solutions from the point of view of their preferences. Rather, it posits that (at least statistically speaking) they behave as if they consciously evaluated the degree to which their preferences are satisfied by every course of action that appears possible in a given situation.

Following Gary Becker and other representatives of the so-called Chicago school of economics, the assumption that human beings make rational choices to maximise their subjectively defined profit started to be applied in the analysis of human behaviour also in other, non-economic spheres of life as a universal model of choice-making in the context of family life, leisure, etc.[60] In this light, human behaviour is influenced by external factors which make the results of one course of action optimal from the perspective of the positive and negative preferences of the agent.

On this view, law influences the decisions made by its addressees in that it renders particular behaviour types more or less "profitable." This encourages rationally acting individuals to more often select courses of action which, as a result of legal regulations, bring desirable effects (e.g., enrichment, access to legal protection, or other benefits) and rarely choose options which entail high costs (penalty, risk, etc.). Thus, legal regulations effectively control human behaviour by influencing decision factors: they raise or lower costs and benefits entailed by the behaviour they regulate.

The most straightforward examples of this mechanism include tax loads and tax incentives, but the same situation can be observed in other fields of legal regulation as well. From the perspective of law and economics, by stipulating punishment for a particular act, a criminal provision increases its "costs," a successful practice provided the costs are higher than the anticipated profit from an offence.[61] The degree to which positive and negative preferences are expected to be satisfied is a quotient of the expected profit or loss and the estimated probability that it will be incurred. Thus, the effectiveness of a legal regulation depends on both the legal consequences that follow from its content and the extent to

---

60 See G. Becker and G.N. Becker, *The Economics of Life: From Baseball to Affirmative Action to Immigration, How Real-World Issues Affect Our Everyday Life* (Columbus, OH: McGraw Hill, 1997).

61 For more detail, see B. Brożek, "Ekonomiczna analiza prawa karnego" [An Economical Analysis of Criminal Law], in *Analiza ekonomiczna w zastosowaniach prawniczych* [Economical Analysis in Legal Applications], ed. J. Stelmach and M. Soniewicka (Warszawa: Wolters Kluwer, 2007), pp. 86ff.

which these consequences are in fact enforced (both factors contributing to the subjective expectations concerning the actual consequences of an action regulated by a given norm).[62]

An important concept in the economic analysis of law is the notion of economically efficient allocation of resources (goods, services, rights), that is one that corresponds to the preferences of particular individuals. It is an economic term that has two slightly different meanings. Efficient allocation in the Pareto sense refers to the situation when it is impossible to improve the position of one individual without making the position of another individual worse. Thus, reallocation of resources is Pareto efficient only if it results in an improvement in the situation of an individual or a group of individuals (that is, better satisfaction of their preferences) without making others' position worse. In other words, an efficient reallocation of resources takes place if there is at least one individual who prefers the new situation and no individual who prefers the situation prior to the change.

In contrast to Pareto efficiency, allocation is efficient in the Kaldor-Hicks sense if it is impossible to improve the situation of one individual to an extent that would compensate for the deterioration in the situation of others. Thus, reallocation is Kaldor-Hicks efficient if the resulting improvement in the position of one individual is more substantial than the deterioration in the position of others, whose losses can be compensated by the gains. In other words, a change is Kaldor-Hicks efficient if there is at least one individual who prefers the new allocation and if it is possible to compensate others for its negative results to such an extent that there is no individual who actually prefers the former allocation.

The criteria of allocation efficiency provide the basic tool for an economic evaluation of legal regulations and their modifications. Legislation is here treated as an instrument to maximise social wealth understood as a degree of satisfaction of individual preferences of those who belong to a given community. Changes in law are desirable if they increase the allocation efficiency of resources, as it is defined in economics. The Kaldor-Hicks criterion is weaker than the Pareto criterion in that every Pareto-efficient change is at the same time Kaldor-Hicks efficient, but the reverse does not hold. The Kaldor-Hicks criterion is also more relevant in practice, because it is very difficult to propose changes

62 Although the regularities that follow from the assumption of rationality are only statistical, they are sufficient for the economic analysis of law, since legal regulations are abstract and general in nature and are meant to regulate behaviours of whole groups of addressees in recurring situations of a particular type.

(e.g., in legislation) which would satisfy the Pareto criterion, that is, which would improve the situation of some individuals without making anybody else worse off.

The economic analysis of law may be understood as a theory describing or explaining the legal phenomenon, or as a normative theory that aims at critique and optimisation of legal regulations. Within the descriptive approach, the very existence of legal order may be perceived as a rational reaction to the obstacles in the efficient allocation of resources in society. These obstacles result from two major factors: the so-called collective action problem and the problem of transaction costs.

The collective action problem consists in that in many cases, undertaking a joint effort may bring the participants more benefits than individual action, but the benefits depend on the cooperative behaviour of all individuals. At the same time, from the point of view of a participant, the most cost-effective behaviour is to avoid cooperation and the costs it entails in order to benefit "for free" from the cooperative behaviour of others (the situation of a stowaway passenger). This situation can be illustrated by the prisoner's dilemma, known from game theory: even if it is in the best interests of two prisoners to cooperate, given the lack of certainty as to how the other will behave, it may be subjectively rational for each of them not to cooperate. In this way, a prisoner may avoid the risk of having to bear all the costs, with the other prisoner (the stowaway) seizing all the benefits.

The most straightforward example of the collective action problem may be the global emission of CO_2, resulting in catastrophic changes in the climate that affect everyone. Each country would benefit most if all other countries, except itself, limited the emission of CO_2; in this case, it would benefit from the effects of the action without having to accept the costs for its own economy. The worst possible scenario, in turn, would be to limit the emission of CO_2 by its own economy (thus bearing the costs of the change), with no such measures being taken by other countries, which may aim at benefiting from a stowaway situation and avoiding the risk of having to pay the bills of others (other stowaways). Thus, as long as there is no guarantee that other countries introduce the limits too, it is rational for each individual country to continue the emission rather than limit it, much like in the prisoner's dilemma. A similar configuration of gains, costs, and risks can be found in many other contexts, and this is why legal regulations enforcing cooperation and reducing uncertainty as to the behaviour of others provide rational mechanisms for removing obstacles in taking collective actions that benefit everyone.[63]

---

63 The example of CO_2 emission and climate change also illustrates a special problem of collective action, known as "the tragedy of the commons." If limited resources are

Another type of problems in the efficient allocation of resources addressed by law is connected with the Coase theorem, a very important concept in law and economics. By way of simplification (and ignoring controversies as to its proper understanding), the Coase theorem states that if the transaction costs are null, the allocation of resources between rationally acting subjects will achieve the optimum state regardless of the initial allocation of rights and obligations that follow from legal rules.[64] However, in real-life situations, the transaction costs are not null, and so the optimum allocation of resources may depend on the rule that distributes particular rights and obligations. Thus, it is the task of law to distribute them in such a way so as to maximise the chance of achieving economically efficient allocation of resources despite the incurred transaction costs. According to Richard Posner,

> [t]he most ambitious theoretical aspect of the economic approach to law has been the proposal of a unified economic theory of law in which law's function is understood to be to facilitate the operation of free markets and, in areas where the costs of market transactions are prohibitive, to "mimic the market" by decreeing the outcome that the market could be expected to produce if market transactions were feasible.[65]

Law is here treated as an instrument for efficient allocation of resources in the domains of civil law, protection of property, and free exchange of goods, as well as constitutional and criminal law. Offence is perceived as a way of profiting (that is, furthering one's preferences) at somebody else's cost, which does not contribute to social wellbeing. Penalty constitutes an additional cost and transforms the decision situation of a rational subject so that committing an offence

---

shared, it is rational for each individual user to exploit them to the greatest extent (before they are used up by others); at the same time, however, the collapse of the resources will result in all the users being worse off compared to a situation when they use the resources prudently.

64 As J. Stelmach, B. Brożek, and W. Załuski put it, "Efficient allocation of the ownership right to particular property (or rights that follow from the ownership right) will occur always and only if the transaction costs are null, regardless of to whom the right (or rights that follow from it) was initially allocated by law or court's decision." The authors comment, however, that although the Coase theorem states that the lack of transaction costs will guarantee economically efficient allocation of resources as a result of the sole logic of voluntary bargaining, the initial distribution of rights and obligations does play a role in pursuing other values than economic efficiency (e.g., fairness of resource allocation). See Stelmach, Brożek, Załuski, *Dziesięć…*, pp. 110–114.

65 R. Posner, *Frontiers of Legal Theory* (Cambridge, MA: Harvard University Press, 2001), p. 5.

instead of making an "honest deal" does not pay off. This is, in fact, the objective of the doctrine and rules of liability and penal procedure that have evolved with criminal law. Hence,

> criminal law, though generally considered the domain par excellence of moral rather than economic thinking in law, has an impressive economic logic .... Although judges and legislators do not often speak the language of economics ... they often do reason implicitly in economic terms and economic analysis is therefore helpful in explaining the basic structure of law, including the criminal law.[66]

Although Posner maintains that the content of real law (in particular, the doctrines and rules of common law) reflects the search for the most efficient way to secure social wealth, it is more common to treat law and economics as a tool for evaluation, critique, and improvement of law. From this perspective,

> legal rules are to be judged by the structure of incentives they establish and the consequences of people altering their behavior in response to those incentives.[67]

In this way, it is possible to establish whether a particular legal solution offers a structure of incentives which makes rational individuals react in a way that maximises social wellbeing (sometimes understood more narrowly, not as a total satisfaction degree of the preferences of all individuals, but as a sum of material wealth produced in a given society). This approach offers a very different perspective on the functioning and sense of legal norms.

For example, in this light, appeal measures in the civil procedure may be treated as an instrument that helps reduce social costs of erroneous court decisions. Such measures should therefore reduce the number of wrong decisions, at the same time keeping the costs of their verification as low as possible. For example, one may propose that an obligatory verification of all decisions by a court of higher jurisdiction would eliminate the majority of errors. However, this procedure would be extremely costly, because the process of verification would also apply to decisions whose correctness is unquestionable. It is then necessary to introduce appropriate "filtering mechanisms," which make it possible to verify only these decisions that raise substantial doubts. Such mechanisms include costs of initiating appeals, discouraging verification of decisions where the probability of error is low. Of course, as a result, some errors will remain (because the

---

66 R. Posner, "An Economic Theory of Criminal Law," *Columbia Law Review* 85 (1985), p. 1230.

67 D. Friedman, *Law's Order. What Economics Has to Do with Law and Why It Matters* (Princeton, NJ: Princeton University Press, 2001), p. 11.

appeal procedure will not be initiated), but, *summa summarum*, this solution may be socially more profitable, as the related losses are smaller than the costs of unnecessary verification of a great number of correct decisions.

The most important point is then to shape the legal regulation in such a way so as to achieve an optimal balance of gains (correct court decisions) and losses (costs of the judiciary, duration of the procedure, etc.). This may mean that, in many areas, it "pays off" to tolerate a certain degree of imperfection in the operation of law if further improvements entail an increase in the social costs that exceeds the gained profit. The same situation, but on a more general level, can be observed in the case of any instances of breaking the law, such as traffic offences, corruption, or tax evasion. The fact that they occur is an obvious wrong (social cost), which law should, in principle, eliminate. However, there is a certain limit beyond which the social gains that follow from further elimination of wrongs (e.g., from fighting a particular type of crime) are visibly out of proportion to the costs they entail (the expansion of the apparatus or institutions, nuisance caused to citizens, who have to bear additional duties and suffer additional limitations, the scope of control, etc.).

The normative tasks of law and economics include, first and foremost, an assessment whether and to what extent the present or proposed legal rules in fact lead to the maximisation of social wellbeing (that is, are economically efficient).[68] An important asset of such legislative analyses is undoubtedly their potential to expose many instances of the actual social effects of law being different than the intentions of the authors. Very often various legal rules and actual circumstances interact to give rise to a pattern of incentives which encourages rational individuals to behave in a different way than that envisaged by the authors of norms, who acted in good faith but without a proper understanding of the situation. As a result, rules that are meant to improve the situation of employees, consumers, victims of crime, or members of a particular social group in fact have a detrimental effect, which can be explained and foreseen on the basis of the pattern

---

68 An interesting example of an economic analysis of the civil procedure can be found in a study on class actions by M. Niedużak. According to the author, enabling class actions provides a solution to a special case of collective action, where the claims of individual plaintiffs are so small that bringing individual lawsuits would be too expensive. As a result, the total of rational individual decisions leaves all plaintiffs in a worse situation than a collective action, whose costs are shared among the members of the group. Some norms of Polish law limit the economic efficiency of this model. See M. Niedużak, *Postępowanie grupowe. Prawo i ekonomia* [Group Proceedings. Law and Economics] (Warszawa: C.H. Beck, 2014).

of incentives and its influence on the behaviour of rational subjects, seeking to maximise their profits and minimise the costs.[69]

Law and economics belong to the most controversial models within modern jurisprudence. Its enthusiasts claim that it is "the most important development in legal scholarship of the twentieth century."[70] At the same time, however, its fundamental assumptions and achievements are the object of fierce criticism and rejection (often combined with the lack of understanding and suspicion) by a large number of legal scholars. The fundamental and most frequently invoked point of criticism concerns the fact that economic efficiency and maximisation of well-being are here treated as the only aim of law. It has often been pointed out that law serves other values too, such as justice, freedom, dignity, etc. This is why it should be perceived and evaluated not only, and not most importantly, from the point of view of economic efficiency.[71] Another point of criticism is the empirical inadequacy of the assumption of rationality of human behaviour. Systematic departures of human decisions and choices from predictions based on the rational individual model, discovered by experimental research, have given rise to behavioural law and economics. According to this line of research, the study of law should be based not on the rationality assumption but on a more realistic model of human behaviour, provided by empirical studies of human reactions to various stimuli.

Leaving aside the problem of whether this criticism is justified or sufficient to dismiss the research tools offered by law and economics as useless, what is truly interesting and important for the present discussion lies elsewhere. Law and economics are attempts to propose a methodologically sound approach to

---

69 For a large number of examples, see, e.g., Friedman, *Law's Order*..., p. 11.

70 B. Ackerman, quoted in R. Cooter and T. Ulen, *Law and Economics*, 6th ed. (Boston: Addison-Wesley, 2012), p. 2.

71 See a thorough discussion in W. Załuski, "Cel prawa według Law & Economics" [The Goal of Law According to Law & Economics], *Wielowymiarowość prawa* [Multidimensionality of Law], ed. J. Czapska, M. Dudek, and M. Stępień (Toruń: Wydawnictwo Adam Marszałek, 2014), pp. 299f. It is worth mentioning that according to proponents of law and economics, justice as a value may not in fact be different from efficiency (the pursuit of optimisation of resources allocation). As Friedman argues, there is a certain "surprising correspondence between justice and efficiency. In many cases, principles we think of as just correspond fairly closely to rules that we discover are efficient. Examples range from 'thou shalt not steal' to 'the punishment should fit the crime' to the requirement that criminal penalties be imposed only after proof beyond a reasonable doubt. This suggests a radical conjecture – that what we call principles of justice may actually be rules of thumb for producing an efficient outcome, rules we have somehow internalized;" Załuski, *Law's Order*..., *p.* 22.

law understood as norms that influence human behaviour. Law and its operation can be explained in terms of causal dependencies between stimuli that influence the behaviour of addressees and the actual effects of particular regulations. On this understanding, law is construed as an element of social reality which is explained in causal terms and comprises various categories of facts (legal norms, law-applying institutions, behaviours of subjects of law, and the effects of these behaviours for the degree of satisfaction of their subjective preferences). The task of jurisprudence is to study these facts and the cause-effect relationships between them, including legal norms and the operation of institutions that create and apply them.

As in legal realism and critical legal studies, also in this case, certain positivist assumptions are accepted concerning what law is. Namely, it is implicitly identified with norms introduced and enforced by appropriate state institutions (whether parliaments or courts that set precedents). At the same time, however, law and economics assumes that it is possible not only to draw a clear line between legal and non-legal norms but also to formulate the content of law in a way that allows for its full and uniform understanding, and thus, for influencing the behaviour of addressees to bring the same effects. Hence, in contrast to classical legal realism and critical legal studies, the economic model either ignores the indeterminacy of law or treats it as a feature which can be eliminated in the course of dogmatic-practical analysis and clarification of legal texts. Also on this approach, the scientific study of law is not meant to replace or compete against legal science. Rather, it is complementary and assumes that legal science fulfils its dogmatic-explanatory objectives appropriately (if not perfectly).

4.4. The biological-evolutionary model

In recent decades, one of the most dynamically developing approaches to the study of law sets it in the context of the natural biological predispositions of humans, giving rise to a variety of practices as well as social and cultural institutions. Seen in this light, human nature is understood in biological terms as a product of an evolutionary pressure to survive and spread genes responsible for properties that reinforce reactions conducive to survival.[72] In the case of species with a complex nervous system (that is, at least in the case of mammals and birds), the wide adaptability of behavioural reactions and the ability to

72 For more detail and an accessible discussion, see Pinker, *The Blank Slate*….

adjust them to specific environmental conditions result from various forms of consciousness.[73]

On the level of elementary consciousness phenomena, emotional processes that trigger behavioural reactions conducive to survival play a major role.[74] On the basis of these processes, some species have developed tendencies to behave in ways which can be described as empathic, altruistic (especially towards related individuals), showing attachment to others, ability to cooperate, and reciprocity, etc. Especially interesting and important are findings indicating that the rudimentary sense of fairness also occurs in some non-human species.[75] If this sense is combined with appropriately developed cognitive abilities, one may speak of proto-normative phenomena in communities of some animal species (especially in chimpanzees and other great apes).[76]

The gradual discovery of proto-normative behaviours among hominids and the growing understanding of the emotional mechanisms that underlie the formation of normative experiences stimulate and encourage the search for the biological roots of morality and law known from human cultures.[77] In the context of the present advancement of knowledge, theories that treat morality – and, as a result, the legal order – as a product of culture only, whose task is to tame

---

73 See, e.g., W. Pisula, "Poziomy świadomości" [Levels of Awareness], *Przegląd Filozoficzny* [Philosophical Review] 2/94 (2015), pp. 383–397; see also, e.g., C. Koch, *The Quest for Consciousness: A Neurobiological Approach* (Denver, CO: Roberts and Company Publishers, 2004).

74 The most important scholars who studied the role of emotional processes in consciousness include J. Panksepp and J. LeDoux. See, e.g., J. Panksepp, "Affective Consciousness: Core Emotional Feelings in Animals and Humans," *Consciousness & Cognition* 14 (2005), pp. 30f; J. LeDoux, *The Synaptic Self* (New York: Penguin, 2002).

75 See, e.g., F. de Waal, *Primates and Philosophers. How Morality Evolved* (Princeton, NJ: Princeton University Press,2006), pp. 42f.

76 See, e.g., S. Ehrlich, *Wiążące wzory zachowania. Rzecz o wielości systemów norm* [The Binding Schema of Conduct. On the Plularity of Norm Systems] (Warszawa: PWN, 1995), pp. 34f.

77 *See,* e.g., M. Weiss, *Etyka a ewolucja. Metaetyczny kontekst etyki ewolucyjnej* [Ethics and Evolution. The Metaethical Context of Evolutionary Ethics] (Poznań: Wydawnictwo Poznańskie, 2010); A. Elżanowski, "Prawdziwie darwinowska etyka" [A Truly Darwinist Ethic], *Lectiones & Acroases Philosophicae* 3 (2010), pp. 13f; H. Gommer, *A Biological Theory of Law* (Seattle: Createspace, 2011); T. Pietrzykowski, "The roots of normativity. From neuroscience to legal theory," in *Studies in the Philosophy of Law*, Vol. 7, *Legal Philosophy and the Challenges of Biosciences*, ed. J. Stelmach, M. Soniewicka, and W. Załuski (Kraków: Wydawnictwo: Wydawnictwo Uniwersytetu Jagiellońskiego 2010), pp. 97–122.

natural, amoral ("animal-like") inclinations of humans, must be regarded as outdated.[78] Theories that attempt to explain the origins of law in terms of purely cultural bonds counteracting natural human predispositions comprise views which Wojciech Załuski dubbed as the Hobbes model and the Hayek model.[79]

According to the first model, law is identified with a set of norms which are to tame the unbridled aggression and egoism of humans, who, without law and order introduced and enforced by the overlord, would wage a war against everyone. In the Hayek model, in turn, law makes it possible to overcome collectivist predispositions dominant in pre-legal communities, which preclude organised and effective cooperation beyond the relatively small community scale. Załuski juxtaposes these two models with the Darwin model, based in the up-to-date knowledge of the biological-evolutionary foundation of human behaviour.

Załuski points out that the Darwin model supports a moderately optimistic view of human nature, which comprises two main elements. The first is "imperfect prudence," referring to the ability to take care of one's wellbeing by setting long-term goals and focusing on plans that help to achieve them. However, this attitude is systematically disturbed by the propensity to disproportionately prefer immediately available benefits over those more remote in time (that is, by hyperbolic discounting of expected reward). The other element of the moderately optimistic view of human nature is the propensity to narrow altruism to relative and reciprocal altruism. At the same time, it is worth bearing in mind that although the biologically determined psychic dispositions that evolved as a result of natural selection are

> the main factor generating our behaviours, our ability to think in abstract terms and to find motivation in cultural factors often leads us to act in a way which runs against out psychic dispositions shaped by natural selection.[80]

The rise of complex normative orders in human communities was possible thanks to the development of abstract and counterfactual thinking, as well as linguistic communication (that is, abilities which were, most probably, closely interconnected). As a result of these developments, cooperation within human communities moved beyond relationships based on personal bonds, possible only in relatively isolated and small (approximately 150-person) groups.

---

78 For criticism of the theories of morality that construe it as a "thin layer" of cultural norms constraining amoral, animal-like inclinations of humans, see in particular de Waal, *Primates…*, pp. 7f.

79 W. Załuski, *Ewolucyjna filozofia prawa* [The Evolutionary Philosophy of Law] (Kraków: Wolters Kluwer, 2009), pp. 19f.

80 Ibid., p. 56.

Expanding it involved a growing need to create and follow norms regulating social interactions, so as to counteract the increased risk of "stowaway passengers" profiting from the situation (as Hendrik Gommer remarks, the bigger the scale of cooperation, the stronger the need for such social norms).[81] Normative models of behaviour that emerge from attempts to regulate this cooperation base to a large extent on biologically determined emotional dispositions, such as anger, shame, gratitude, conformism, or respect for the hierarchy that governs a particular community.

From the biological-evolutionary perspective, law is therefore, as Załuski puts it, an emergent entity which supervenes on social practices of cooperation and on recognition these practices receive as models of prescribed behaviour.[82] The cooperative practices and the grounds for treating them as normatively valid models that ought to be followed are manifestations of natural human dispositions, shaped in the course of evolution of the human species and its ancestors.

The biological-evolutionary approach towards the study of law seeks to explain (or to provide a substantial part of the explanation for) the origin of law, the mechanisms of its operation, and the needs and goals it serves and that provide the reason for it.[83] It is then an attempt to build a theory of the legal phenomenon that would rest on solid foundations of empirical natural sciences and do justice to the so far accumulated knowledge of the biological and psychological factors governing human behaviour (including those connected with the creation, application, and enforcement of social norms). This view differs in important respects from the traditional natural legal approaches in that it seeks to provide, first of all, a causal explanation of the legal phenomenon rather than to base or justify it by referring to an objective moral order. Thus, it can be said that one deals here with naturalist rather than natural legal theories.[84]

Nevertheless, biological-evolutionary theories are often used not only to explain the legal phenomenon as a whole but also to analyse concrete legal solutions. In this form, they can be treated as arguments for or against particular regulations. This application of biological-evolutionary ideas raises much more

81 Gommer, *A Biological…*, p. 44.

82 Załuski, *Ewolucyjna…*, pp. 95f.

83 See ibid.

84 Even biological-evolutionary theories of the origins of morality point to the need for a critical ethical evaluation of these sets of "positive morality" norms which derive from a propensity to behave in ways that do not deserve unconditional approval (e.g., a bias in favour of in-group members, aggression, revenge, conformism, or exaggerated emphasis on honour); cf. Elżanowski, "Prawdziwie," pp. 50f.

controversies, because it carries the risk of naturalist error. This concerns in particular the risk of a too hasty identification of the "naturalness" of a particular behaviour with its ethical merits and of the biological explanation of particular dispositions with their justification. Still, it seems that well thought-out biologically oriented *de lege ferenda* arguments may easily avoid such dangers.[85]

An interesting example of such controversies is the discussion on the biological bases of rape and the related dispute concerning appropriate legal measures.[86] There are important evolutionary arguments in favour of the view that, on certain conditions, enforcing procreation may – in the case of males whose genetic material favours such behaviour – be an effective adaptive strategy to achieve a relative reproductive success. This would imply that there are mechanisms responsible for some males being "naturally" more predisposed to sexual aggression.

Supporters of the biological theory of rape reject socio-cultural explanations, influential especially in feminist circles. Seen in this perspective, sexual aggression towards women is, in fact, a learnt behaviour, with models transmitted within a broader "rape culture" (comprising trivialisation, blaming the victim for provoking or expecting aggression on the part of the rapist, and, finally, regarding the state of social dominance of men over women as "natural"). Rape is here viewed not as a strictly sexual act (as biological explanations would suggest), but as an act of subordinating the victim, of humiliation and reification, and of gaining control and power over her body.

Opting for the biological explanation of sexual aggression, Owen Jones draws attention to potential far-reaching consequences of a correct or misguided description of legally regulated behaviour for law and its effectiveness. In the light of the biological theory of rape, the so-called chemical castration of offenders may be an efficient penalty method, lowering their sexual drive. By contrast, according to socio-cultural theories, this legal measure is useless and irrational, because rape follows from other than sexual drives. Referring to a wrong theory may thus lead to a grossly misguided choice of penalty instruments and, as a result, to a large number of tragedies that might have been avoided.

---

85 *De lege ferenda* arguments based on biological dispositions to behave in particular ways may bring to mind empirical-behavioural versions of law and economics; cf. D. Elliott, "Law and Biology. The New Synthesis?" *Saint Louis University Law Journal* 41 (1997), p. 610.

86 O. Jones, "Sex, Culture and the Biology of Rape," *California Law Review* 87 (1999), pp. 827f; R. Thornhill and C. Palmer, *A Natural History of Rape: Biological Bases of Sexual Coercion* (Cambridge, MA: MIT Press 2000).

The biological theory may also lead to conclusions regarding the relationship between fighting against rape and prostitution policy. If sexual aggression is a form of relieving sexual desire, it may be expected that the risk of rape would decrease proportionally to the increase in the availability of consensual sexual activity. And conversely, an increase in sexual violence may be a side-effect of a rigorous elimination of prostitution. By contrast, the socio-cultural theory leads to very different conclusions, with both prostitution and rape treated as symptoms of the same attitude, namely, the reification of women. On this view, both must be eliminated, and any degree of tolerance with respect to one could also support the other practice.

Jones observes that in the light of the biological theory, severe penalisation of rape is fully justified. The biological bases of sexual aggression indicate that potential offenders may experience a strong, irresistible temptation to commit the act, to only a very limited extent modifiable by imposed cultural models.[87] Thus, it is only through appropriately strong deterring stimuli that the behaviour of a large number of potential rapists can be effectively influenced. By contrast, socio-cultural theories would rather argue in favour of using preventive cultural methods (that is, changing models provided by rape culture), which, if the theory they are based on collapses, may prove totally ineffective.

The discussion demonstrates that the biological-evolutionary approach to law may be useful not only as a theory explaining the foundations of the legal phenomenon as such, but also as an important source of support for hypotheses concerning the origin, operation, and effectiveness of concrete legal solutions. However, for this kind of argumentation to be correct, one must bear in mind the principle repeatedly invoked by Jones: "is" does not imply "ought," description is not prescription, and explanation is not justification.[88] As long as this principle is maintained, the understanding of the biological-evolutionary bases of law-regulated phenomena may be invaluable for legislation. On the one hand, it helps avoid well-meant but often naive and ultimately counterproductive utopian

---

87 Proponents of the law and biology movement argue that in this case, law is supposed to serve as an "evolutionary prosthesis," helping to deal with the shortage of naturally developed dispositions towards desirable behaviour and to counteract the propensity to behaviour which is not ethically acceptable; see Elliott, "Law...," pp. 606–607.

88 O. Jones, "Time-Shifted Rationality and the Law of Law's Leverage: Behavioral Economics Meets Behavioral Biology," *Northwestern University Law Review* 95 (2001), p. 1168.

aspirations.[89] On the other, it makes it possible to treat law as an instrument, or "lever," in shaping the decision situation, so that nature and psychobiological mechanisms determining human reactions can be used to the best effect.[90]

Just like other models discussed in this chapter, this form of reflection on law is not meant as an alternative to legal dogmatics; rather, it rests on it, attempting to explain the origin, content, and operation of norms formulated by legal science (as well as reasons for their failure to operate). In practice, legal scholars who represent this approach to the study of law assume a particular view of legal norms. Only on this basis is it possible to investigate what psychosocial mechanisms – and of what evolutionary origin – underlie legal orders that have developed in various societies.

On the basis of these mechanisms, it is also possible to predict the results, or lack thereof, of particular legal regulations. Representatives of this approach do not seek answers to questions concerning the content of norms; they merely assume that such answers exist. Thus, the science of law they pursue is a distinct research area, much like the models discussed earlier, all of them, in a way, "living off" legal science, which is directly concerned with explaining the content of valid norms.

4.5 The socio-behavioural model

The study of law that refers to sociological concepts and methods was initiated, on the one hand, by the co-founders of sociology as a science, such as Durkheim and Weber, and on the other, by jurists interested in this research perspective, including Eugen Ehrlich, Georges Gurvitch, and Leon Petrażycki (who looked for the key to understanding social phenomena mainly in psychological processes[91]).

Further development of the sociology of law proceeded in several directions. Attempts have been made to provide a general description of law, or its selected aspects, as an element of a broader social reality, referring to general sociological theories. As an example, one may invoke Durkheim's considerations on law as a special (organised) way of enforcing social morality. A similar concept can be

---

89 Gommer, *A Biological...*, p. 130.

90 W. Załuski, *Ewolucyjna...*, p. 132; for more detail on the role of law as a lever which makes use of the natural inclinations of humans, see Jones, "Time-Shifted...," p. 1187.

91 Still, as A. Podgórecki observes, "it is misleading to label Petrażycki as psychological theorist since his interest was mainly in sociological questions," and his explanation of the foundations of the social order as a complex network of relations between intuitive law and official law remains "the most synthetic [theory] ever presented in the sociology of law" (Podgórecki, "Unrecognized...," pp. 184, 198).

found in the theory of relationship between the type of law (repressive, restitutive), on the one hand, and the type of social solidarity (mechanical, organic) and social function of sanctions, on the other, as well as in the theory of the impact of social evolution on the ways of penalising offenders.[92] Weber's views on the concept and evolution of the rationality of law, its role in social development, and the types of valid government it involves (legitimation of power) may serve as another well-known example.[93] Also theories of law as an autopoietic social subsystem (Niklas Luhmann, Günther Teubner) have sociological roots, as do theories of the evolution of law from repressive systems, through autonomy, to responsiveness (Philip Nonet, Peter Selznick).[94]

Another direction in the sociological study of law is empirical study of concrete, usually closely defined problems connected with the practice of legal order and its operation: attitudes, beliefs, and behaviour of its members. Such investigations apply research methods used by general sociology (as pointed out by Krzysztof Pałecki, there are no special socio-legal research methods other than those known from general sociology).[95] The most popular are surveys, followed by interviews, observation, and text analysis.[96] Empirical studies of this kind were

---

92 See A. Kojder, "Czytając Durkheima" [Reading Durkheim], in *Prawo, władza, społeczeństwo, polityka. Księga pamiątkowa prof. Krzysztofa Pałeckiego* [Law, Power, Society, Politics. Prof. Krzysztof Pałecki's Memorial Book] (Toruń: Adam Marszałek, 2006), pp. 286f.; for more detail, cf. R. Cotterrell, *Emile Durkheim - Law in a Moral Domain* (Edinburgh: Edinburgh University Press, 1999).

93 See A. Kojder, "Sprawcze siły racjonalizacji prawa. Zarys socjologii prawa Maxa Webera" [Causal Forces of the Rationalization of Law. An Outline of Max Weber's Sociology of Law], in *Okolice socjologicznej tożsamości. Księga pamiątkowa Wojciecha Sitka* [The Periphery of Sociological Identity. Wojciech Sitek's Memorial Book], ed. Z. Kurcz and I. Taranowicz (Wrocław: Wydawnictwo Uniwersytetu *Wrocławskiego,* 2010), pp. 51f.

94 P. Nonet and P. Selznick, *Law and Society in Transition. Toward Responsive Law* (New Brunswick, NJ: Transaction Publishers, 2009), p. 73f.; the concept of responsiveness is used in investigations into the operation of administration by M. Stępień, *Responsywna administracja publiczna* [A Responsive Public Administration] (Toruń: Adam Marszałek 2008).

95 K. Pałecki, "O przedmiocie socjologii prawa raz jeszcze" [On the Subject of the Sociology of Law Once Again], in *Prawo w zmieniającym się społeczeństwie. Księga pamiątkowa z okazji 70-lecia urodzin Profesor Marii Boruckiej-Arctowej* [A Memorial Book on the 70th Anniversary of the Birth of Professor Maria Borucka-Arctowa], ed. G. Skąpska (Kraków: Adam Marszałek 1992), p. 33.

96 On the sociological methods in the study of law, see Z. Ziembiński, *Socjologia prawa jako nauka prawna* [Sociology of Law as a Legal Science] (Warszawa: PWN, 1975), pp. 59f.;

already undertaken by American realists, although they played a peripheral role in this model of legal research. Among the main representatives of legal realism, Underhill Moore carried out such analyses on a relatively big scale, investigating banking practices and the operation of parking rules in New Haven. Still, in general, realists' efforts to bring together jurisprudence and social sciences yielded moderate effects; "as if someone had invented the square wheel; some movement of the horse cart was possible, but not much."[97] Also, in retrospect, the cooperation of another prominent realist Karl Llewellyn with the anthropologist E. Adamson Hoebel and their research into the non-state legal system of the Cheyenne tribe are usually regarded as not particularly successful.[98]

Among Polish empirical socio-legal studies, of particular interest are those dealing with the problem of legal awareness,[99] the practice of lay justice,[100] and sociological aspects of the application of family law.[101] A slightly different line of research comprises criminological studies into the social factors in crime, pathology, and social deviance. Interesting investigations have also been carried out into socio-legal aspects of social exclusion and dysfunction at the junction of political power and administration or economy.[102]

M. Borucka-Arctowa, "Podejście socjologiczne" [Sociological Approach], in *Metody badania prawa* [Methods of Studying Law], ed. A. Łopatka (Warszawa: Ossolineum, 1971), pp. 76f.

97 J. Schlegel, *American Legal Realism and Empirical Social Science* (Chapel Hill: The University of North Carolina Press, 1995), p. 211.

98 K. Llewellyn and E.A. Hoebel, *The Cheyenne Way. Conflict and Case Law in Primitive Jurisprudence* (Norman, OK: University of Oklahoma Press, 1941).

99 A. Gryniuk, *Świadomość prawna. Studium teoretyczne* [Legal Awareness. A Theoretical Study] (Toruń: Uniwersytet Mikołaja Kopernika, 1979); M. Borucka-Arctowa, *Świadomość prawna a planowe zmiany społeczne* [Legal Awareness and Planned Social Change] (Wrocław: Ossolineum, 1981). Empirical research into legal awareness of selected social groups is also carried out abroad; see, e.g., S. Merry, *Getting Justice and Getting Even. Legal Consciousness Among Working Class Americans* (Chicago: University of Chicago Press,1993).

100 *Ławnicy. Rezultaty badań empirycznych* [Jurors. Results of an Empirical Study], ed. A. Siemaszko (Warszawa: Instytut Wymiaru Sprawiedliwości, 1994).

101 K. Pałecki, *Społeczne wyznaczniki skutecznego oddziaływania prawem na stosunki rodzinne* [Social Markers of Effective Impact of Law on Family Relations], (Kraków: Uniwersytet Jagielloński, 1977); J. Górecki, *Rozwód. Studium socjologiczno-prawne* [Divorce. A Sociological and Legal Study] (Warszawa: PWN, 1965).

102 *Prawo i wykluczenie. Studium empiryczne* [Law and Exclusion. An Empirical Study], ed. A. Turska (Warszawa: C.H. Beck, 2010); K. Gadowska, *Dysfunkcje administracji* [Dysfunctions of Administration] (Kraków: Wydawnictwo Uniwersytetu

This brief overview of the various types of empirical studies carried out for several past decades, fragmentary as it is, illustrates the view that the problems they address

> form a rather incoherent picture, and an attempt to systematise the subject matter of such studies is far from convincing. On the one hand, there are no sharp contours defining what counts as a socio-legal problem; on the other, the incompleteness and fragmentariness of the topics addressed... is more than obvious.[103]

These faults are well visible in the context of the proposed scope of socio-legal research, that is, explanation of normative behaviour (undertaken because of an existing legal norm), which forms the social roots of law, the reasons for and mechanisms of legal change (the dynamics of law), the social phenomena that take place in legal institutions (the operation of law), and the social consequences of law (its effectiveness and function).[104] At the same time, sociological theories are expected to refer to data from empirical research, generalised to hypotheses explaining the phenomena that comprise the object of the sociology of law.[105]

Ziembiński's opinion remains valid if one considers broader theoretical concepts proposed in socio-legal literature, referring to various aspects of the operation of law. As an example, one may invoke Adam Podgórecki's three-level hypothesis concerning the operation of law,[106] various versions of the social mirror thesis mentioned above, or a variety of concepts evolving within the legal pluralism approach (such as Leopold Pospisil's legal levels, a network of legal spaces proposed by Boaventura de Sousa-Santos, and various perspectives on the polycentric nature of law).[107]

Jagiellońskiego, 2015); eadem, *Zjawisko klientelizmu polityczno- ekonomicznego. Systemowa analiza powiązań sieciowych na przykładzie przekształceń sektora górniczego w Polsce* [The Phenomenon of Political-Economic Clientelism. A Systemic Analysis of Network Relations Based on the Example of Transformations in the Mining Sector in Poland] (Kraków: Wydawnictwo Uniwersytetu Jagiellońskiego, 2002), p. 218.

103 Ziembiński, *Socjologia prawa*..., p. 141.

104 Pałecki, "O przedmiocie...," p. 35.

105 Ibid., p. 34.

106 For more detail, see J. Kwaśniewski, "Hipoteza trójstopniowego działania prawa" [The Hypothesis of the Three-Stage Operation of Law], in A. Kojder and Z. Cywiński, eds., *Socjologia prawa. Główne problemy i postacie* [Sociology of Law. Key Problems and Figures] (Warszawa: Wydawnictwa Uniwersytetu Warszawskiego, 2014), pp. 122f.

107 On the problem of pluralism in general, see J. Winczorek, "Pluralizm prawny wczoraj i dziś. Kilka uwag o ewolucji pojęcia" [Legal Pluralism Then and Now. Remarks on the Evolution of the Term], in *Pluralizm prawny* [Legal Pluralism], ed. D. Bunikowski

Studies into the conditions and factors influencing the actual process of solving decision problems related to the application of law have been developing intensively for the past decades. They are usually located at the junction of sociology and psychology (cognitive sciences). As an example, one may invoke Eileen Braman's experiments on motivated reasoning in legal decision-making. They aimed to determine the extent to which prior moral and political preferences of subjects (related to such issues as homosexuality or abortion) were likely to influence their perception of the legal situation (including strictly procedural elements, with no direct moral underpinning). With this goal in mind, the subjects were asked to solve neutral, technical legal problems that would indirectly influence the ultimate result of a legal case, making it more or less convergent with non-legal preferences of the subjects.

The research has confirmed that in cases where there is a wider margin of decision, such preferences do play an important role in the perception and resolution of problems apparently unrelated to moral considerations. Interestingly, the results obtained by Braman also suggest that this influence varies not only according to the degree of controversy or unclarity of a particular case (which might have been expected), but also according to non-legal preferences, which may motivate the reasoning.[108]

The significance of the experiments carried out by Braman, and of other similar studies on the psychological aspects of legal reasoning and decision-making, consists not only in the empirical verification of common-sense beliefs of jurists (and speculative considerations by Jerome Frank and other realists). What is perhaps more important, the research has exposed the extra-conscious nature of many processes: jurists are subjectively certain that in their decision-making, they are guided only by "neutral" legal reasons, objective legal rules, and impartial perception of the facts of the case. In this light, interpreting the relationship between, on the one hand, legal reasoning and decisions and, on the other, non-legal preferences and opinions in terms of "sincerity" of argumentation appears grossly oversimplified. What turns out to be essential is that people remain largely unaware of the degree to which their own understanding of the situation, perception of particular solutions, and arguments supporting them are entangled with their subjective axiological, ideological, or political perspectives. Thus,

---

and K. Dobrzeniecki (Toruń: Interdyscyplinarne Koło Naukowe Doktorantów UMK, 2009); Dupret, *Droit…*, pp. 54f.

108 See E. Braman, *Law, Politics and Perception: How Policy Preferences Influence Legal Reasoning* (Charlottesville, VA: University of Virginia Press, 2009); cf. also Pietrzykowski, *Intuicja…*, pp. 267f.

the influence of such factors may be – and usually is – independent of the subjectively sincere belief that in making a decision, one takes into consideration only objective and strictly legal reasons.

The studies correspond with intensive research into empirical correlations between decisions made by judges as to the application of law and concrete circumstances or personal non-legal preferences or beliefs that can be established. In this context, one may invoke the widely discussed idea of "judicial attitudinal model," proposed and developed by Jeffrey Segal and Harold Speath.[109] It is based on an analysis of the behaviour of the American Supreme Court justices (voting) in selected types of cases. Segal and Speath made an attempt to classify their personal ideological positions from the most liberal to the most conservative ones (basing on the available information unrelated to the context of the court). Next, they compared the findings with the decisions the justices made in cases with a relatively strong "ideological load" (e.g., in cases that concerned the extent of state intervention in civil liberties). The results have shown that the knowledge of the ideological stance of the justice allows for much more accurate predictions regarding his or her decisions (the resolution of the case) than the so-called legal model, where such predictions are based solely on legal arguments relevant to the case.

In other words, according to Segal and Speath, on the basis of legal arguments only, it is impossible to successfully predict the judge's decision (the probability of making a correct prediction being below 50%); by contrast, using knowledge about his or her ideological position, it is possible to predict the decision with 70% accuracy. Although the attitudinal model has been raising serious controversy and remains an object of criticism,[110] the data on which it is based provide a considerable support for speculations and conjectures of legal realists as to the role that ideological and political preferences of justices play in the way they decide concrete cases.

***

Sociological and psychological studies, which analyse law as empirically available behaviour patterns and experiences, philosophical-legal lines of critical

---

109 J. Segal and H. Speath, *The Supreme Court and the Attitudinal Model* (Cambridge: Cambridge University Press, 1993); J. Segal and H. Speath, *The Supreme Court and the Attitudinal Model Revisited* (New York: Cambridge University Press, 2002).

110 See, e.g., M. Bailey and F. Maltzman, *The Constrained Court. Law, Politics and the Decisions Justices Make* (Princeton, NJ: Princeton University Press, 2011).

legal studies and law and economics, as well as earlier directions of legal realism offer very different perspectives on law. However, what they all have in common is the fundamental viewpoint that law is a kind of social practice, constituted by interconnected facts which can and should be systematically studied and explained with appropriate empirical methods. Behaviour and decisions of people who participate in the creation, application, interpretation, and observance of law form the factual dimension of the legal phenomenon and are equally important as an area of legal research as considerations about the content and mutual relations of the norms of a legal system. The latter are the province of legal science, which plays an important role here, because what is regarded as the content of valid norms in the practical operation of the legal order becomes the actual point of reference for beliefs, behaviour, and decisions, which, in turn, are the object of interest for the science of law.

Finally, it must be noted that many views and theories developing within the science of law rather than legal science may be, and often are, invoked in dogmatic and practical discourse as well. They can provide arguments to strengthen a particular stance on the way law should be understood and applied, or offer a foundation for observations *de lege ferenda*, making a case for a change in law. In this respect, the findings of the science of law may overlap with considerations of legal science, aiming at a reconstruction of the content of norms which are, or should be, part of valid law.

5 Naturalisation and legal sciences

In his polemics with Eugen Ehrlich, Hans Kelsen, the founder of normativism, rejected the idea of developing empirical legal science that assumed that law as a phenomenon belonged to the realm of facts and, hence, adopted the perspective and methods of social sciences. At the same time, he fiercely criticised Ehrlich's attempt to distinguish law from other rules on the basis of empirically identified types of "legal facts" and recorded reactions to violations of various kinds of social norms. According to Kelsen, law belongs to the realm of duty (*Sollen*) rather than to the realm of being (*Sein*). Thus, legal science is not a science of facts but of the content of norms which give rise to specific legal obligations.

The view that the study of law consists in the empirical study of facts rather than of the content of norms which comprise the legal system must result in the unfounded identification of being and duty. This, in turn, as Kelsen argues, is the gravest possible methodological error. The true scope of legal science is the realm of duty, with the content specified by valid legal norms which prescribe that in certain circumstances particular types of behaviour must occur. The description of actual behaviour of subjects of law may, on some occasions, be helpful for the jurist, but it is not – and cannot be – the object of legal science in the proper understanding of the term.

It has been pointed out in the literature that Kelsen's violent criticism of Ehrlich's ideas significantly slowed down the development of the sociology of law. It created a barrier of mistrust of sociological empirical findings and their usefulness for the main task of legal science, that is, for the study of the normative content of valid law. In his later years, Kelsen openly regretted his overly radical opposition against Ehrlich and the negative effects it had for the perception of the role of sociology in legal studies.[1]

Looking at Kelsen's polemic with Ehrlich from a greater historical distance and through the prism of the later development of legal thought, one comes to the conclusion that, in spite of their beliefs to the contrary, they promoted not two competing and incompatible visions of jurisprudence but complementary and legitimate types of legal studies. The two perspectives are very different – both in their objectives and in their methods and findings – but they complement each

1 S. Machura, "Eugen Ehrlich's Legacy in the Contemporary German Legal Sociology," in *Eugen Ehrlich's Sociology of Law*, ed. K. Papendorf, S. Machura, and A. Hellum (Münster: LIT Verlag, 2014), pp. 51–52.

other in offering various types of scientific reflection on law, equally useful and necessary. Seen in this light, Kelsen's normativism, arguing for "purification" of jurisprudence so that it is concerned exclusively with the description of the content of valid legal norms, appears as an ideal type of legal science (as here understood). On the other hand, calls for strictly empirical investigations into the ways in which certain social norms determine actual behaviour of individuals, the internal experiences they produce, and the impact of these experiences on the observable behavioural reaction patterns to recurrent circumstances comprise the model of jurisprudence as the science of law.

On this understanding, the scope of legal science is the content of valid legal norms (that is, norms that belong to the legal system). This means that its scientific character is strictly connected with methods and criteria of validation, interpretation, and systematisation, which make it possible to draw conclusions as to who, in what circumstances, and how should behave in view of valid regulations. By contrast, the science of law aims at a description and explanation of processes and mechanisms of the operation of law, defined as the entirety of experiences, behaviour, and cultural artefacts that comprise the factual substratum of the legal phenomenon.

From this perspective, it would seem that jurisprudence can develop into a *scientific* study of law along two different paths. It can respect methodological requirements of humanities investigations into the content of a particular type of norms, or it can propose empirically verifiable (falsifiable) explanations of facts constituting the legal order and of mutual dependencies between them. These two approaches are by no means mutually exclusive; rather, they offer complementary perspectives that differ in goals and research methods. These differences, in turn, are of immediate significance for the debate on naturalisation. What is more, ignoring them makes it virtually impossible to arrive at plausible conclusions concerning the need for naturalisation of legal studies and the boundaries within which legal studies can comply with the modern tendencies and calls for naturalisation.

In the simplest terms, naturalism refers to a view which asserts that everything that exists is a product of nature, unaffected by any inexplicable "supernatural" factors. Thus, the naturalist picture of the world does not admit any "'supernatural' or other 'spooky' kinds of entity."[2] Nature – and everything that

2 D. Papineau, "Naturalism," in *Stanford Encyclopedia of Philosophy*, ed. E.N. Zalta, Winter 2016 Edition; available at https://plato.stanford.edu/archives/win2016/entries/naturalism/.

exists – can be accounted for using methods which are suitable for discovering and investigating the laws that govern natural phenomena.[3] This refers both to the world of non-living entities and to living creatures, including the human being perceived as a product of hundreds of millions of years of biological evolution. It is in its course that the structures of the homo sapiens nervous system were formed, providing the biological foundation for human intellectual and behavioural capacities. The specific conditions in which these structures operate are also the key to understanding the mechanisms of creating a complex social and cultural reality, including a legal order.

In this broad understanding, ontological naturalism is sometimes deemed trivial and treated as a view which in fact cannot be challenged, at least as long as everything that exists is *ex definitione* a product of nature. Still, much like the tautology of Parmenides of Elea, this apparently trivial thesis of ontological naturalism is invoked to draw radical and controversial conclusions, which refer primarily to the human being. Naturalism leads (or, at least, may lead) to the rejection of the belief that human beings have a metaphysically unique status relative to nature and break from the laws that govern it. Instead, they are perceived as merely one of its species, whose specific characteristics are nothing else but a result of adaptation and a response to evolutionary pressure from environmental conditions which have accompanied humans and their biological ancestors for millions of years. These processes gave rise to a unique combination of features and abilities thanks to which humans evolved linguistic communication enabling advanced forms of cooperation, development and transmission of complex cultural models, and production and use of complicated tools (technology).[4]

These features were not mysteriously "bestowed" on humans in a *deus ex machina* fashion. Both the genealogy and the operation of the human body – and, most importantly, the nervous structures – can be completely described and accounted for as products of complex biological processes. Inner experiences and other psychological phenomena are results of neurophysiological activity of particular brain structures. Thus, according to a naturalist maxim, human mind is "not spirit, but brain." Consciousness and the ability to react emotionally and think rationally are fully natural phenomena which developed thanks to the evolution of the nervous system and its capacities. Capabilities to

---

3 Cf. S. Goetz and Ch. Taliaferro, *Naturalism* (Cambridge: CUP, 2008), pp. 8f.; cf. Also *Contemporary Philosophical Naturalism and its Implications*, ed. B. Bashour and H. Muller (London: Routledge, 2014).

4 For more detail, see, e.g., R. Dunbar, *Human Evolution* (Pelican Books 2014).

cooperate, communicate, build social relations, and grant conventional, culture-based senses to various entities reflect the anatomic and functional complexity of the human brain. At the same time, they are constrained by the brain's limitations. Most of such abilities have simpler counterparts in other animal species, where the brain structures are related to the human nervous system (as in other mammals) or where functional equivalents occur (as, e.g., in birds).

The level of development of some mental abilities and the way they are integrated in human mind are unique among animals. Still, they are merely products of the specific evolutionary path of humans. Although the abilities that underlie speech, conscious abstract thinking, and the development of culture and technology are distinctive for human beings, specific characteristics of other species, which went through a different evolutionary path, are equally unique products of evolution. Most importantly, however, all typically human abilities – ones that have made it possible for the human being to dominate the planet and create civilisation, culture, science, and, last but not least, law – are equally "natural" (that is, explicable in terms of natural laws and processes) as predispositions, instincts, and ways of life characteristic of other species. Also the ability of humans to "transcend" their natural needs and inclinations results from the presence of brain structures developed in the course of evolution, in particular, prefrontal cortical areas responsible for so-called executive functions.[5]

Thus, the appeal for naturalisation of the picture of the world, embracing not only nature as such but also culture and "human spirit," is, in fact, an inexorable consequence of the aspiration to ultimately demystify it by removing illusions and myths created by humans about other creatures and about themselves, in particular, about their "supranatural" position in the world (the status of "Man"). Versions of such ontological or metaphysical naturalism differ widely in specific (and often fundamental) points.[6] For the purposes of this discussion, only the

5 E. Goldber, *The Executive Brain. Frontal Lobes and the Civilized Man* (Oxford: OUP, 2001); J. LeDoux, *The Synaptic Self* (London: Macmillan, 2002), pp. 176f. On the natural abilities of the human being to act "against nature," see also two interesting contributions which offer very different perspectives on the problem: psychological and philosophical; see K. Stanovich, *The Robot's Rebellion. Finding Meaning in the Age of Darwin* (Chicago, IL: University of Chicago Press, 2004) and J. McDowell, *Reason and Nature* (Münster: Lit Verlag, 1999).

6 For more detail, see J. Stelmach, "Stare i nowe interpretacje naturalizmu prawniczego" [Old and New Interpretations of Legal Naturalism], in *Naturalizm prawniczy. Interpretacje* [Legal Naturalism. Interpretations], eds. J. Stelmach, B. Brożek, Ł. Kurek, and K. Eliasz (Warszawa: Wolters Kluwer, 2015), p. 13f.

most elementary distinction will be outlined, the one between radical and moderate versions of ontological naturalism.

In its radical version, naturalism is associated with a monistic view of reality, usually connected with the belief that all kinds of phenomena can be reduced to processes that occur at the most basic, physical level of organisation. Thus, in its standard form, radical naturalism is a reductionist monism and a type of physicalism. Psychological and sociological terms provide a different description of phenomena that occur on a higher level of complexity of matter, but their findings are, in principle, fully translatable into the physicalist language. Ultimately, all phenomena occur on the level of physical interactions and processes. They can simply be construed in terms that refer to macroscale events involving complex objects, their groups, and interactions among them.[7]

In its moderate version, naturalism is not strictly reductionist and accepts that there might be phenomena which, while constituted by entities and processes on the physical-chemical level, cannot be fully reduced to them. Every level of organisation of matter needs an appropriate language (e.g., the language of physics, chemistry, or biology) because of the possible emergence of additional, level-specific properties or phenomena. These additional elements are not fully reducible to the language used to describe more elementary levels and can be grasped only in terms of concepts that make sense on a particular level of complexity.

As an illustration, one may think of the property of liquidity, an example used by John Searle, one of the foremost supporters of the moderate version of naturalism. Liquidity refers to a type of organisation of a large number of molecules of water or other liquids. If described on the individual level, the molecules are no more "liquid" than any other molecules. This demonstrates that liquidity is a real-life property which can be described only on the level of organisation where it actually emerges.

Searle takes a similar approach to describe the relation between consciousness as an emergent property, on the one hand, and the biochemical activity of nervous system cells, on the other. Mental phenomena emerge on the level of interactions that are complex enough and occur thanks to synaptic links between neurons. No single neural cell is more "conscious" than any somatic cell. However, if the number of neural cells is large enough and if the electric and chemical signals they transmit are sufficiently complex, a new phenomenon

7 Cf., e.g., L.R. Baker, *Naturalism and the First-Person Perspective* (Oxford: Oxford University Press, 2013), p. 7f.

emerges, that is, conscious subjective experience. Searle refers to this approach to the ontology of consciousness as biological naturalism. On this view,

> consciousness is a biological phenomenon like any other. It is true that it has special features, most notably the feature of subjectivity, as we have seen, but that does not prevent consciousness from being a higher-level feature of the brain in the same way that digestion is a higher-level feature of the stomach, or liquidity a higher-level feature of the system of molecules that constitute our blood.[8]

Looking for a solution to the problem of the mind and body relation, we must avoid, on the one hand, the faith in the metaphysical "spiritual substance" and, on the other, reductionism which openly contradicts facts and ignores the occurrence of conscious experiences: real, although subjective and absent on the elementary levels of complexity of matter. According to Searle, we have to acknowledge that:

> consciousness, with all its subjectivity, is caused by processes in the brain, and ... conscious states are themselves higher-level features of the brain .... Of course, consciousness is still special among biological phenomena. Consciousness has a first-person ontology and so cannot be reduced to, or eliminated in favor of, phenomena with a third-person ontology. But that is just a fact about how nature works. It is a fact of neurobiology that certain brain processes cause conscious states and processes. I am urging that we should grant the facts without accepting the metaphysical baggage that traditionally goes along with the facts.[9]

It is worth pointing out that the concept of personhood developed by Lynne Rudder Baker rests on similar assumptions. She claims that the relation between a person (a conscious individual) and a body (the physical substance) consists in the person being constituted by the organism (the body), in a special sense of the term "to constitute." A person is thus constituted by the body but cannot be reduced to it.[10]

The claim that for a description of reality to be accurate, it has to include the non-reductive first-person perspective leads Baker to what she calls near-naturalism. It differs from "scientific naturalism," among others, in the fact that its naturalist ontology takes into consideration the sphere of subjective experiences of conscious individuals. It also treats medium-sized objects, such as

8 J. Searle, *Mind, Language and Society: Philosophy in the Real World* (New York: Basic Books, 1999), pp. 51–52.

9 Ibid., p. 52.

10 L.R. Baker, *Persons and Bodies. A Constitution View* (Cambridge: Cambridge University Press, 2000).

people, animals, or artefacts, as real-life entities, no less legitimate than electrons or other objects that can be described in the language of physics.[11]

In modern analytic philosophy, the interdependence between phenomena on different levels of organisation of matter is often captured by the concept of supervenience. Popularised mainly by Donald Davidson and Jaegwon Kim, it is usually understood as a non-reductive dependence that can be expressed in the following way: every change on the higher level of organisation (the supervening level) must be accompanied by a change on a more elementary level (the supervened level). At the same time, the reverse is not necessarily the case. Not every change on the supervened (lower) level must entail a variation on the supervening level.

This concept is used by some authors to describe the relation between mental (supervening) states and neurophysiological "neural events" (supervened states, or neurophysiological activity). It was also applied by Załuski in his model of law, where law supervenes on the empirical level of behaviour and beliefs of participants in a legal order.[12] There is a unidirectional dependence between the state of law (its content) and the beliefs and behaviour of people, but there is no equivalence. No change in the content of law is possible without a change in beliefs or behaviour. At the same time, changes in beliefs and behaviour need not be accompanied by a change on the supervening level of the content of law (which is why it cannot be regarded as identical with anybody's beliefs or behaviour).

The concepts of emergence and supervenience loosen tight naturalist ontology in such a way that it allows for the presence of properties and entities which cannot be reduced to a strictly physical level, at the same time avoiding radical dualism and positing a sphere of phenomena independent of the material world.

Complementing naturalist ontology with mental states and cultural artefacts that depend on them, including the normative legal order, seems particularly important for the prospects of naturalisation of jurisprudence. It offers a new perspective, which treats legal phenomena and concepts as real-life entities and a fully legitimate and self-contained object of study. At the same time, investigations of this kind cannot proceed in isolation; they must match knowledge of the laws that govern events and processes occurring on the level on which law supervenes, that is, on the level of people's experiences and behaviour.

Ontological naturalism is usually distinguished from methodological naturalism. According to the latter, methods of natural sciences (that is, sciences that

---

11 Baker, *Naturalism…*, pp. 207–208.

12 Załuski, *Ewolucyjna…*, pp. 96f.

study "nature") are the only credible way of gaining knowledge about reality.[13] Any attempt to make sense of reality, if it is to be called scientific, must consist in the study of facts and relations between them, regardless of what type of facts or what part of reality it is concerned with.

Methodological naturalism may follow from ontological naturalism. Nevertheless, it is not inherently connected with it, so an approach marked by methodological naturalism need not rest on metaphysical naturalist assumptions. The fact that there exists a domain of phenomena distinct from those governed by laws operating on the level of nature does not mean that there must be special methods, fundamentally different from those used by natural history, to study them scientifically. Radical ontological naturalism is obviously conducive to methodological naturalism: once we accept the monistic and physicalist view of reality, it is difficult to question the usefulness of natural science methods in searching for a complete explanation of all types of phenomena. However, weaker versions of ontological naturalism appear fully compatible with both naturalist and anti-naturalist methodological approach.

Accepting that there are other types of phenomena on higher levels of organisation of matter leaves open the problem of methods that are appropriate for their description and study. One may believe that the same methods are equally suitable to describe any domain of reality. Still, the opposite view is also possible, namely, that different types of phenomena (regardless of their mutual dependencies) should be studied with methods corresponding specifically to their characteristics.

In practice, however, ontological naturalism and methodological naturalism go hand in hand and complement each other, one might say, naturally. In its radical version, consistent naturalism claims that whatever exists is ultimately explicable in terms of phenomena and processes occurring on the lowest levels of organisation of matter. A thorough study of these processes – using appropriate natural science methods – will provide a complete explanation of all types of facts: psychological, social, and cultural. It merely offers a different type of description of phenomena that ultimately occur on the physical level.

More moderate versions of naturalism accept that certain types of properties and entities emerge on higher levels of organisation and require a language and methods of analysis adjusted to their specific character, impossible to explain in terms and laws that describe reality on the physical level. All findings and claims

13 For more detail, see, e.g., J. Stelmach, "Naturalistyczny i antynaturalistyczny model teorii prawa" [The Naturalistic and Anti-Naturalistic Models of Legal Theory], *Studia Prawnicze* [Legal Studies] 3–4 (1984).

concerning higher-level phenomena must be compatible (consistent) with the laws governing the lower levels of organisation. Thus, explanations of social and cultural phenomena cannot be at odds with knowledge about the psychological aspects of human life, which, in turn, cannot contradict data on neurobiological processes in the brain. And neurobiological data must tally with the laws of physics, chemistry, and physiology. In a naturalist view, possible inconsistencies are signals of error or incompleteness of findings provided by one of the branches of knowledge.

Irrespective of the degree of radicalism, each version of naturalism seems to rest on a minimum assumption: the belief that there is at least some continuity and consistency in the chain of explanations from the most elementary levels of description of reality (that is, phenomena that occur on the physical-chemical level) to the highest levels of complexity, where other properties and entities emerge. These entities comprise developed forms of consciousness produced by human brain thanks to the incredibly high number of combinations of synaptic links between tens of billions of neurons (their number significantly exceeds the estimated number of atoms that build the universe). They also comprise products of culture and social phenomena that emerge as a result of communication and cooperation among a large number of human beings (including cultural transmission across generation).

Despite the growing distance between the level of physical and chemical processes, on the one hand, and the most sophisticated manifestations of civilisation and the cultural development of humanity ("the human spirit"), on the other, naturalism is based on the assumption that the two levels are interconnected by inseverable ties. These bonds need not (although they may) take the form of a unidirectional deterministic relationship. What is important is that everything that takes place on the higher levels of complexity is a "natural" product of processes and relations that occur on the more fundamental levels. In this way, everything that exists can be studied and explained as part of a consistent, multilevel scientific picture of the world, even though the picture itself is still fragmentary, and is likely to remain so for a long time (perhaps indefinitely).

Recent decades have seen impressive advancement in natural sciences, which provide an increasingly more complete and internally coherent picture of the world. As a result, voices have been raised to argue that this complex description should also take into account mental phenomena and processes, together with their symptoms and products that comprise the sociocultural domain of reality. Such an advanced picture consists of a largely coherent description of processes that take place in the universe as we know it. It is these processes that led to the formation of our solar system, biogenesis, and evolution of organisms equipped with a nervous system of such complexity as to be able to have subjective conscious states, providing the basis for social and cultural phenomena, morality, politics, aesthetic experiences, etc. Wilson, one of the most prominent modern biologists, puts it as follows:

> The natural sciences have constructed a webwork of causal explanation that runs all the way from quantum physics to the brain sciences and evolutionary biology. There are gaps in this fabric of un-known breadth .... Yet I think it fair to say that enough is known to justify confidence in the principle of universal rational consilience across all the natural sciences. The explanatory network now touches the edge of culture itself. It has reached the boundary that separates the natural sciences on one side from the humanities and humanistic social sciences on the other.[14]

It is worth noting that during the twenty years that have passed since Wilson wrote these lines, research into the evolutionary foundations and neurophysiological mechanisms of cultural phenomena – such as language, morality, art, religion, and politics – has made important progress. Fast-expanding empirical knowledge about the relationships between events on the neurobiological level, on the one hand, and the content of states of consciousness and behaviour, on the other, brings not only discoveries but also technological possibilities which have until recently been unimaginable. These new vistas concern both the generation of artificial sensations and experiences in people[15] and attempts to control animal behaviour.[16]

The most important impulse to look for the links between the humanities and natural history has come from the dynamic development of neuroscience, an interdisciplinary research programme that studies the functioning of the brain and the relationships between the brain and psychological and behavioural phenomena. Achievements of this programme seem to be the final stage in the long process of breaking away from religious Cartesian dualism, according to which

---

14 E.O. Wilson, *Consilience: The Unity of Knowledge* (New York: Knopf, 1998), p. 136.

15 Various experiments of this kind concern generation of emotions and religious or sensory sensations by artificial activation of particular cerebral cortical areas and remote control of a computer or other devices directly steered by thoughts (the Brain Gate system recognises the pattern of neural activity that corresponds to a particular intention and transmits an appropriate signal to a receiver device that is controlled by such signals, etc.).

16 Spectacular examples include robo-rats, whose movement is controlled by signals transmitted directly to their brains by implanted electrodes, or taming bulls in the bullfighting ring using brain stimulation by Jose Delgado several decades ago.

the world consists of two distinct domains: that of matter and that of "spirit" (consciousness and culture).

This inevitably brings us back to the problem of the nature and distinctiveness of the humanities and social sciences, including legal studies. I firmly believe that a discussion of legal studies must take into account the distinction introduced in the previous chapters, namely, that between jurisprudence as legal science and as the science of law. The need, sense, and limits of possible naturalisation look radically different in these two cases.

Naturalisation of the science of law seems to be an unavoidable consequence of the developing paradigm of interdisciplinary research into human behaviour, including the psychological processes that underlie it and various factors that influence them. These obviously include external circumstances, such as social interactions, internalised normative models, and stimuli produced by the expected risks and profits that follow, among others, from the legal environment. The complex web of such interrelated circumstances and the mechanisms of problem solving and decision making provides the best available explanation for human behaviour, at least to the extent that it can be causally explained (for example, on the level of statistical regularities).

There is no reason why the behaviour of participants in a legal order should not be studied in a similar way as other types of human behaviour and social practices that arise from them. This kind of analysis requires taking into account external factors together with the ways in which they initiate and influence the course of internal processes in the human mind and the behaviour thus determined. The course of this behaviour and its results depend on both external stimuli and internal resources: individual procedural memory (schemata and habits), episodic (autobiographic) memory, and semantic memory (the accumulated set of individual beliefs about the external world). There is no reason to suppose that human decisions and behaviour in legal contexts are substantially different in nature from those taking place in other contexts. What makes them different is the type of data and external factors that play crucial role in them.

It seems that, in the long run, there is no other scientifically credible approach to explain human behaviour in a possibly holistic way. The only promising perspective is an integrated research programme combining, on the one hand, knowledge about internal biological-psychological mechanisms that govern the workings of the brain and, on the other, sociological, cultural and historical knowledge about the influence contingent external circumstances have on these mechanisms. At the same time, it is clear that the whole configuration of factors that come into play in a particular situation will often be too complex and complicated to explore and explain in its entirety. Still, even relatively small steps in the right direction are scientifically more valuable than chaotic wanderings in the vast expanse of random speculations and guesses.

As any other social-cultural practice, from the point of view of an external observer, the legal order is a complex set of inner experiences, behaviour patterns these experiences determine and by which they are influenced, and specific cultural artefacts that are created and function in their context (in particular, texts considered "legal," including acts of law, judgements, procedural writs, etc.). They are closely interconnected by multilateral causal relationships, and taking them into consideration in their entirety seems indispensable to a holistic description and understanding of any legal event or fact, to say nothing of the whole legal order and its operation.

This is why law as a linguistic fact comprises only one aspect of a broader phenomenon, whose nature is determined by human inner experiences and behaviour. The legal character of a norm and its content (the way it is understood) are inseparably connected with the beliefs and actions of people who regard it as a valid model of "ought" behaviour. Thus, I think it is impossible to identify law with a linguistic phenomenon without taking into account the relevant experiences and behaviour of participants in a legal order, who treat a particular text as a binding legal norm. Similarly, it is impossible to isolate "legal" experiences and behaviour patterns from the ways in which they refer to the artefacts of the legal culture. Legal texts are the main type of such artefacts, and their normative status is usually a result of a convention that grants it to formal acts of law-making.

In view of the mutual relationships between legal text and the inner experiences and behaviour types that determine its character, it seems more apt to call them aspects of the legal phenomenon, following Ziembiński's terminology, rather than its distinct levels. At the same time, because of the complexity of the processes that determine the shape of the legal order in the empirical sense of the term, they can be studied mostly in parts, through an ad hoc fragmentation (for research purposes), which makes it possible to formulate a meaningful and solvable research problem.

Seen in this light, the theory of distinct levels of the legal phenomenon may be useful only from the methodological point of view, and not from the ontological one. It draws attention to the problem of the choice of appropriate methods that correspond to the research problem at hand. Still, from the perspective of the study of law as an empirical phenomenon, the idea that linguistic, psychological, and sociological problems can be studied in isolation seems to have very limited applicability and must be approached with caution.

A general theory of law – aiming to provide a possibly complete explanation for the legal order as a kind of social practice and to offer partial explanations regarding the factors involved in the establishing, understanding, and application of law, together with its impact on the addressees – requires taking into account the bulk of data on the human being made available by interdisciplinary behavioural sciences. Moreover, this kind of knowledge must be adapted to the specific context of human conduct shaped by the normative legal order. Conducive to the pursuit of these research goals of the science of law (which form an idealised model that gives a sense of direction rather than a checklist of realistic expected results) are investigations into the psychological aspects of decision-making processes of jurists, evolutionary roots of human predisposition to create and apply normative models of behaviour, the processes of understanding and linguistic communication, the applicability of the economic utilitarian model of human behaviour, etc.

All these research endeavours bring to mind the story of blind men who try to learn how an elephant looks like by feeling different parts of its body and drawing hasty conclusions that the whole animal must look like a trunk, a tail, or a hind paw. While such investigations often require different methods, concepts, and theories, they all aim to reveal, each in its own way, the regularities that underlie the complex whole of the empirical legal phenomenon.

Thus, it seems that in the long term, the study of law as a special type of social practice may not, and perhaps cannot, steer away from a naturalist and interdisciplinary research approach. If it did, it would risk breaking the intrinsic links that bind together the explanations of human behaviour in legal contexts with the more general and more fundamental research into psychological and behavioural processes. In order to be scientific, the science of law must assume that the reality of the legal order is constituted by psychological and social facts (inner experiences, attitudes, behaviour, and cultural artefacts that result from them). Beyond them, there is no other, "ideal," non-empirical aspect of law, an aspect that would not depend (at least in the sense of supervenience) on the entirety of relevant mental processes and their behavioural symptoms observable among participants in the legal order.

The study of law is, therefore, a study of these kinds of psychological and sociological facts, their origin, their nature, and the relations that hold between them. The specifically legal context of the inner experiences, attitudes, and behaviour of participants in the legal order has no impact on the suitability of applied research methods. *Ex hypothesi*, they do not differ from those used to study facts of the same type in non-legal areas and contexts. Facts comprising the empirical fabric of the legal phenomenon are products of the same cognitive and decision-making processes which are at work in the case of inner experiences, attitudes, and behaviour that constitute other types of social practice, such as, for instance, religion, politics, and morality. This is why the science of law is to a large extent "immersed" in sciences that seek to explain the functioning of the mind, the origin of and factors determining its processes, and the transformation of these processes into various forms of external behaviour. The fact that certain types of behaviour occur in specifically legal context does not imply that they do not follow general regularities studied by cognitive and behavioural sciences.

The object of the science of law situates it in a broader spectrum of empirical sciences that study the human mind and behaviour; hence, it must find its proper place in the "tree of knowledge." The trunk of the tree is formed by natural sciences, including evolutionary biology and neurobiology, while the crown is shaped by a variety of phenomena studied by disciplines that focus on society and culture.[17] In the long run, anti-naturalist models of the science of law would lead to its isolation. As a result, it would ignore the findings and discoveries that provide the essential tools to explain the psychological and social mechanisms of creating and maintaining a legal reality. In other words, the science of law must fit the web of possibly coherent explanations of interrelated levels of reality. This is why it must be naturalist, interdisciplinary, and closely integrated with relevant non-legal disciplines, or it will not exist at all (at least as a science).

It is worth emphasising that the arguments for ontological and methodological naturalism of the science of law are radically different from the naturalism of natural law and the century-long iusnaturalist tradition. Natural law models assume that there is a certain natural *duty* that determines and justifies legal obligations. By contrast, naturalism as understood here (it may be called realistic for distinction's sake) takes a very different view. Each existing "duty" is a set of facts (inner experiences, attitudes, and behaviour of individual people), whose origin and content can be causally explained. There is no other domain of objective normativity that is not a set of such experiences or behaviour of concrete individuals and social groups they form.

Normativity can be a supraindividual phenomenon in that the acceptance and implementation of "ought" models of behaviour may be more or less widespread. From the point of view of an individual, they may form a certain objective sociocultural reality. However, the origin of this reality and the ways in which it shapes

17 For this reason, the science of law cannot be reduced to the sociology of law (as proposed, among others, by Ehrlich), at least as long as the latter remains a discipline of "chimeric origin, from bits and pieces of science and the humanities ... the stronghold of the Standard [anti-naturalist] Social Science Model (SSSM)" (Wilson, *Consilience*..., p. 204).

the inner experiences and behaviour of individuals are fully explicable in terms of complex processes that take place in their minds and that result from complex chains of social interactions, internalisation of cultural models, and factors emerging from concrete, biological characteristics of the processes of perception, understanding, and decision-making.

Thus, the status of duty is ultimately reduced to causally interconnected facts (even if this relation can be seen as an instance of supervenience rather than reduction). It does not exist, nor can it be modified, in any other form or way than by the content of a person's decisions, attitudes, beliefs, and expectations manifest in various types of external behaviour, both individual and group-level. In the case of legal duty (normativity), these types of behaviour are additionally formalised by explicit mention in texts regarded as authoritative sources of models (that is, in texts which become a specific cultural artefact recognised as a source of law).

Realistic naturalism construes normativity as the content of inner experiences which trigger particular behaviour.[18] As a result, it rejects the dualism of being and obligation, where the latter is understood as an independent, quasi-empirical domain of *Sollen*.[19] Of course, this does not mean that it treats obligation as a logical result of reasoning based on premises limited to descriptive statements. On this view, normativity is merely another type of fact (or a set of facts) that exists objectively, that is, independently of the will and beliefs of individuals (although it cannot exist independently of the will and beliefs of all individuals or of a sufficiently big group of people).

Normativity is objective in the same sense as for every individual, it is an objective fact that others have beliefs and preferences, some of which may exert various kinds of pressure on his or her own decisions, making him or her act in a particular way or adopt certain beliefs. Models of behaviour accepted and implemented by others may thus constitute a fact with actual "normative force" in relation to individuals who are in the process of acculturation or socialisation, and in the context of legal normativity, they are a source of additional pressure connected with the risk of coercion by the organised apparatus of the state.

---

18 For more detail, see a comprehensive discussion in B. Brożek *Normatywność prawa* [Normativity of the Law] (Warszawa: Wolters Kluwer, 2012).

19 In fact, this is not a scientific claim but an act of choosing one among competing views of the world, with ontology being the assumption rather than a result of scientific investigations; for more detail, see J. Stelmach, "A jeśli powinność nie istnieje?" [And What If Duty Does Not Exist?] in A. Brożek, B. Brożek, and J. Stelmach, *Fenomen normatywności* [The Phenomenon of Normativity] (Kraków: Copernicus Center Press, 2013), p. 206.

In contrast to the iusnaturalist tradition, in this case, the domain of psychological and social facts provides an explanation for the origin, presence, and dynamics of norms rather than a source of objectively significant obligations.[20] At the same time, the content of normative experiences is not generated arbitrarily, in a *deus ex machina* way. The set of actual needs common to human beings and individual goals and aspirations these needs determine form the foundation for at least some culture-based models of behaviour. Also instrumental dependencies invoked by norms aiming to satisfy these needs and expectations are objective in nature and independent of the will of individuals or communities which on their basis generate normative standards of behaviour. Thus, irrespective of the specific cultural elaboration, often highly diversified, ontologically subjective aims and normative experiences are to a large extent based on objective human needs. Those, in turn, are to some extent determined by the species features and specific living conditions of particular individuals and societies.

The minimum extent to which the science of law must be naturalist involves three assumptions. Firstly, its scope is the legal order understood as the entirety of facts which comprise its empirical aspect. These include external behaviour of the participants in the legal order triggered by processes that take place in their minds. The explanation of these facts must refer to sociological, psychological, and evolutionary-biological laws that govern their occurrence. Thus, the science of law must be interdisciplinary and adapt to its own purposes the findings and tools of many other disciplines.

The second crucial assumption is that "normativity" is construed as an ontologically subjective (in the sense of Searle) product of inner experiences and behaviour of individual human beings. The origin and content of special mental representations of reality – that is, models of "ought" behaviour – and the courses of action they determine can in principle be explained as a type of psychological and social facts. Normativity as a socially objectified construct is dependent and secondary in relation to these facts.

Finally, the object of the science of law is the study of facts (attitudes, internal experiences, and behaviour) that comprise a special part of social reality: the legal order. A naturalist science of law should aim to explain the reasons for

20 For more detail on the neurobiological underpinnings of normative experiences, see T. Pietrzykowski, "The roots of normativity. From neuroscience to legal theory, in *Studies in the Philosophy of Law*, Vol. 7, *Legal Philosophy and the Challenges of Biosciences*, ed. J. Stelmach, M. Soniewicka, and W. Załuski (Kraków: Wydawnictwo: Wydawnictwo Uniwersytetu Jagiellońskiego 2010), pp. 97f.

these facts and their mutual relationships (adapting for this purpose the relevant findings of more fundamental sciences). It does not aim to propose any models of behaviour that could possibly derive "from nature." This is the fundamental difference between a naturalist science of law and iusnaturalist theories, whose objective is to identify norms that operate by nature (that is, facts which might provide the grounds for the binding force of norms).

The degree of naturalisation of the science of law may differ according to the strength of assumptions. The most important dividing line seems to be whether the assumption of free will is accepted or rejected. Moderate naturalism treats decisions taken by individuals as legitimate elements of the ultimate explanation of their behaviour. According to it, further search for factors determining (in the causal sense) the content of such decisions is neither necessary nor possible (it treats these decisions as a manifestation of "free will"). The free and undetermined will of a conscious subject may thus fill the gap between factors that determine his or her situation and the way of behaviour.[21] Moderate naturalism does not exclude the possibility that some or even most of his or her actions are to various extents automated and fully explicable in terms of specific factors. At the same time, it accepts that at least some of his or her behaviour follows from free decision, which, *ceteris paribus*, might have been different.

In contrast to so understood moderate naturalism, radical naturalism rejects the assumption of free will. In consequence, all behaviour, irrespective of the subjective impression of agency, is treated as determined by concrete external circumstances, combined with the internal state of the decision-making subject. Seen in this light, no decision might, *ceteris paribus*, have been different than what it was. Its content (and the very process of making it) is just another fact that needs to be causally explained, as is the behaviour it triggers, together with its external consequences.

The situation looks very different in the case of naturalisation of jurisprudence construed as legal science. The task of legal science is primarily to establish the content of valid law. Thus, it is concerned with the problems of validation, interpretation, and systematisation in order to determine what actions are commanded, forbidden, or permitted by law. To achieve this goal, legal science interprets both texts and other types of behaviour of subjects who make and apply

21 Cf. J. Searle, *Rationality in Action* (Cambridge, MA: The MIT Press, 2001), pp. 62f.

law. In short, its major and most important findings concern what particular legal norms "say" and how they should be "correctly" understood and applied.

Investigations of this type, in principle, aim to establish the meaning of texts and events to whom these texts attribute a certain conventional character (e.g., of offence). They consist in acts of interpretation based on formalised and non-formalised rules determining how facts *should* be understood. As a result, they are by nature anti-naturalist. As long as the juxtaposition between naturalism and anti-naturalism as two methodological approaches is meaningful, legal science will remain a classic example of an anti-naturalist discipline.

Irrespective of the existing controversy concerning the choice of the appropriate methods of legal science, its object, tasks, and role prevent it from being transformed into a discipline free from the specifically anti-naturalist element of interpretation (the act of meaning-ascription on the basis of adopted rules). It cannot be limited to recording and describing "raw facts" and to detecting relationships or associations between them. As long as solving broadly understood dogmatic legal problems lies at the core of legal science, its tasks will comprise ascribing meaning to legal text and arguing in favour of one of a number of possible senses as "the only appropriate" way of understanding.

Moreover, a servant of legal practice, its goals are for the most part idiographic and short-term, as it aims to establish the content of a momentary legal system, on a particular occasion and at a given point in time.[22] Legal science is thus immediately applicable in legal practice (perhaps even indispensable to it as an essential source of support); however, the price to be paid is the necessarily provisional character of its findings. This does not mean, of course, that the concepts, legal constructs, and normative solutions it develops cannot be of a more universal value; indeed, they often reach far beyond the contingent content of current legislation. Still, its major tasks are connected with the exegesis of the content of norms that are valid at a given point in time.

Thus, legal science is an essentially interpretive undertaking, closely connected with the current and changeable form of legal material and needs of legal practice. This makes it fundamentally immune to calls for methodological naturalisation. Of course, it does not mean that legal science cannot refer to empirical findings of natural and social sciences as factors which are relevant and

---

22 For more detail on the "momentary legal system," see the classical approach in J. Raz, *The Concept of a Legal System* (Oxford: Oxford University Press, 1980), pp. 189f.

therefore taken into account in interpretive decisions.[23] Nevertheless, they only play an ancillary role; they have no impact on the essence of legal science and its tasks, which comprise ascribing meaning to the lawmaker's statements and producing statements concerning the validity or non-validity of certain models of behaviour.

Calls for naturalisation may be somewhat more relevant to those findings of legal science which are sociotechnical rather than strictly interpretive in nature.[24] It is now generally recognised that – contrary to Kelsen's views – political-legal issues fall within the actual scope of legal science. Investigations by legal dogmatists, or their results, often comprise considerations regarding the optimum ways of achieving set aims or values (those approved by the scholars or attributed to the lawmaker). They may serve both as arguments for a particular interpretation of the rules or as arguments *de lege ferenda*.

In the former case, they take the form of teleological interpretation or refer to the expected consequences of adopting various possible ways of understanding a norm. In the latter case, they provide arguments to demonstrate that the set objectives of a particular regulation, or any other desirable values, call for a different shape of the norm, one that would better serve its goals. Such statements also refer, explicitly or implicitly, to cause-effect regularities, as it is these regularities that underlie the possible future social effects of a given law.

In this respect, legal science may and should refer to relevant empirical knowledge and well-established scientific theories rather than base on intuitive, groundless speculations ("life experience," "common sense," etc). All such considerations pursued within this discipline are an appropriate domain of naturalisation and call for an interdisciplinary approach. In this case, naturalisation would consist in taking into account relevant theories concerning the cause-effect regularities of social phenomena relevant for law and accommodating them within the body of legal science.

However, even in this non-dogmatic and non-interpretive area of legal science, the possible scope of naturalisation is rather of secondary importance from

---

23 Cf. interesting discussions in K. Płeszka and T. Gizbert-Studnicki, "Empirisches Wissen als Grundlage der teleologischen Interpretation," in *Praktische Vernunft und Rechtsanwendung*, ed. H.J. Koch (Stuttgart: ARSP, 1994, Beiheft 53), pp. 185f. and K. Płeszka, *Uzasadnianie decyzji interpretacyjnych przez ich konsekwencje* [Justifying Interpretive Decisions by Their Consequences] (Kraków: Universitas, 1996).

24 For more detail on the sociotechnical problems in legal sciences, see Z. Ziembiński, *Szkice z metodologii szczegółowych nauk prawnych* [Sketches in the Methodology of Particular Legal Sciences] (Warszawa–Poznań: Polska Akademia Nauk, 1983), pp. 28f.

the point of view of the entirety of its tasks. Also, it overlaps to a large extent with the problem of naturalisation of methods and approaches in such non-legal sciences as sociology and psychology. This results from the fact that their findings are potentially the basic source of knowledge which might be useful to legal science in finding effective and reliable solutions to sociotechnical problems addressed by jurisprudence.

The fact that the prospects of methodological naturalisation of legal science are strictly limited does not mean that it must be based on ontological anti-naturalism. As pointed out by Jan Woleński, naturalisation of the ontological foundations of legal science is, in fact, necessary and legitimate. According to Woleński, in its present shape, legal science rests on the philosophically dubious assumption that norms are linguistic entities which somehow "exist" on the logical-linguistic plane of the legal phenomenon. By contrast, from a naturalist perspective, norms are, or can be, perceived as:

> decisions expressed in the form of deontic sentences in the first person, that is, in the form of (**) "I resolve that this should be the case." Schema (**) expresses performativity and is itself a performative utterance. This is an approach to the imperative theory of norms, one which holds that each norm is a command, resolution, decision, etc. … Ultimately, the reality of law comes down to inner human experiences, individual or group actions, and acts of verbal communication. Law is not a complex ontological structure; it is always a collection of decisions, usually recorded by means of commonly accepted means of communication.[25]

From the point of view of ontological naturalism, norms are effects of the lawmaker's decisions construed as acts of norm-making. If the conditions for successful norm-making are satisfied (that is, if appropriate actions and performative utterances take place), the normative utterance that expresses the content of the act (the lawmaker's decision) is accepted by other participants in the legal order as a valid model of behaviour. Similar models determine the way in which people designated by norms as "law-applying organs" react to cases of violation of these accepted models of behaviour.

Fear of such reactions and acceptance of the lawmaker's decisions – because of the content of the introduced norms or because of the recognition that the lawmaker is empowered to introduce them – are the two main factors determining

---

25 J. Woleński, "Naturalizm w teorii prawa" [Naturalism in Legal Theory], in *W poszukiwaniu dobra wspólnego. Księga jubileuszowa Profesora Macieja Zielińskiego*, [In Search of the Common Good. Professor Maciej Zieliński's Anniversary Book], ed. A. Choduń and S. Czepita (Szczecin: Wydawnictwo Naukowe Uniwersytetu *Szczecińskiego*, 2010), pp. 910–911.

the social effectiveness of law. They transform a system of "formally valid" law (that is, valid according to the criteria established by itself) into a real, operating legal order. The lawmaker's decisions and the decisions taken by law-applying institutions (officials of the legal order) determine and express models of behaviour that are recognised by other participants in the legal order as valid and normatively significant. In my opinion, this naturalist ontological perspective provides a rational and legitimate foundation for any scientifically acceptable way of thinking about law. At the same time, with regard to methodology, it does not ignore the need to take account of "the humanistic coefficient," which turns legal science into a discipline that makes sense of intentional and conventional behaviour (that is, a discipline that applies first and foremost humanistic methodology).

This, I think, leads to the conclusion that legal science may and should rest on the assumptions of ontological naturalism, at the same time remaining anti-naturalist in its methodology. The actions it interprets – acts of creating, understanding, applying, and obeying law – must be described in a way that takes into account the essential moment of hermeneutic understanding. At the same time, they may and should be investigated as facts constituting the legal order, an element of empirical socio-cultural reality. Still, this perspective, characteristic of the science of law, cannot replace interpretive legal science. The latter is part of the legal order rather than its ultimate explanation.

Epilogue: Legal sciences and the philosophy of law

Even in their broadest understanding, legal science and the science of law are not able to cover the variety of problems and possible approaches that comprise the entirety of law-oriented reflection, interests, and perspectives. Of importance are not only various auxiliary sciences but, first and foremost, the ongoing discussion on the fundamental philosophical assumptions on which any kind of law must rest, as must the practice of its study. This is why metalegal philosophical problems are an indelible part of reflection on law and jurisprudence, irrespective of the possible aphilosophical approach they might more or less forcefully declare.

Such assumptions may – and often do – partly differ depending on contingent historical and cultural factors. Nevertheless, each legal order and the practice of its study rest on a set of ontological, epistemological, axiological, and methodological beliefs. Together, they form a certain picture of the world, providing the background – often unnoticed and unquestioned – for lawmakers' decisions and findings of scholars who study them. It consists of various, as Searle puts it, "background presuppositions" which underlie the problems addressed and solved in legal theory and practice.[1]

Wróblewski rightly observes that, irrespective of whether or not legal models explicitly refer to specific philosophical ideas that form their background presuppositions, the latter can always be "assigned" to them.

> The rejection of traditional philosophy and disbelief in the need for a philosophical approach themselves follow from certain methodological-philosophical premises which, *ex hypothesi*, make it possible to distinguish apparent problems (*Scheinprobleme*) from real problems.[2]

Such background presuppositions form the foundation for both normative-dogmatic legal science and the empirical-descriptive, naturalist science of law.

---

1 J. Searle, *Mind, Language and Society: Philosophy in the Real World* (New York: Basic Books, 1999), pp. 12f.

2 J. Wróblewski, "Postawa filozoficzna i afilozoficzna we współczesnej teorii prawa" [A Philosophical and Aphilosophical Approach in Modern Legal Theory], in Wróblewski, *Pisma wybrane* [Selected Works], ed. M. Zirk-Sadowski (Warszawa: Wolters Kluwer 2015), p. 36.

Some metascientific beliefs, not necessarily unarguable, are also indispensable to the kind of thinking that

> rejects speculation and stays close to "facts" and solving disputes "by facts alone;" one that emphasises concrete empirical investigations (in the narrower or broader sense of the term) and discredits problems which cannot be solved in this way.[3]

One of the major tasks of the philosophy of law is to reconstruct and problematise such presuppositions, to verify their accuracy and coherence, and to determine their relation to the arguments and views that rest on them. Seen in this light, the philosophy of law is an indispensable complement of legal science and the science of law, as it addresses issues which are, in a sense, preliminary and metaparadigmatic in nature.

Of course, it would be impossible to draw a neat line between this domain and the problems addressed directly by legal science and the science of law. To some extent, they must overlap. True, the main focus of each of these law-related disciplines and the perspectives they assume to look at similar problems are fundamentally different. Still, the findings each of them obtains may be of huge importance for the others, which is why practicing them in isolation would be detrimental and difficult to accept.

The position of the philosophy of law in relation to legal science and the science of law may be illustrated, following Jerzy Zajadło, with the famous *bon mot* of Bertrand Russell, who commented on the more general relation of philosophy and science in the following way:

> the only difference between science and philosophy is that science is what you more or less know and philosophy is what you do not know. Philosophy is that part of science which at present people choose to have opinions about, but which they have no knowledge about.[4]

On this view, philosophical considerations both precede and go ahead of knowledge generated within the paradigms of particular legal sciences. In other words, the domain of philosophical reflection comprises problems for which there is yet no verified, systematically accumulated knowledge, obtained with well-established research methods.

---

3 Ibid., p. 40.

4 B. Russell, "The Philosophy of Logical Atomism," in *Bertrand Russell on Metaphysics. Selections from the Writings of Bertrand Russell*, ed. S. Mumfold (London–New York: Routledge, 2003), p. 119.

At the same time, such problems are not confined to a specific thematic area, and thus may include everything that can have an effect on understanding and pursuing legal studies, as well as on the creation and application of law. As Wilfried Sellars puts it in his well-known definition, "the aim of philosophy … is to understand how things in the broadest possible sense of the term hang together in the broadest possible sense of the term."[5] This is why philosophical considerations cannot avoid a certain degree of speculativeness, nor can they be subjected to the rigours of methodology and evidence. However, this is not to say that philosophical argumentation cannot or should not be evaluated in terms of clarity, precision, rationality, or compatibility with available factual knowledge.

This refers in particular to philosophical problems and enquiries that concern a specific discipline, as in the case of the philosophy of law. In such cases, the abstract level of philosophical considerations is necessarily bound with a relatively well-defined area of knowledge and problems that lie within its scope. Philosophical tools are here used to look for answers to fundamental ontological, epistemological, and axiological questions related to a specific phenomenon, such as law. These answers must correspond (positively or negatively) with factual knowledge about the problems addressed, accumulated by various branches of legal studies. This is why, as Zajadło puts it, in philosophical-legal reflection, it is the philosopher who asks questions and the jurist who answers them (not the other way round).[6]

On this understanding, the most important types of problems addressed by the philosophy of law include, first and foremost, methodological issues. They concern, in particular, the distinction between legal science and the science of law, their characteristic elements, their subdisciplines, and their relation to non-legal disciplines (including, for instance, history, economics, theory of the state, and politics). In addition, the scopes of the philosophy of law and various branches of legal studies in a sense overlap as regards research methods and assumptions characteristic of different types of legal and jurisprudential problems.

Still, the most comprehensive and fundamental issues, pervading all specific concerns, are conceptual problems. They comprise the analysis of the legal conceptual apparatus, starting with the concept of law. Conceptual considerations about what law is are indeed the main axis of the philosophical-legal discussion.

---

5 W. Sellars, "Philosophy and the Scientific Image of Man," in Sellars, *Empiricism and the Philosophy of Mind* (London: Routledge & Kegan Paul, 1963), p. 1.

6 See J. Zajadło, "Aneks. Filozofia prawa. Pyta filozof, odpowiada prawnik" [Annex. Philosophy of Law. A Philosopher Asks, a Lawyer Answers], in Zajadło, *Carl Schmitt* (Gdańsk: Wydawnictwo Arche, 2016), pp. 143, 148.

It seems that the search for "necessary," "significant," and "constitutive" features of law goes in two opposite directions. On the one hand, what is needed is a philosophical discussion and argumentation that construe the legal phenomenon in abstract ontological terms and set it in a more general and holistic picture of the world. On the other hand, and on a more concrete level, one needs a perspective provided by particular branches of law and an understanding of the assumptions on which their findings rest. It seems to me that it is only when these two ways of thinking about law are taken into account and combined that we can start looking for rational and appropriately justified answers to questions about the concept of law and the essential, constitutive elements that comprise its "nature."[7]

Views on the concept of law determine not only what one regards as an appropriate research method for jurisprudence but also what constitutes a well-formulated research problem for legal studies. This is well visible in the radicalism and fierceness of the conflict between Kelsen and Ehrlich. For the latter, the view of law and jurisprudence adopted by Kelsen distorted the problems and the very scope of the legal phenomenon which should be the object of a truly scientific study of law. Norms expressed in legal acts are only a fraction of what is understood by law, with all the social rules which in practice regulate and shape people's behaviour in legal situations. Thus, legal science, focused on the exegesis of legal acts and codes, zooms in on a secondary fragment of the phenomenon it should study. As a result, it does not provide valuable knowledge about law; hence, it fails to fulfil the tasks and role assigned to a scientific study of this domain of reality.

For Kelsen, in turn, the rules regarded by Ehrlich as the main object of jurisprudence (that is "living law") are beyond the scope of legal science in the proper understanding of the term. Legal science is not concerned with people's actual behaviour or with factors that influence their conduct and decisions. It studies the content of obligation created by norms introduced by competent institutions. The legal system consists exclusively of such norms, and their content imputes certain legal consequences to specific circumstances. The task of legal science is to reconstruct the relations that emerge as a result of imputation and acts of

---

7 For more detail, cf. T. Pietrzykowski, "On the Nature and Limits of Conceptual Truths," in *Jurisprudence and Political Philosophy in the 21st Century*, ed. M. Jovanovic and B. Spaic (Frankfurt a.M.: Peter Lang, 2012), pp. 37f.; see also, e.g., *Philosophical Foundations of the Nature of Law*, ed. W. Waluchow and S. Sciaraffa (Oxford–New York: Oxford University Press, 2013).

norm-making – both general and individual – by organs with appropriate norm-making competence.

Thus, the dispute between Kelsen and Ehrlich was in fact conceptual and metalegal in nature. It consisted in different views on what law is, a conflict that led to radically different conclusions regarding the object and nature of a science that should study it. In this sense, the dispute referred to preliminary assumptions and preceded, rather than resulted from, any scientific findings.

The place and importance of conceptual analysis as a method of philosophical study of law have in recent years become an object of special interest and vivid discussion, especially in the context of the postulated naturalisation of jurisprudence.[8] The ongoing debate focuses in particular on such key terms as "concept," "essence," "nature," and "necessity." Thus, it largely concerns conceptual analysis of the nature and place of conceptual analysis itself. The most important questions raised are connected with what is meant by "concept," "essence," "nature," and "necessary properties" of an object to which a concept refers.

The discussion is usually dominated by proposals situated between radical realism and nominalism. Concepts are rarely treated as Plato's objectively existing ideas or reduced to the meanings of words that function purely by virtue of linguistic conventions. Much more convincing is identifying concepts with a type of psychological facts, that is, subjective mental representations of specific objects or their classes, produced in the minds of individuals. They translate into relatively consistent predispositions to categorise reality, which is an important aspect of perception of and orientation in the world.

However, this view seems to be compatible only with the version of conceptual analysis that Frank Jackson calls "modest." On this understanding, conceptual analysis is not treated as a method of obtaining knowledge about objective, external reality but only as a rational reconstruction of the social picture – "our ordinary conceptions" – of its selected fragment. These ordinary conceptions form a "folk theory" of a particular domain or phenomenon, manifest in the accepted ways of taking about it by using relevant terms. Establishing what the concepts of everyday language refer to may be a valuable, if not indispensable, point of departure for investigations into the kind of reality denoted by these

---

8 See, e.g., B. Leiter, *Naturalizing Jurisprudence: Essays on American Legal Realism and Naturalism in Legal Philosophy* (Oxford-New York: Oxford University Press, 2007), pp. 121f.; K. Himma, "Reconsidering a Dogma: Naturalistic Turn, Conceptual Analysis and Legal Philosophy," in *Law and Philosophy*, ed. M. Freeman and R. Harrison (Oxford: Oxford University Press, 2007).

concepts. Still, such investigations require moving beyond conceptual analysis, which should not be rashly identified with gaining knowledge about reality; conceptual analysis provides information about pictures people have of reality, reflected in the way they use words to describe it. The assumption that the reconstruction of concepts provides knowledge about reality to which they refer is, according to Jackson, "immodest," as it sets tasks for conceptual analysis that it cannot achieve.[9]

The aim of modest conceptual analysis is not only a reconstruction of the criteria and usage of terms by speakers of a language. It also aims at exposing the presuppositions – at least those that can be reconstructed – that are indispensable for the terms to function in the way they do in everyday language, their relation to other concepts, their logical consequences, etc. Various aspects of concepts and representations they convey may not be clear for those who use them. This is why even a modest version of conceptual analysis can contribute significantly to knowledge of the true content of "our everyday concepts" and the "folk theories" of the fragments of reality that they express.

It seems that only a consistently modest version of conceptual analysis can avoid the accusations of essentialism, that is, the belief that there is an "essence" of objects that can be grasped through an analysis of the concepts that refer to them (in this case, concepts must mean more than the established linguistic usage). Irrespective of the strengths and weaknesses of essentialism as such, it is certainly highly problematic to accept it as an obvious assumption of conceptual analysis which needs no proof (which often happens in the philosophy of law). This is why legal theories resting on the a priori belief that linguistic intuition and practice alone are a sufficient and credible source of knowledge about the "essence" of entities and phenomena are philosophically dubious.

As it is aptly pointed out in contemporary philosophical-legal literature, even a modest version of conceptual analysis adopts a debatable (if not utterly untenable) assumption that the concepts analysed form classical categories. It is only in the case of a classical category that all the objects it holds (and to which a given concept refers) are marked, *ex definitione*, by the same set of necessary and sufficient properties, which is what turns them into designata of the concept.[10] This assumption does not take into account concepts which may refer to radial

9 For more detail, see F. Jackson, *From Metaphysics to Ethics: A Defence of Conceptual Analysis* (Oxford: Clarendon Press, 1998), pp. 42f.

10 T. Gizbert-Studnicki, A. Dyrda, and A. Grabowski, *Metodologiczne dychotomie. Krytyka pozytywistycznych teorii prawa* [Methodoligcal Dychotomies. A Critique of Positivst Legal Theories] (Warszawa: Wolters Kluwer, 2016), pp. 35f.

categories, denoting objects connected through Wittgensteinian "family resemblances," or "essentially contested concepts," described by Walter B. Gallie.[11]

In the philosophy of law, conceptual analysis is used both in considerations about the "essence" or "nature" of law and in relation to other key terms of legal language and the language of law (such as be in effect, norm, act, person, system, responsibility, etc). Its aim is to establish the properties thanks to which a given object is a *designatum* of a particular concept. This refers in particular to properties which are cognitively nontrivial and which are not obvious or recognisable at first glance, that is to properties whose identification requires a certain degree of analytical effort.[12] The results of conceptual analysis should identify a set of such significant properties which apply to all *designata* of a given concept, and only to them.[13]

In the case of legal concepts, the distinction between modest and immodest versions of conceptual analysis runs into additional difficulties, resulting from conventional aspects of law. It can be argued that certain norms are legal in nature because of the beliefs or attitudes of participants in the legal order. Thus, norms are "legally valid" if they satisfy the conventionally accepted criteria of validity (that is, criteria comprising the rule of recognition which functions in the community).[14] However, if this is the case, the analysis of the concept of law adopted by participants in the legal order consists not only in the examination of their beliefs or representations but also in the examination of the very phenomenon these beliefs constitute. The point is that the phenomenon is not distinct from its representations reflected in linguistic practice (that is, the ways the concept of law is used). On the contrary, it is to a large extent shaped by these representations and linguistic practice.

A similar argumentation may apply to other legal concepts, referring to entities that exist by virtue of linguistic conventions and related practices of granting to real-life objects and phenomena an additional legal sense of "court," "act," "derogation," "personal chattels," etc. Thus, it can be argued that an analysis of concepts used in legal language and the language of law, together with the ways in which they are understood and applied, reveals more than just how the phenomena they refer to are perceived. It reveals what these phenomena in fact are,

11 Ibid., pp. 125f.
12 Ibid., pp. 43, 47.
13 Ibid., pp. 38, 47.
14 Cf. T. Pietrzykowski, "John Searle i ontologia prawa" [John Searle and the Onthology of Law], *Studia Prawnicze* [Legal Studies] 1–2 (2009), pp. 7f.

as they are nothing beyond that (much like Ross' *tû-tû*). What they are is determined by how they are perceived. In the case of conventional social practices, such as law, this line of thinking blurs the distinction between the modest and immodest versions of conceptual analysis.[15]

Preliminary philosophical assumptions underlie not only any law-oriented research activity but also law itself. Each legal order rests on certain metalegal ontological, axiological, and epistemological presuppositions adopted by law-makers; without them, law-making and the content of norms would be meaningless. In this sense, each existing legal order has its own "philosophy of law" manifest in the content of norms it comprises and in the ways of norm-making and norm application. This philosophy is to a large extent part of a more general legal culture, with the culturally dominant picture of the world providing the background without which it would be very difficult, if possible at all, to understand the shape of a particular legislation.

For a person immersed in a given culture, the assumptions that form this background are often mere truisms or are simply taken for granted and thus ignored. They become visible only when, for some reason, they are explicitly formulated. It is much easier to discern the close connection between law and its cultural background in the case of legal orders which are culturally or historically remote, that is, which are rooted in substantially different pictures of the world. Their content and operation may then appear "strange," with their rationality restored only after one takes into account the beliefs dominant in a given culture, which are their point of departure and reference.

Thus, the task of the philosophy of law is also a reconstruction of this philosophical underpinning of the legal order and, if necessary, its problematisation, analysis, and criticism. Only when it is brought to light is it possible to verify the internal coherence of its assumptions, their rationality, and their compatibility with available empirical knowledge of the world and consciously professed values.[16] These assumptions are not always spontaneously or quickly adapted to changing knowledge of the world. Because they consist to a large extent in not fully acknowledged or articulated "common sense beliefs," they often turn out to be contradictory or inconsistent. Seen in this light, the philosophy of law may and often does act as an instrument of criticism, aiming to confront and verify the fundamental assumptions of the legal order, which otherwise may continue

15 Gizbert-Studnicki, Dyrda, and Grabowski, *Metodologiczne...*, p. 186.
16 Cf., e.g., R. Dworkin, *Taking Rights Seriously* (London: Bloomsbury, 1997).

to be accepted blindly and without reflection in spite of their apparent inconsistency or groundlessness.[17]

This kind of criticism may refer to beliefs concerning the existence or cognisability of various entities which are significant for the content and shape of law (such as, for instance, "the dignity of the human person," "the principles of social justice," etc.). However, it is of major importance first and foremost to the axiological and ideological beliefs underlying concrete legal solutions. Its elements are present in the work of many of the foremost philosophers of law, such as Kelsen, Hart, Petrażycki, and Ross, to name but a few. In fact, some strands of legal philosophy treat it as a *raison d'etre* of any socially valuable reflection on law. This refers in particular to Critical Legal Studies and various directions of critical-emancipatory legal research that sprouted from this school (including racial, feminist, and gender theories which expose the oppressive elements of ideological assumptions underlying contemporary legal orders).

These research strands treat law almost exclusively as a manifestation of ideological-axiological assumptions which are, in principle, contingent and express the interests and privileges of socially dominant groups. Thus, while pretending to be axiologically neutral and universally rational, the legal order is, in a sense, an instrument of social domination, placing groups which are culturally or economically dominant (and, hence, which have a major influence on the actual shape of the legal order) in a position of privilege. It is the task of the critical philosophy of law to deconstruct a facade of formalist objectivism and apolitical "autonomy" of law and to expose its ideological entanglements and bias. Only when various prejudice, stereotypes, and limitations inherent in legal awareness are brought to light and fully revealed is it possible to refute or reform them, enabling legal emancipation of discriminated groups (the fact that they receive unequal treatment may not be fully realised not only by the groups who discriminate against them but also by the marginalised groups themselves, influenced by the prevalent culture-bound schemata).[18]

---

17 The main areas of philosophical-legal reflection and their role in relation to problems addressed by legal science and the science of law can be captured in an acronym MACCA (Methodology, Analysis of Concepts, Criticism, Axiology).

18 An attempt at this kind of critical approach towards philosophical assumptions underlying the modern concept of legal subjecthood has been made in T. Pietrzykowski, *Personhood Beyond Humanism: Animals, Chimeras, Autonomous Agents and the Law* (Springer, 2018).

The attitude that in its radical version takes the form of Critical Legal Studies is to a certain extent inseparable from any deeper reflection on the philosophical underpinnings of law. The philosophy of law is an area where the foundations of both law and legal studies confront a more general picture of the world, a picture which underlies them and warrants their coherence. Thus, it investigates and considers whatever constitutes the basis for the legal order and jurisprudence and provides a link between the latter and other areas of knowledge. This refers in particular to disciplines whose findings are directly or indirectly used in legal studies or in the practice of law making and application. On this understanding, apart from cognitive and critical tasks, the philosophy of law also plays an important integrating role, both with respect to various types of legal research and perspectives (that is, within legal studies) and with respect to other disciplines, thus preventing isolation of the legal picture of the world from the advances of relevant non-legal knowledge.

***

The domain of philosophical reflection and argumentation related to the problems of methodology, conceptual analysis, legal criticism, and axiological aspects of the existence, content, and operation of the legal order extends far beyond the scope of both legal science and the science of law. The development of the latter two approaches obviously provides the context for the philosophy of law and affects the problems it addresses. Still, jurisprudence cannot replace legal philosophy, nor can it make it seem superfluous. Otherwise, its struggles would resemble Baron Munchausen's attempts to pull himself out of a mire by his own hair. At the same time, the meaning and scope of possible naturalisation of the philosophy of law are different than in the case of legal science or the science of law.

As we have seen above, the methodology of legal science (irrespective of the ongoing controversies and doubts) is in principle anti-naturalist. Thus, in this case, the calls for naturalisation do not appear well-justified or properly targeted. They may refer, at most, to rather peripheral considerations within its specific sub-disciplines. The relation between legal science and ontological naturalism, though, seems somewhat more complicated. On the one hand, legal science is based on the assumption that – at least for the purpose of establishing their causes and legal effects – all events may be accounted for in terms that do not involve any supranatural factors (that is, factors beyond reality composed of psychological and behavioural facts and the relations between them). Seen in this light, it embodies a naturalist picture of the world, where everything that occurs is perceived as an element in an explicable cause-and-effect chain of events which does not allow any other factors.

On the other hand, the paradigm of legal science rests firmly on the assumption of free will, which belongs to key factors of the legal description of reality. The view that people, at least in principle, are subjects responsible for their decisions and choices means that a possible naturalist approach, combined with the existing paradigm of legal science, would have to be explicitly non-determinist. In this respect, it would have to be a "weak" version of naturalism, where some events depend on something else than merely a determinist chain of causes, and where "decision," "will," "intention," and "choice" are the ultimate key factors of the legal description and explanation of reality, themselves not further analysed.

Can legal science rest on the assumptions of fully determinist naturalism? It seems unlikely, although efforts to redefine the way of thinking about the role and operation of law are sometimes undertaken. Perhaps the best-known attempt of this kind in recent decades has been the model proposed by the leading representative of behaviourist psychology Burrhus Skinner in *Beyond Freedom and Dignity*.[19] Nevertheless, such proposals must be treated as grossly premature, if ever possible to successfully implement. At the present stage of knowledge and philosophical discussion about the picture of the world and its naturalisation, projects of this kind targeted at legal science seem neither necessary nor practicable.

In contrast to legal science, the science of law, empirical and interdisciplinary as it is, must rest on naturalist methodological assumptions. From this perspective, law consists in human inner experiences and behaviour; in order to understand their origin, their dynamics, and the processes in the course of which they constitute the legal order as a special kind of social practice, they must be treated as phenomena explicable in terms of cause-and-effect relationships and regularities. Research into the formation of beliefs about law, reactions to incentives created by legal regulations, the processes of legal decision-making, and behaviour triggered by law (its representations) calls for a strictly naturalist approach, combining the methodology of empirical cognitive sciences, sociology, neuroscience, modern linguistics, etc.

Because the social practice that provides the empirical footing for the legal order is extremely complex, it must be studied in fragments, with a focus on selected aspects. Nevertheless, it should fit at least the minimally naturalist paradigm, taking into account mutual dependencies and aiming to gradually bring coherence to the obtained results. *Ex hypothesi*, the methodological shape of the science of law, as defined here, cannot be but naturalist in character. In contrast

---

19 B. Skinner, *Beyond Freedom and Dignity* (New York: Knopf, 1971).

to legal science, this seems to be the condition of success for the science of law, if it is to be a truly scientific attempt to explain various aspects of law as a social phenomenon.

This perspective is inherently combined with ontological naturalism (at least local, that is, in the context of the legal order), according to which the origin of law and the mechanisms that govern it can be fully accounted for in terms of cause-and-effect regularities. There is no place here for any factors that lie outside so understood "nature" (of the human being, society, human mind that was formed by biological evolution, etc.). However, this approach need not entail a broader, or "global," ontological naturalism, referring to the general outlook on the world. There is no reason why such a picture of the world could not be reconciled with various anti-naturalist metaphysical beliefs which are not connected with the operation of the legal order.

Questions regarding the possibility, scope, or significance of naturalisation of the philosophy of law are part of a much more fundamental discussion about naturalisation of various areas of philosophical reflection, apparently triggered by Willard V. Quine's call for "naturalised epistemology."[20] From this standpoint, "first philosophy," concerned with the most fundamental issues that precede and condition all empirical sciences, should be replaced by "second philosophy," that is, a continuation and an extension of knowledge accumulated by other sciences.[21] In the most radical version, its tasks would then be reduced to what, in the context of the Vienna Circle, Feyerabend ironically referred to as clinging onto science's coat-tails.

A discussion of calls for this kind of philosophical reform is far beyond the scope of the present considerations or the author's expertise. My closing remarks will therefore be confined to three observations. First, the problem of naturalisation of the philosophy of law cannot be separated from the prospects of naturalisation of philosophy in general. Second, the discussion about the latter is still at too early a stage to attempt any broader range application of its results to the philosophy of law. In fact, this application may never be possible. This does not mean, however, that philosophy is in a position to disregard knowledge produced by empirical sciences; in particular, it cannot ignore it or compete against it.

---

20 W.V. Quine, "Epistemology Naturalized," in *Ontological Relativity and Other Essays* (New York: Columbia University Press, 1969).

21 See, e.g., P. Maddy, *Second Philosophy: A Naturalistic Method* (Oxford: Oxford University Press, 2007).

Doing philosophy "in the context of science" necessarily comprises problems which go beyond empirical knowledge, obtained in the course of experiments or observations that satisfy rigorous methodological criteria. The tasks of philosophical reflection also include analysis, verification, and criticism of calls for naturalisation of various research areas and of objections to such calls. Thus, in the debate about the need for and boundaries of naturalisation of different areas of reflection on reality, philosophy must play the role of an arbitrator rather than a party in the dispute. The same is true, I think, of the philosophy of law.

Third, one should distinguish between the problem of global naturalisation of philosophy (including the philosophy of law) and local naturalisation of specific philosophical problems or their categories. If the former triggers obvious, fundamental doubts, the latter involves a process – well known from the antiquity – of delimiting, within the field of speculative philosophy, an area that can be studied empirically. The same process has led to naturalisation of, for instance, astronomy, medicine, physics, chemistry, and, to a large extent, psychology. This is the perspective that makes it possible, and indeed necessary, to discuss the prospects of naturalisation of selected issues addressed by the philosophy of law; in fact, it implies a transformation of philosophical problems into problems that lie within the scope of the science of law or other auxiliary disciplines of jurisprudence.

Bibliography

Albert, H. *Rechtswissenschaft als Realwissenschaft. Das Rechts als Soziale Tatsache und die Aufgabe der Jurisprudenz,* Nomos, Baden Baden 1993

Andreski, S. *Max Weber's Insights and Errors.* London: Routledge & Kegan Paul, 1984.

Aristotle. *On Interpretation.* Trans. E. M. Edghill. Available at http://classics.mit.edu/Aristotle/interpretation.html; accessed 6.05.2019.

Bacon, F. *The New Organon.* Eds. L. Jardine and M. Silverthorne. Cambridge: Cambridge University Press, 2000.

Boulanger, C. "The Comparative Sociology of Legal Doctrine: Thoughts on a Research Program". *German Law Journal, 21*(7) 2020, 1362–1377

Bailey, M., Maltzman, F. *The Constrained Court. Law, Politics and the Decisions Justices Make.* Princeton, NJ: Princeton University Press, 2011.

Baker, L.R. *Naturalism and the First-Person Perspective.* Oxford: Oxford University Press, 2013.

Baker, L.R. *Persons and Bodies. A Constitution View.* Cambridge: Cambridge University Press, 2000.

Baum, L. *The Puzzle of Judicial Behavior.* Ann Arbor: University of Michigan Press, 1998.

Becker, G., Becker, G.N. *The Economics of Life: From Baseball to Affirmative Action to Immigration, How Real-World Issues Affect Our Everyday Life.* Columbus, OH: McGraw Hill, 1997.

Borucka-Arctowa, M. "Podejście socjologiczne" [Sociological Approach]. In *Metody badania prawa* [Methods of Studying Law], ed. A. Łopatka. Warszawa: Ossolineum, 1971.

Borucka-Arctowa, M. *Świadomość prawna a planowe zmiany społeczne* [Legal Awareness and Planned Social Change], Wrocław: Zakład Narodowy im. Ossolińskich, 1981.

Botts, T. "Legal Hermeneutics," IEP. Available at http://www.iep.utm.edu/leg-herm/.

Braman, E. *Law, Politics and Perception: How Policy Preferences Influence Legal Reasoning.* Charlottesville, VA: University of Virginia Press, 2009.

Brożek, B. "Derywacyjna koncepcja wykładni z perspektywy logicznej" [Derivative Concept of Interpretation from a Logical Perspective]. *Ruch Prawniczy, Ekonomiczny i Socjologiczny* [The Legal, Economic and Sociological Movement], 1 (2006).

Brożek, B. "Ekonomiczna analiza prawa karnego" [An Economical Analysis of Criminal Law]. In *Analiza ekonomiczna w zastosowaniach prawniczych* [Economical Analysis in Legal Applications], ed. J. Stelmach and M. Soniewicka. Warszawa: Wolters Kluwer, 2007.

Brożek, B. *Normatywność prawa* [Normativity of the Law]. Warszawa: Wolters Kluwer, 2012.

Brożek, B. "On Tû-Tû." *Revus. Journal for Constitutional Theory and Philosophy of Law* 27 (2015).

Bydlinski, F. *Grundzüge der juristischen Methodenlehre*. Wien: UTB GmbH, 2012.

Carnap, R. *Philosophy and Logical Syntax*. London: Kegan Paul, Trench, Trubner & Co. Ltd., 1935.

Champeil-Desplats, V. *Methodologies du Droit et des Sciences du Droit*. Paris: Dalloz, 2014.

Chiba, M. "Other phases of legal pluralism in the contemporary world." *Ratio Juris* 11/3 (1998).

Comte, A. *The Positive Philosophy of Auguste Comte*. Vol. 1. Trans. H. Martineau. Kitchener: Batoche Books, 2000.

Conley, J., O'Barr, W. "Legal Anthropology Comes Home: A Brief History of the Ethnographic Study of Law." *Loyola of Los Angeles Law Review* 27/1 (1993). Available at http://digitalcommons.lmu.edu/llr/vol27/iss1/4.

Contemporary Philosophical Naturalism and its Implications. Eds. B. Bashour and H. Muller. London: Routledge, 2014.

Cooter, R., Ulen, T. *Law and Economics*. 6th ed. Boston: Addison-Wesley, 2012.

Cotterrell, R. *Emile Durkheim – Law in a Moral Domain*. Edinburgh: Edinburgh University Press, 1999.

Danner, R. "Law Libraries and Laboratories: The Legacies of Langdell and His Metaphor." *Law Library Journal* 107/1 (2015).

Dennett, D. "Explaining the 'Magic'of Consciousness." *Journal of Cultural and Evolutionary Psychology* 1/8 (2003).

Dunbar, R. *Human Evolution*. Pelican Books, 2014.

Dupret, B. *Droit et sciences sociales*. Paris: Armand Colin, 2006.

Dworkin and His Critics. Ed. J. Burley. Oxford–Malden, MA: Blackwell, 2004.

Dworkin, R. *Taking Rights Seriously*. London: Bloomsbury, 1997.

Dworkin, R. *Law's Empire*. Cambridge, MA: Harvard University Press, 1986.

Dworkin, R. *Justice in Robes*. Cambridge, MA: Harvard University Press, 2006.

Ehrlich, E. "Die Erforschung das Lebendes Rechts." In Ehrlich, *Recht und Leben. Gesammelte Schriften zur Rechtstatsachenforschung und zur Freirechtslehre*, ed. M. Rehbinder. Berlin: Duncker & Humblot, 1967.

Ehrlich, E. *Fundamental Principles of the Sociology of Law*. Trans. W. L. Moll. Cambridge, MA: Harvard University Press, 1936.

Ehrlich, E. "Gesetz und Lebendes Recht." In Ehrlich, *Gesetz und Lebendes Recht*, ed. M. Rehbinder. Berlin: Duncker & Humblot, 1986.

Ehrlich, S. "Kilka uwag w sprawie metodologii nauk prawnych" [Comments on the Methodology of Legal Sciences]. *Państwo i Prawo* [State and Law] 11 (1964).

Ehrlich, S. *Wiążące wzory zachowania. Rzecz o wielości systemów norm* [The Binding Schema of Conduct. On the Plularity of Norm Systems]. Warszawa: PWN, 1995.

Eliasz, K. *Realistyczna koncepcja prawa Alfa Rossa* [A Realistic Concept of Alf Ross's Law]. Warszawa: Wolters Kluwer, 2016.

Elliott, D., "Law and biology. The new Synthesis?" *Saint Louis University Law Journal* 41 (1997).

Elżanowski, A. "Prawdziwie darwinowska etyka" [A Truly Darwinist Ethic], *Lectiones & Acroases Philosophicae* 3 (2010).

Evald, J. *Alf Ross. A Life*. Copenhagen: DJØF Publishing, 2014.

Feyerabend, P. *Against Method*. London: Verso, 1993.

Feyerabend, P. *Science in a Free Society*. London: New Left Books, 1978.

Foucault, M. *Discipline and Punish*. Trans. A. Sheridan. New York: Pantheon Books, 1977.

Frank, J. *Courts on Trial. Myth and Reality in American Justice*. Princeton, NJ: Princeton University Press, 1954.

Frank, J. *Law and the Modern Mind*. New York: Anchor Books, 1963.

Friedman, D. *Law's Order. What Economics Has to Do with Law and Why It Matters*. Princeton, NJ: Princeton University Press, 2001.

Gadowska, K. *Dysfunkcje administracji* [Dysfunctions of Administration]. Kraków: Wydawnictwo Uniwersytetu Jagiellońskiego, 2015.

Gadowska, K. *Zjawisko klientelizmu polityczno- ekonomicznego. Systemowa analiza powiązań sieciowych na przykładzie przekształceń sektora górniczego w Polsce* [The Phenomenon of Political-Economic Clientelism. A Systemic Analysis of Network Relations Based on the Example of Transformations in the Mining Sector in Poland]. Kraków: Wydawnictwo Uniwersytetu Jagiellońskiego, 2002.

Garcia-Salmones, M. "On Kelsen's Sein: An Approach to Kelsenian Sociological Themes." *No Foundations. An Interdisciplinary Journal on Law and Justice* 8 (2011).

Geier, M. *Der Wiener Kreis*. Hamburg: Rowohlt, 1992.

Gizbert-Studnicki, T. "Das hermeneutische Bewußtsein der Juristen." *Rechtstheorie* 18 (1987).

Gizbert-Studnicki, T. "Vorverständnisbegriff in der juristischen Hermeneutik." *Archiv für Rechts- und Sozialphilosophie* 73 (1987).

Gizbert-Studnicki, T., Dyrda, A., Grabowski, A. *Metodologiczne dychotomie. Krytyka pozytywistycznych teorii prawa* [Methodoligcal Dychotomies. A Critique of Positivst Legal Theories]. Warszawa: Wolters Kluwer, 2016.

Gizbert-Studnicki, T., Klinowski, M. "Are Legal Concepts Embedded in Legal Rules?" *International Journal of Semiotics and Law* 25 (2012).

Goetz, S., Taliaferro, Ch. *Naturalism*. Cambridge: CUP, 2008.

Goldber, E. *The Executive Brain. Frontal Lobes and the Civilized Man*. Oxford: OUP, 2001.

Gommer, H. *A Biological Theory of Law*. Seattle: Createspace, 2011.

Gorazda, M. *Filozofia ekonomii* [The Philosophy of Economy]. Kraków: Copernicus Center Press, 2014.

Górecki, J. *Rozwód. Studium socjologiczno- prawne* [Divorce. A Sociological and Legal Study]. Warszawa: PWN, 1965.

Grabowski, A. "*Clara non sunt interpretanda* vs. *omnia sunt interpretanda*. A Never-Ending Controversy in Polish Legal Theory?" *Revus. Journal for Constitutional Theory and Philosophy of Law* 26 (2015).

Green, M. "Legal Realism as Theory of Law." *William and Mary Law Review* 46 (2005).

Gryniuk, A. *Świadomość prawna. Studium teoretyczne* [Legal Awareness. A Theoretical Study]. Toruń: Uniwersytet Mikołaja Kopernika, 1979.

Guastini, R. "A realistic view on law and legal cognition." *Revus. Journal for Constitutional Theory and Philosophy of Law* 27 (2015).

Guest, S. "How to Criticize Ronald Dworkin's Theory of Law." *Analysis* 69/2 (2009).

Guest, S. *Ronald Dworkin*. Stanford: Stanford University Press, 1991.

Hage, J. "The Method of a Truly Normative Legal Science." In *Methodologies of Legal Research. Which Kind of Method for What Kind of Discipline?*, ed. M. Van Hoecke. Oxford: Hart Publishing, 2013.

Hägerström, A. *Philosophy and Religion*. London: Allen & Unwin, 1964.

Hall, A. R. *The Scientific Revolution, 1500–1800: The Formation of the Modern Scientific Attitude*. London: Longmans, Green, 1954.

Hart, H.L.A. *The Concept of Law*. 2nd ed. Oxford: Clarendon Press, 1994.

Hart, H.L.A. *Essays in Jurisprudence and Philosophy*. Oxford: Clarendon Press, 1983.

Head, M. *Evgeny Pashukanis. A Critical Reappraisal.* Abingdon: Routledge-Cavendish, 2008.

Hodges, M.A. *Wilhelm Dilthey: An Introduction.* Ann Arbor: University of Michigan, 2010.

Heller, M., Życiński, J. *Wszechświat - maszyna czy myśl? Filozofia mechanicyzmu - powstanie, rozwój, upadek.* [The Universe - Machine or Thought? The Philosophy of Mechanicism - Rise, Development, Decline]. Kraków: Polskie Towarzystwo Teologiczne, 1988.

Himma, K. "Reconsidering a Dogma: Naturalistic Turn, Conceptual Analysis and Legal Philosophy." In *Law and Philosophy*, ed. M. Freeman and R. Harrison. Oxford: Oxford University Press, 2007.

Holmes, O.W. *Collected Legal Papers.* New York: The Lawbook Exchange, 2006.

Jackson, F. *From Metaphysics to Ethics: A Defence of Conceptual Analysis.* Oxford: Clarendon Press, 1998.

Jones, O. "Sex, Culture and the Biology of Rape." *California Law Review* 87 (1999).

Jones, O. "Time-Shifted Rationality and the Law of Law's Leverage: Behavioral Economics Meets Behavioral Biology." *Northwestern University Law Review* 95 (2001).

Jørgensen, S. *Pluralis Juris. Towards a Relativistic Theory of Law.* Aarhus: Det Laerde Selskab, 1982.

Kelly, J.M. *A Short History of Western Legal Theory.* Oxford: Clarendon Press, 1992.

Kelsen, H. *Pure Theory of Law.* Trans. M. Knight. Berkeley: University of California, 1967.

Kelsen, H. *The Political Theory of Bolshevism. A Critical Analysis.* Clark, NJ: The Lawbook Exchange, 2007/1948.

Kirchmann, J. Von. *Die Wertlosigkeit der Jurisprudenz als Wissenschaft. Ein Vortrag gehalten in der Juristischen Gesellschaft zu Berlin.* Berlin, 1848.

Klink, B. von. "Facts and Norms. The Unfinished Debate Between Eugen Ehrlich and Hans Kelsen." *Tilburg Working Paper Series on Jurisprudence and Legal History* 06–03 (28 August 2006).

Koch, C. *The Quest for Consciousness: A Neurobiological Approach.* Denver, CO: Roberts and Company Publishers, 2004.

Kojder, A. "Czytając Durkheima" [Reading Durkheim]. In *Prawo, władza, społeczeństwo, polityka. Księga pamiątkowa prof. Krzysztofa Pałeckiego* [Law, Power, Society, Politics. Prof. Krzysztof Pałecki's Memorial Book]. Toruń: Adam Marszałek, 2006.

Kojder, A. "Leon Petrażycki." In *Socjologia prawa. Główne problemy i postacie* [Sociology of Law. Key Problems and Figures], ed. A. Kojder and Z. Cywiński. Warszawa: Wydawnictwo Uniwersytetu Warszawskiego, 2014.

Kojder, A. "Sprawcze siły racjonalizacji prawa. Zarys socjologii prawa Maxa Webera" [Causal Forces of the Rationalization of Law. An Outline of Max Weber's Sociology of Law]. In *Okolice socjologicznej tożsamości. Księga pamiątkowa Wojciecha Sitka* [The Periphery of Sociological Identity. Wojciech Sitek's Memorial Book], ed. Z. Kurcz and I. Taranowicz. Wrocław: Wydawnictwo Uniwersytetu *Wrocławskiego*, 2010.

Kotarbiński, T. "Myśl przewodnia metodologii Franciszka Bacona. Program Bacona" [The Guiding Thought of Francis Bacon's Methodology. Bacon's Program]. In Kotarbiński, *Szkice z historii filozofii i logiki* [Sketches from the History of Philosophy and Logic]. Warszawa: Państwowe Wydawnictwo Naukowe, 1979.

Koterski, A. *Spór o zdania protokolarne. "Erkenntnis" i "Analysis" 1932–1940* [Dispute over Protocol Phrases. "Erkenntnis" and "Analysis" 1932–1940]. Warszawa: Aletheia, 2002.

Kowalski, J., Lamentowicz, W., Winczorek, P. *Teoria państwa i prawa* [Theory of State and Law]. Warszawa: PWN, 1986.

Kuhn, T. *The Structure of Scientific Revolutions*. 2nd ed. Chicago: University of Chicago Press, 1970.

Kwaśniewski, J. "Hipoteza trójstopniowego działania prawa" [The Hypothesis of the Three-Stage Operation of Law]. In A. Kojder and Z. Cywiński, eds., *Socjologia prawa. Główne problemy i postacie* [Sociology of Law. Key Problems and Figures]. Warszawa: Wydawnictwa Uniwersytetu Warszawskiego, 2014.

Lacey, N. *A Life of H.L.A. Hart. The Nightmare and the Noble Dream*. Oxford: Oxford University Press, 2004.

Lagerspetz, K. *The Opposite Mirrors. An Essay on the Conventionalist Theory of Institutions*. Dordrecht: Kluwer Academic Publishers, 1995.

Lakatos, I. "History of Science and its Rational Reconstructions." *Boston Studies in the Philosophy of Science* 8 (1971).

Lakatos, I. *The Methodology of Scientific Research Programmes*. Cambridge: Cambridge University Press, 1978.

Lang, W., Wróblewski, J., Opałek, K. *Teoria państwa i prawa* [Theory of State and Law]. Warszawa: PWN, 1979.

Larenz, K. *Über die Unentbehrlichkeit der Jurisprudenz als Wissenschaft*. Berlin: Walter de Gruyter & Co., 1966.

Larenz, K., Canaris, R. *Methodenlehre der Rechtwissenschaft*. Heidelberg–Berlin: Springer, 1992.

LeDoux, J. *The Synaptic Self.* New York: Penguin, 2002.

Legal Hermeneutics: History, Theory, and Practice. Ed. G. Leyh. Berkeley: University of California Press, 1992.

Leiter, B. "Legal Realism and Legal Positivism Reconsidered." *Ethics* 111(2001).

Leiter, B. *Naturalizing Jurisprudence: Essays on American Legal Realism and Naturalism in Legal Philosophy.* Oxford-New York: Oxford University Press, 2007.

Leszczyński, J. *Pozytywizacja prawa w dyskursie dogmatycznym* [Positivization of Law in Dogmatic Discourse]. Kraków: Universitas, 2010.

Llewellyn, K. "Remarks on the theory of appellate decisions and the rules or canons of about how statutes are to be constructed." *Vanderbild Law Review* 3 (1950).

Llewellyn, K. *The Bramble Bush.* New York: Oceana, 1951.

Llewellyn, K., Hoebel, E.A. *The Cheyenne Way. Conflict and Case Law in Primitive Jurisprudence.* Norman, OK: University of Oklahoma Press, 1941.

Ławnicy. Rezultaty badań empirycznych [Jurors. Results of an Empirical Study]. Ed. A. Siemaszko. Warszawa: Instytut Wymiaru Sprawiedliwości, 1994.

Łopatka, A. "Wprowadzenie" [Introduction]. In *Metody badania prawa* [Methods of Studying Law], ed. A. Łopatka. Warszawa: Zakład Narodowy im. Ossolińskich, 1973.

MacCormick, N. *H.L.A.Hart.* London: Edward Arnold, 1981.

MacCormick, N. *Institutions of Law,* Oxford: Oxford University Press, 2007.

Machura, S. "Eugen Ehrlich's Legacy in the Contemporary German Legal Sociology." In *Eugen Ehrlich's Sociology of Law,* ed. K. Papendorf, S. Machura, and A. Hellum. Münster: LIT Verlag, 2014.

Mackor, A.R. "Explanatory Non-Normative Legal Doctrine. Taking the Distinction Between Theoretical and Practical Reason Seriously." In *Methodologies of Legal Research. Which Kind of Method for What Kind of Discipline?,* ed. M. Van Hoecke. Oxford: Hart Publishing, 2013.

Maddy, P. *Second Philosophy: A Naturalistic Method.* Oxford: Oxford University Press, 2007.

Magee, B. *Confessions of a Philosopher.* New York: Random House, 1997.

Malinowski, B. *Crime and Custom in Savage Society.* 1959.

Malinowski, B. *Zwyczaj i zbrodnia w społeczności dzikich. Życie seksualne dzikich* [Crime and Custom in Savage Society. The Sexual Life of Savages. Warszawa: PWN, 1984.

McDowell, J. *Reason and Nature.* Münster: Lit Verlag, 1999.

Menand, L. *The Metaphysical Club. The Story of Ideas in America.* New York: Farrar, Straus and Giroux, 2001.

Merry, S. *Getting Justice and Getting Even. Legal Consciousness Among Working Class Americans.* Chicago: University of Chicago Press, 1993.

Metody badania prawa [Methods of Studying Law], Ed. A. Łopatka. Warszawa–Wrocław–Kraków–Gdańsk: Zakład Narodowy im. Ossolińskich, 1973.

Mindus, P. *A Real Mind. The Life and Work of Axel Hägerström.* Dordrecht: Springer, 2009.

Motyka, K. *Wpływ Leona Petrażyckiego na polską teorię i socjologię prawa* [Leon Petrażycki's Influence on Polish Theory and Sociology of Law]. Lublin: Redakcja Wydawnictw KUL, 1993.

Nelken, D. "Ehrlich's Legacies: Back to the Future in the Sociology of Law?" In *Living Law. Reconsidering Eugen Ehrlich*, ed. M. Hertogh. Oxford: Hart Publishing, 2009.

Niedużak, M. *Postępowanie grupowe. Prawo i ekonomia* [Group Proceedings. Law and Economics]. Warszawa: C.H. Beck, 2014.

Nonet, P., Selznick, P. *Law and Society in Transition. Toward Responsive Law.* New Brunswick, NJ: Transaction Publishers, 2009.

Noras, A.J. *Historia neokantyzmu* [History of Neo-Kantianism]. Katowice: Wydawnictwo Uniwersytetu Śląskiego, 2012.

Noras, A.J. *Kant i Hegel w sporach filozoficznych osiemnastego i dziewiętnastego wieku* [Kant and Hegel in the Philosophical Disputes of the Eighteenth and Nineteenth Centuries]. Katowice: Wydawnictwo Uniwersytetu Śląskiego, 2007.

Nowacki, J. "Luki w prawie. Ideologia" [Gaps in the Law. Ideology]. In *Studia z teorii prawa* [Studies in Legal Theory]. Kraków: Zakamycze, 2003.

Nowak, L. *Interpretacja prawnicza. Studium z metodologii prawoznawstwa* [Legal Interpretation. A Study in the Methodology of Jurisprudence]. Warszawa: PWN, 1973

Nowak, L. *Próba metodologicznej charakterystyki prawoznawstwa* [An Attempt at a Methodological Characterization of Jurisprudence]. Poznań: Uniwersytet im. Adama Mickiewicza, 1968.

Olivecrona, K. *Law as Fact.* London: Stevens & Sons, 1971.

Olszewska-Dyoniziak, B. *Bronisław Malinowski.* Zielona Góra: WSP, 1996.

Opałek, K. "Teoria Petrażyckiego a współczesna teoria prawa" [Petrażycki's Theory and Modern Legal Theory]. In *Z zagadnień teorii prawa i teorii nauki Leona Petrażyckiego* [Elements From Leon Petrażycki's Theory of Law and Theory of Science], ed. K. Opałek. Warszawa: PWN, 1969.

Pałecki, K. "O przedmiocie socjologii prawa raz jeszcze" [On the Subject of the Sociology of Law Once Again]. In *Prawo w zmieniającym się społeczeństwie. Księga pamiątkowa z okazji 70-lecia urodzin Profesor Marii Boruckiej-Arctowej* [A Memorial Book on the 70th Anniversary of the Birth of Professor Maria Borucka-Arctowa], ed. G. Skąpska. Kraków: Adam Marszałek, 1992.

Pałecki, K. *Społeczne wyznaczniki skutecznego oddziaływania prawem na stosunki rodzinne* [Social Markers of Effective Impact of Law on Family Relations]. Kraków: Uniwersytet Jagielloński, 1977.

Panksepp, J. "Affective consciousness: Core emotional feelings in animals and human." *Consciousness & Cognition* 14 (2005).

Papineau, D. "Naturalism." In *Stanford Encyclopedia of Philosophy*, ed. E.N. Zalta, Winter 2016 Edition. Available at https://plato.stanford.edu/archives/win2016/entries/naturalism/.

Paszukanis, J. *Ogólna teoria prawa a marksizm* [The General Theory of Law and Marxism]. Trans. L. Lisiakiewicz. Warszawa: PWN, 1985.

Pawlowski, H.M. *Methodenlehre für Juristen. Theorie der Norm und des Gesetzes.* Heidelberg: C.F. Müller, 1999.

Peczenik, A. "Petrażycki o dogmatyce prawa - krytyka czy obrona?" [Petrażycki on the Dogma of Law - Critique or Defense?] In *Z zagadnień teorii prawa i teorii nauki Leona Petrażyckiego* [Elements From Leon Petrażycki's Theory of Law and Theory of Science], ed. K. Opałek. Warszawa: PWN, 1969.

Petrażycki, L. *O pobudkach postępowania i istocie moralności i prawa* [On the Motives of Conduct and the Nature of Morality and Law]. Warszawa: Oficyna Naukowa, 2002.

Petrażycki, L. *Teoria prawa i państwa w związku z teorią moralności* [The Theory of Law and the State in Relation to the Theory of Morality]. Vol. I. Warszawa: PWN, 1959.

Philosophical Foundations of the Nature of Law. Ed. W. Waluchow and S. Sciaraffa. Oxford–New York: Oxford University Press, 2013.

Pickering, M. *August Comte: An Intellectual Biography*. Vol. 3. Cambridge: Cambridge University Press, 2009.

Pietrzykowski, T. *Etyczne problemy prawa* [Ethical Problems of the Law]. Warszawa: LexisNexis, 2011.

Pietrzykowski, T. *Intuicja prawnicza. W stronę zewnętrznej integracji teorii prawa* [Legal Intuition. Toward an External Integration of Legal Theory]. Warszawa: Difin, 2012.

Pietrzykowski, T. "John Searle i ontologia prawa" [John Searle and the Onthology of Law]. *Studia Prawnicze* [Legal Studies] 1–2 (2009).

Pietrzykowski, T. *Personhood Beyond Humanism: Animals, Chimeras, Autonomous Agents and the Law.* Cham: Springer, 2018.

Pietrzykowski, T. "On the Nature and Limits of Conceptual Truths." In *Jurisprudence and Political Philosophy in the 21st Century*, ed. M. Jovanovic and B. Spaic. Frankfurt a.M.: Peter Lang, 2012

Pietrzykowski, T. "The Roots of Normativity. From Neuroscience to Legal Theory." In *Studies in the Philosophy of Law*, Vol. 7, *Legal Philosophy and the Challenges of Biosciences*, ed. J. Stelmach, M. Soniewicka, and W. Załuski. Kraków: Wydawnictwo: Wydawnictwo Uniwersytetu Jagiellońskiego, 2010.

Pietrzykowski, T. "Wielkość i błąd teorii Leona Petrażyckiego" [The Greatness and Error of Leon Petrażycki's Theory]. In Pietrzykowski, *Intuicja prawnicza. W stronę zewnętrznej integracji teorii prawa* [Legal Intuition. Toward an External Integration of Legal Theory]. Warszawa: Difin, 2012.

Pinker, S. *The Blank Slate: The Modern Denial of Human Nature.* New York: Viking, 2002.

Pisula, W. "Poziomy świadomości" [Levels of Awareness]. *Przegląd Filozoficzny* [Philosophical Review] 2/94 (2015).

Płeszka, K. *Uzasadnianie decyzji interpretacyjnych przez ich konsekwencje* [Justifying Interpretive Decisions by Their Consequences]. Kraków: Universitas, 1996.

Płeszka, K. *Wykładnia rozszerzająca* [Extensive Interpretation]. Warszawa: Wolters Kluwer, 2010.

Płeszka, K., Gizbert-Studnicki, T. "Empirisches Wissen als Grundlage der teleologischen Interpretation." In *Praktische Vernunft und Rechtsanwendung*, ed. H.J. Koch. Stuttgart: ARSP, 1994, Beiheft 53.

Podgórecki, A. "Unrecognized father of sociology of law." *Law and Society Review* 15 (1980–1981).

Popper, K. *Conjectures and Refutations.* New York: Basic Books, 1962.

Popper, K. *The Logic of Scientific Discovery.* London: Routledge, 2005.

Posner, R. "An Economic Theory of Criminal Law." *Columbia Law Review* 85 (1985).

Posner, R. *Frontiers of Legal Theory.* Cambridge, MA: Harvard University Press, 2001.

Prawo i wykluczenie. Studium empiryczne [Law and Exclusion. An Empirical Study]. Ed. A. Turska, Warszawa: C.H. Beck, 2010.

Priel, D. "Were the Legal Realists Legal Positivists?" *Law and Philosophy* 27 (2008).

Quine, W.V. "Epistemology Naturalized." In *Ontological Relativity and Other Essays*. New York: Columbia University Press, 1969.

Raz, J. *The Authority of Law.* Oxford: Clarendon Press, 1983.

Raz, J. *The Concept of a Legal System.* Oxford: Oxford University Press, 1980.

Reimann, M. "Nineteenth Century German Legal Science." *Boston College Law Review* 31/4 (1990).

Ross, A. *On Law and Justice.* Clark, NJ: The Lawbook Exchange, 2004.

Ross, A. *"Tû-Tû." Harvard Law Review* 70 (1957).

Rott-Pietrzyk, E. "Agent jako rzekomy pełnomocnik" [The Agent as Alleged Representative]. *Przegląd Prawa Handlowego* [Commercial Law Review] 9 (2005).

Russell, B. "The Philosophy of Logical Atomism." In *Bertrand Russell on Metaphysics. Selections from the Writings of Bertrand Russell*, ed. S. Mumfold. London–New York: Routledge, 2003.

Schallon, S. "Zur Dedeutung Heinrich Rickerts 'Die Grenzen der Naturwissenschaftliche Begriffsbildung.'" In Schallon, *Rickert. Texte zur Praktischen Philosophie.* London: Turnshare, 2009.

Schlegel, J. *American Legal Realism and Empirical Social Science.* Chapel Hill: The University of North Carolina Press, 1995.

Schlick, M. "Meaning and Verification." *The Philosophical Review* 45/4 (1936).

Searle, J. *Making the Social World. The Structure of Human Civilisation.* Oxford: Oxford University Press, 2010.

Searle, J. *Rationality in Action.* Cambridge, MA: The MIT Press, 2001.

Searle, J. *Mind, Language and Society: Philosophy in the Real World.* New York: Basic Books, 1999.

Segal, J., Speath, H. *The Supreme Court and the Attitudinal Model.* Cambridge: Cambridge University Press, 1993.

Segal, J., Speath, H. *The Supreme Court and the Attitudinal Model Revisited.* New York: Cambridge University Press, 2002.

Sellars, W. "Philosophy and the Scientific Image of Man." In Sellars, *Empiricism and the Philosophy of Mind.* London: Routledge & Kegan Paul, 1963.

Shapiro, S. "What is the Internal Point of View?" *Fordham Law Review* 75 (2004).

Singer, P., de Lazari-Radek, K. *The Point of View of the Universe. Sidgwick and Contemporary Ethics.* Oxford: Oxford University Press, 2014.

Sinha, S. *Jurisprudence.* St. Paul, MN: West Publishing, 1993.

Skinner, B. *Beyond Freedom and Dignity.* New York: Knopf, 1971.

Smits, J.M. *The Mind and Method of the Legal Academic.* Cheltenham–Northampton: Edward Elgar Publishing, 2012.

Sokal, A., Bricmont, J. *Fashionable Nonsense: Postmodern Intellectuals' Abuse of Science*. New York: Picador, 1998.

Somek, A. *The Indelible Science of Law*, International Journal of Constitutional Law, 7 (2009), 424–41.

Stanovich, K. *The Robot's Rebellion. Finding Meaning in the Age of Darwin.* Chicago, IL: University of Chicago Press, 2004.

Stark A., *Interdisziplinarität der Rechtsdogmatik*, Mohr Siebeck, Tübingen 2020.

Stelmach, J. "A jeśli powinność nie istnieje?" [And What If Duty Does Not Exist?] In A. Brożek, B. Brożek, and J. Stelmach, *Fenomen normatywności* [The Phenomenon of Normativity]. Kraków: Copernicus Center Press, 2013.

Stelmach, J. "Naturalistyczny i antynaturalistyczny model teorii prawa" [The Naturalistic and Anti-Naturalistic Models of Legal Theory]. *Studia Prawnicze* [Legal Studies] 3–4 (1984).

Stelmach, J. "Stare i nowe interpretacje naturalizmu prawniczego" [Old and New Interpretations of Legal Naturalism]. In *Naturalizm prawniczy. Interpretacje*, [Legal Naturalism. Interpretations], eds. J. Stelmach, B. Brożek, Ł. Kurek, and K. Eliasz. Warszawa: Wolters Kluwer, 2015.

Stelmach, J. *Współczesna filozofia interpretacji prawniczej* [Modern Philosophy of Legal Intepretation]. Kraków: Wydawnictwo Uniwersytetu Jagiellońskiego, 1999.

Stelmach, J., Brożek, B. *Metody prawnicze* [Legal Methods]. Kraków: Zakamycze, 2004.

Stelmach, J., Brożek, B., Brożek, A. *Fenomen normatywności* [The Phenomenon of Normativity]. Kraków: Copernicus Center Press, 2013.

Stelmach, J., Brożek, B., Załuski, W. *Dziesięć wykładów o ekonomii prawa* [Ten Lectures on the Economy of Law]. Warszawa: Wolters Kluwer, 2007.

Stępień, M. *Responsywna administracja publiczna* [A Responsive Public Administration]. Toruń: Adam Marszałek, 2008

Sulikowski, A. *Konstytucjonalizm a nowoczesność. Dyskurs konstytucyjny wobec tryumfu i kryzysu moderny* [Constitutionalism and Modernity. Constitutional Discourse in the face of the Triumph and Crisis of Modernism]. Wrocław: Wydawnictwo Uniwersytetu Wrocławskiego, 2012.

Sulikowski, A. "O możliwościach postmodernizacji nauki prawa konstytucyjnego" [On the Postmodernization Possibilities of Constitutional Law]. *Państwo i Prawo* [State and Law] 12 (2010).

Sunstein, C. "How Star Wars Illuminates Constitutional Law;" available at http://papers.ssrn.com/sol3/papers.cfm?abstract_id=2604998.

Tamanaha, B. *A General Jurisprudence of Law and Society.* Oxford: Oxford University Press, 1999.

Teubner, G. "Global Bukowina. Legal Pluralism in the World-Society." In *Global Law Without a State*, ed. G. Teubner. Aldershot: Dartmouth, 1997.

The Legacy of Ronald Dworkin. Ed. W. Waluchow and S. Sciaraffa. Oxford: Oxford University Press, 2016.

Thornhill, R., Palmer, C. *A Natural History of Rape: Biological Bases Of Sexual Coercion.* Cambridge, MA: MIT Press 2000.

Tobor, Z. *W poszukiwaniu intencji prawodawcy* [The Search for the Legislator's Intentions]. Warszawa: Lex a Wolters Kluwer, 2013.

Waal, F. de *Primates and Philosophers. How Morality Evolved.* Princeton, NJ: Princeton University Press, 2006.

Walicki, A., *Marksizm i skok do królestwa wolności* [Marxism and the Leap into the Realm of Freedom]. Warszawa: PWN, 1996.

Weber, M. *Economy and Society*. Ed. and trans. G. Roth and C. Wittich. New York: Bedminster, 1968.

Weber, M. "Science as Vocation." In *The Vocation Lectures*, trans. R. Livingstone, ed. D. Owen and T. Strong. Illinois: Hackett Books, 2004.

Weiss, M. *Etyka a ewolucja. Metaetyczny kontekst etyki ewolucyjnej* [Ethics and Evolution. The Metaethical Context of Evolutionary Ethics]. Poznań: Wydawnictwo Poznańskie, 2010.

Wilson, E.O. *Consilience: The Unity of Knowledge.* New York: Knopf, 1998.

Winczorek, J. "Pluralizm prawny wczoraj i dziś. Kilka uwag o ewolucji pojęcia" [Legal Pluralism Then and Now. Remarks on the Evolution of the Term]. In *Pluralizm prawny* [Legal Pluralism], ed. D. Bunikowski and K. Dobrzeniecki. Toruń: Interdyscyplinarne Koło Naukowe Doktorantów UMK, 2009.

Windelband, W. "Geschichte und Naturwissenschaft." Rede zum Antritt des Rektorats der Kaiser-Wilhelms-Universität Straßburg gehalten am 1. Mai 1894; available at http://philosophierer.blogspot.com/2014/09/wilhelm-windelband-geschichte-und.html

Windelband, W. "History and Natural Science." Trans. J. Lamiell. *Theory and Psychology* 8 (1894/1998).

Wittgenstein, L. *Tractatus Logico-Philosophicus.* London: Kegan Paul, Trench, Trubner & Co., Ltd, 1922. Available from Project Gutenberg at https://www.gutenberg.org/ebooks/5740.

Woleński, J. "Naturalizm w teorii prawa" [Naturalism in Legal Theory]. In *W poszukiwaniu dobra wspólnego. Księga jubileuszowa Profesora Macieja Zielińskiego* [In Search of the Common Good. Professor Maciej Zieliński's

Anniversary Book], ed. A. Choduń and S. Czepita. Szczecin: Wydawnictwo Naukowe Uniwersytetu *Szczecińskiego*, 2010

Wróblewski, J. "Paradygmat dogmatyki prawa a prawoznawstwo" [The Paradigm of Legal Dogma and Jurisprudence]. In Wróblewski, *Pisma wybrane* [Selected Works], ed. M. Zirk-Sadowski and T. Bekrycht. Warszawa: Wolters Kluwer, 2015.

Wróblewski, J. "Postawa filozoficzna i afilozoficzna we współczesnej teorii prawa" [A Philosophical and Aphilosophical Approach in Modern Legal Theory]. In Wróblewski, *Pisma wybrane* [Selected Works], ed. M. Zirk-Sadowski. Warszawa: Wolters Kluwer, 2015.

Wróblewski, J., Lang, W., Zawadzki, S. *Teoria państwa i prawa* [Theory of State and Law]. Warszawa: PWN, 1979.

Zajadło, J. "Aneks. Filozofia prawa. Pyta filozof, odpowiada prawnik" [Annex. Philosophy of Law. A Philosopher Asks, a Lawyer Answers]. In Zajadło, *Carl Schmitt*. Gdańsk: Wydawnictwo Arche, 2016.

Załuski, W. "Cel prawa według Law & Economics" [The Goal of Law According to Law & Economics]. In *Wielowymiarowość prawa* [Multidimensionality of Law], ed. J. Czapska, M. Dudek, and M. Stępień. Toruń: Wydawnictwo Adam Marszałek, 2014.

Załuski, W. *Ewolucyjna filozofia prawa* [The Evolutionary Philosophy of Law]. Kraków: Wolters Kluwer, 2009.

Zieliński, M. *Wykładnia prawa. Zasady, reguły, wskazówki* [Interpreting Law. Principles, rules, guidelines]. Warszawa: LexisNexis, 2012.

Ziembiński, Z. In Z. Ziembiński, A. Redelbach, and S. Wronkowska, *Zarys teorii państwa i prawa* [An Outline of the Theory of State and Law]. Warszawa: PWN, 1993.

Ziembiński, Z. *Metodologiczne zagadnienia prawoznawstwa* [Methodological Issues of Jurisprudence]. Warszawa: PWN, 1974.

Ziembiński, Z. "Przepis prawny a norma prawna" [Legal Provisions and Legal Norms]. *Ruch Prawniczy, Ekonomiczny i Socjologiczny* [The Legal, Economic and Sociological Movement] 1 (1960).

Ziembiński, Z. *Socjologia prawa jako nauka prawna* [Sociology of Law as a Legal Science]. Warszawa: PWN, 1975.

Ziembiński, Z. *Szkice z metodologii szczegółowych nauk prawnych* [Sketches in the Methodology of Particular Legal Sciences]. Warszawa–Poznań: Polska Akademia Nauk, 1983.

Zippelius, R. *Juristische Methodenlehre*. München: Beck, 1994.

Zirk-Sadowski, M. "Pozytywizm prawniczy a filozoficzna opozycja podmiotu i przedmiotu poznania" [Legal Positivism and the Philosophical Opposition of the Cognitive Subject and Object]. In *Studia z filozofii prawa* [Studies in Philosophy of Law], ed. J. Stelmach. Kraków: Wydawnictwo Uniwersytetu Jagiellońskiego, 2001.

Zirk-Sadowski, M. *Wprowadzenie do filozofii prawa* [Introduction to Philosophy of Law]. Warszawa: Wolters Kluwer, 2011.

Index

DIA-LOGOS
Schriften zu Philosophie und Sozialwissenschaften
Studies in Philosophy and Social Sciences

Edited by
Piotr W. Juchacz

Dia-Logos. Studies in Philosophy and Social Sciences is a peer-reviewed book series publishing valuable monographs and edited volumes on various aspects of philosophy and social sciences. The series is intended to be an interdisciplinary forum of deliberation according to our firm belief that challenges of the contemporary world require common and multilevel research. The *Dia-Logos* series does not represent a single ideology or school of thought, but it is open to different trends and various styles of reflection, trying to understand better the contemporary world. We invite the submission of manuscripts of monographs and edited volumes from academic philosophers and social scientists.

Vol. 1 Piotr W. Juchacz/Roman Kozłowski (Hrsg.): Freiheit und Verantwortung. Moral, Recht und Politik. 2002.

Vol. 2 Norbert Leśniewski/Ewa Nowak-Juchacz (Hrsg.): Die Zeit Heideggers. 2002.

Vol. 3 Marek Kwiek (ed.): The University, Globalization, Central Europe. 2003.

Vol. 4 Ewa Czerwińska-Schupp (Hrsg.): Philosophie an der Schwelle des 21. Jahrhunderts. Geschichte der Philosophie, Philosophische Anthropologie, Ethik, Wissenschaftstheorie, Politische Philosophie. 2003.

Vol. 5 Danuta Sobczyńska / Pawel Zeidler / Ewa Zielonacka-Lis (eds.): Chemistry in the Philosophical Melting Pot. 2004.

Vol. 6 Marek Kwiek: Intellectuals, Power, and Knowledge. Studies in the Philosophy of Culture and Education. 2004.

Vol. 7 Marek Kwiek: The University and the State. A Study into Global Transformations. 2006.

Vol. 8 Andrzej Przylebski (Hrsg.): Das Erbe Gadamers. 2006.

Vol. 9 Ewa Czerwińska-Schupp (ed.): Values and Norms in the Age of Globalization. 2007.

Vol. 10 Tadeusz Buksiński (ed.): Democracy in Western and Post-Communist Countries. Twenty Years after the Fall of Communism. 2009.

Vol. 11 Marek Zirk-Sadowski / Mariusz Golecki / Bartosz Wojciechowski (eds.): Multicentrism as an Emerging Paradigm in Legal Theory. 2009.

Vol. 12 Bartosz Wojciechowski: Philosophical Approach to the Interculturality of Criminal Law. 2010.

Vol. 13 Marek Nowak / Michał Nowosielski (eds.): (Post)transformational Migration. Inequalities, Welfare State, and Horizontal Mobility. 2011.

Vol. 14 Tadeusz Buksiński (ed.): Religions in the Public Spheres. 2011.

Vol. 15 Bartosz Wojciechowski / Piotr W. Juchacz / Karolina M. Cern (eds.): Legal Rules, Moral Norms and Democratic Principles. 2013.

Vol. 16 Ewa Nowak / Dawn E. Schrader / Boris Zizek (eds.): Educating Competencies for Democracy. 2013.

Vol. 17 Tadeusz Buksiński (ed.): Identities and Modernizations. 2013.

Vol. 18 Karolina M. Cern: The Counterfactual Yardstick. Normativity, Self-Constitutionalisation and the Public Sphere. 2014.

Vol. 19 Vito Breda / Lidia Rodak (eds.). Diverse Narratives of Legal Objectivity. An Interdisciplinary Perspective. 2016.

Vol. 20 Marek Woszczek: Platonic Wholes and Quantum Ontology. Translated by Katarzyna Kretkowska. 2015.

Vol. 21 Roman Hauser / Marek Zirk-Sadowski / Bartosz Wojciechowski (eds.): The Common European Constitutional Culture. Its Sources, Limits and Identity. 2016.

Vol. 22 Aigerim Raimzhanova: Hard, Soft, and Smart Power – Education as a Power Resource. 2017.

Vol. 23 Roberto Franzini Tibaldeo / Graziano Lingua (eds.): Philosophy and Community Practices. 2018.

Vol. 24 Marta Soniewicka: After God – The Normative Power of the Will from the Nietzschean Perspective. 2017.

Vol. 25 Tomasz Jarmużek: On the Sea Battle Tomorrow That May Not Happen. A Logical and Philosophical Analysis of the Master Argument. 2018.

Vol. 26 Krzysztof Brzechczyn (ed.): New Perspectives in Transnational History of Communism in East Central Europe. 2019.

Vol. 27 Ewa Nowak: Advancing the Human Self. Do Technologies Make Us "Posthuman"?. 2020.

Vol. 28 Lidia Rodak: Judicial Objectivity. Limits, Merits and Beyond. 2020.

Vol. 29 Tomasz Pietrzykowski: Naturalism and the Frontiers of Legal Science. 2021.

www.peterlang.com

www.ingramcontent.com/pod-product-compliance
Ingram Content Group UK Ltd.
Pitfield, Milton Keynes, MK11 3LW, UK
UKHW021832100926
8556IPUK00004B/299